Pragmatics: Teaching Natural Conversation

Edited by Noël R. Houck and Donna H. Tatsuki

Maria Dantas-Whitney, Sarah Rilling, and Lilia Savova, Series Editors

TESOL Classroom Practice Series

Teachers of English to Speakers of Other Languages, Inc.

Typeset in ITC Galliard and Vag Rounded
by Capitol Communication Systems, Inc., Crofton, Maryland USA
Printed by United Graphics, Inc., Mattoon, Illinois USA
Indexed by Pueblo Indexing and Publishing Services, Pueblo West, Colorado USA

Teachers of English to Speakers of Other Languages, Inc.
1925 Ballenger Avenue, Suite 550
Alexandria, Virginia 22314 USA
Tel 703-836-0774 • Fax 703-836-6447 • E-mail tesol@tesol.org •
http://www.tesol.org/

Publishing Manager: Carol Edwards
Copy Editor: Sarah J. Duffy
Additional Reader: Terrey L. Hatcher
Cover Design: Capitol Communication Systems, Inc.

ISBN 9781931185707
Library of Congress Control No. 2011927483

Table of Contents

Dedication v

Series Editors' Preface vii

Transcription Conventions ix

Chapter 1
Introduction 1
    Noël R. Houck and Donna H. Tatsuki

Chapter 2
Assessing Familiarity With Pragmatic Formulas:
Planning Oral/Aural Assessment 7
    Kathleen Bardovi-Harlig

Chapter 3
No, Thanks. I'm Full! Raising Awareness of Expressions of
Gratitude and Conventional Expressions 23
    Kathleen Bardovi-Harlig and Edelmira L. Nickels

Chapter 4
Oh, I'm So Sorry! Are You All Right? Teaching Apologies 41
    Carmella Lieske

Chapter 5
Have You Paid Someone a Compliment Today? .61
    Jessie Carduner

Chapter 6
Male and Female Complimenting Behavior 79
    Anne McLellan Howard

Chapter 7

Taking Turns and Talking Naturally:
Teaching Conversational Turn-Taking 91
  Donald Carroll

Chapter 8

Teaching Preference Organization: Learning How Not to Say "No" 105
  Donald Carroll

Chapter 9

Pragmatic Competency in Telephone Conversation Openings 119
  Jean Wong

Chapter 10

Pragmatic Competency in Telephone Conversation Closings 135
  Jean Wong

Chapter 11

Responders: Continuers. 153
  David Olsher

Chapter 12

Responders: Change-of-State Tokens, News Markers, and Assessments 171
  David Olsher

Chapter 13

Developing Students' Language Awareness 193
  Maria Dantas-Whitney

References 207

Index 219

Dedication

To Merrinell and Bill,
for their invaluable support in the final stages of this book.

And to Lori, Kanji, and Daniel,
for their laughter, inspiration, and friendship.

Series Editors' Preface

The TESOL Classroom Practice Series showcases state-of-the-art curricula, materials, tasks, and activities reflecting emerging trends in language education and in the roles of teachers, learners, and the English language itself. The series seeks to build localized theories of language learning and teaching based on students' and teachers' unique experiences in and out of the classroom.

This series captures the dynamics of 21st-century ESOL classrooms. It reflects major shifts in authority from teacher-centered practices to collaborative learner- and learning-centered environments. The series acknowledges the growing numbers of English speakers globally, celebrates locally relevant curricula and materials, and emphasizes the importance of multilingual and multicultural competencies—a primary goal in teaching English as an international language. Furthermore, the series takes into account contemporary technological developments that provide new opportunities for information exchange and social and transactional communications.

Each volume in the series focuses on a particular communicative skill, learning environment, or instructional goal. Chapters within each volume represent practices in English for general, academic, vocational, and specific purposes. Readers will find examples of carefully researched and tested practices designed for different student populations (from young learners to adults, from beginning to advanced) in diverse settings (from preK–12 to college and postgraduate, from local to global, from formal to informal). A variety of methodological choices are also represented, including individual and collaborative tasks and curricular as well as extracurricular projects. Most important, these volumes invite readers into the conversation that considers and so constructs ESOL classroom practices as complex entities. We are indebted to the authors, their colleagues, and their students for being a part of this conversation.

This volume offers teachers in the ESOL classroom some of the first published materials for guiding learners past grammar into authentic-sounding (conventional) utterances and sequences, replacing the scripted unnatural or stilted dialogue provided in textbooks. Teachers will find a range of pedagogical activities to put to immediate use in the classroom, as students learn turn-taking, initiations and responses for formal academic and informal conversation, thanking expressions, apologies, compliments and compliment responses, differences in complimenting behavior between men and women, opening and closing telephone conversations, and use of responders such as *oh, uh-huh/mm-hm*, and *yeah.*

Pragmatics: Teaching Natural Conversation, taken together with the previous volume, *Pragmatics: Teaching Speech Acts*, provides teachers with a comprehensive basis for the theoretically sound and pedagogically effective teaching of this important, but often neglected, area of language.

Maria Dantas-Whitney, Western Oregon University
Sarah Rilling, Kent State University
Lilia Savova, Indiana University of Pennsylvania

Transcription Conventions

SPELLING

Orthodox spelling is generally used throughout this volume in lieu of the "spoken representations" commonly used in conversation analysis–style transcripts, with a few high-frequency exceptions (e.g., *wanna* for *want to*; *Hawar yuh?* for *How are you?*).

PROSODIC FEATURES

These conversation analysis transcription conventions have been used throughout this volume to represent intonation and other prosodic features as follows:

At the end of a word, phrase, clause, or sentence

?	Rising intonation
.	Falling intonation
,	Nonfinal intonation (usually a slight rise)
	No punctuation at clause end indicates flat intonation (no pitch change)
< >	The talk between the brackets is spoken at a slower rate
> <	The talk between the brackets is spoken at a faster rate
lo::ng	Lengthening of the prior sound. Multiple colons may be used. The longer the elongation, the more colons that are used.
°soft°	The talk between the degree marks is spoken softly
LOUD	Capital letters indicate loud speech
<u>Emphasis</u>	Underlining indicates added stress or emphasis

OTHER

(?) or ( )   Incomprehensible word or phrase

(all right)   The transcriber is not certain that he or she has heard the word or phrase correctly

[Overlapping speech; bracket is placed at the point at which the overlap begins

> Example:
> J: We'll talk to you [tomorrow.
> M: [Okay.

[[Simultaneous next-turn speaker startup talk

=   The utterance on one line continues without pause where the next = sign picks it up (latches)

y-   Hyphen after an initial sound indicates a cutoff

> Example:
> N: y- your mother is coming, right?

hhh   Audible out-breath or laughter (the more h's, the longer the out-breath or laughter)

.hhh   Audible in-breath (the more h's, the longer the in-breath)

(.)   Very brief silence ("micropause")

(0.4)   The length of a silence, in seconds (e.g., four-tenths of a second)

((lifts glass))   Transcriptionist comment or supplemental information such as embodied aspects of the interaction

CHAPTER 1

Introduction

Noël R. Houck and Donna H. Tatsuki

This is the second of two volumes designed to provide English as a second language (ESL) and English as a foreign language (EFL) teachers with information on pragmatics-based research for the classroom. Whereas the first volume, *Pragmatics: Teaching Speech Acts*, focuses on an area traditionally associated with pragmatics, this volume expands the domain to include conventional expressions. *Pragmatics: Teaching Natural Conversation* emphasizes those that are consistently used in the performance of particular speech acts, as well as characteristics of interactional sequences—from the fluent production of relevant, coherent next turns to the construction of telephone openings and closings. This volume also offers an approach for investigating the discursive practices of the learner's community.

The need for resources for teaching pragmatics to learners who have little opportunity to engage in appropriate linguistic behavior outside the classroom has long been recognized. As R. Ellis (2009) notes, "there is clear evidence that the kind of communication that takes place in the classroom may restrict learners' access to the kinds of interactional acts needed to ensure the development of pragmatic competence" (p. 9). In addition, there is a growing awareness that simply exposing learners to grammatically appropriate sentences is inadequate and that, as Bardovi-Harlig (2001) states, "making contextualized pragmatically appropriate input available to learners from early stages of acquisition onward is the very least that pedagogy should aim to do" (p. 31).

The first half of this volume includes activities based on research on the pragmatic use of formulas, or *conventional expressions* as they are referred to when the focus is on strings of words that are regularly used by a particular speech community (Bardovi-Harlig, 2009). Two strands of research on formulas/conventional expressions in speech have been pursued over the past few decades. In second language acquisition, in contrast to the emphasis on rule-based theories of language, a number of researchers (e.g., N. C. Ellis, 1996, 2007; Nattinger & DeCarrico, 1992; Pawley & Syder, 1983; Schmidt & Frota, 1986; Wray, 2002) have noted that a much larger part of English consists of patterns or memorized chunks than had been previously theorized (c.f., Chomsky, 1959; Dulay, Burt, & Krashen,

1982). For instance, the expression *time is over* is grammatical and acceptable, yet it is rarely used; *time's up* is the conventional pattern.

In a strand related to conventional expressions in speech act production, researchers such as Manes and Wolfson (1981) have pointed out that speech acts such as compliments, which are often thought to be generally spontaneous and creative, are usually performed in English using routines or predictable syntactic patterns. At the same time, other researchers focusing on linguistic and social characteristics of seemingly simple routines such as *thanks/you're welcome* have noticed that these are often not as uncomplicated as they appear (see chapter 3 in this volume). The contributions to this volume are designed to focus teacher attention on conventional expressions and patterns as objects worthy of classroom attention.

The second half of the volume focuses on interaction, which includes turn-taking, initiations and responses, and interactional sequences in both formal academic and informal conversational discourse. Long ignored but crucial to ESL learners, these aspects of conversation have benefited from the research on interaction emanating from conversation analysis (CA), from the earliest studies (Sacks, Schegloff, & Jefferson, 1974; Schegloff, Jefferson, & Sacks, 1977) to more recent work on the relevance of CA concepts to the language classroom (Hellerman, 2008; Mori, 2002; Seedhouse, 2004; Wong & Waring, 2010). Researchers using CA have developed an unrivaled ability to characterize not only conversation but institutional discourse as well. They have looked at aspects of conversation that had been ignored, but which are of crucial relevance to second language learners—areas such as characteristics of fluent turn-taking, systematic variation in response shapes, functions of different response tokens, and organization of sequences.

Teachers attempting to engage learners in oral communication often do not see the need to spend time on language beyond the sentence level; that is, they assume that if students can construct grammatical sentences, they can by extension produce conversational sequences. This is perhaps partly because native speakers feel no need to concentrate on the language involved in activities that are, to them, straightforward. Rather, they tend to rely on textbooks to provide authentic, accurate representations of interaction in the target language. Unfortunately, insights based on research describing characteristics of real language use have been slow to trickle into teaching materials. Thus, when teachers do attempt to teach sequences, they may rely on published language instructional materials that are inadequate, incomplete, or erroneous in their treatment and discussion of pragmatic conversation skills (Bernsten, 2002; Bardovi-Harlig, 2001; Boxer & Pickering, 1995; Grant & Starks, 2001; Vellenga, 2004; Wong, 1984, 2002, 2007). They may not be aware of mismatches between textbook dialogue and real conversation in terms of sequence structure, although they may have a vague sense that the scripted dialogues they are relying on are unnatural or stilted. Complementing the chapters on conventional expressions and conversational sequences, this volume also provides learners with guidance in principled observations of aspects of second language use.

The section on conventional expressions (chapters 2–6) begins with an orientation for teachers on how to assess students' current state of knowledge. The remaining four chapters in the section, as well as four of the chapters on conversational sequences, follow a classic sequencing of tasks. They move from awareness raising to some form of identification, often followed by a discussion of the form and its distribution. Students are then provided with opportunities for guided or controlled production. Two of the chapters on conversational sequencing take an integrated approach to awareness raising and production in that learners learn about the practices as they perform them. In addition, the final chapter guides learners through steps for completing an ethnographic analysis.

Thus, *Pragmatics: Teaching Natural Conversation* extends the boundaries of interest from pedagogical applications of research on linguistic action, launched in *Pragmatics: Teaching Speech Acts*, to classroom applications of new areas of research on authentic talk in interaction. It offers some of the first published materials for guiding learners past grammar into authentic-sounding (conventional) utterances and sequences, as well as resources for observing these aspects of language on their own.

The chapters in *Pragmatics: Teaching Speech Acts* provide information and activities primarily related to the realization of speech acts and the effect of different contexts on the form used to realize the act. This volume focuses more closely on (a) the role of conventional expressions or patterns in expressing actions; (b) the characteristics of longer sequences and the work involved in producing them fluently, coherently, and appropriately, as reported in studies on talk in interaction; and (c) resources for students to use in observing and identifying authentic language patterns.

Chapters 2–6 concentrate on pragmatic formulas used to convey common meanings or acts. Chapter 2, "Assessing Familiarity With Pragmatic Formulas: Planning Oral/Aural Assessment," by Kathleen Bardovi-Harlig, differs from other chapters in the volume in that it provides a means by which teachers can evaluate learners' familiarity with natural conventional expressions such as those used in many English speech acts. A listening-based recognition task provides teachers with a model for determining the differences between learner and native-speaker knowledge of common phrases.

Recent research into the use of conventional expressions by learners of English as a second language has shown noticeable differences between native speakers and English language learners even in such simple expressions as *thank you* and *thanks*. In chapter 3, "No, Thanks. I'm Full! Raising Awareness of Expressions of Gratitude and Conventional Expressions," Kathleen Bardovi-Harlig and Edelmira Nickels present a series of activities designed to improve learners' ability to produce thanking expressions.

Chapter 4, "Oh, I'm So Sorry! Are You All Right? Teaching Apologies," by Carmella Lieske, limits its focus to apologies that result from bumping into someone. After providing a brief overview of the most widely used strategies for performing apologies in general, Lieske concentrates on the particular strategies typically produced by Americans who bump into others and guides learners to produce apologies appropriate to subtle contextual factors.

In chapter 5, "Have You Paid Someone a Compliment Today?," Jessie Carduner provides a resource for teaching compliments and compliment responses in a sequenced set of activities that diagnose students' current ability to produce compliments and responses in English, instructs learners on the conventional nature of most English compliments, provides opportunities to recognize different compliment and compliment response forms, and then presents activities that offer students a chance to produce and respond to compliments.

After reviewing appropriate compliment forms and topics, in chapter 6, "Male and Female Complimenting Behavior," Anne McLellan Howard provides a springboard for discussion about the differences in complimenting behavior between men and women.

In chapter 7, "Taking Turns and Talking Naturally: Teaching Conversational Turn-Taking," the first of six chapters on turn-taking and sequence organization, Donald Carroll makes a case for teaching and practicing the norms of conversational turn-taking in the EFL/ESL classroom. He begins by presenting some common misperceptions about how turn-taking works in conversation and then provides a brief overview of a more accurate description of conversational turn-taking, as revealed by studies in CA. Carroll then offers a series of activities that have been used successfully to sensitize students to the practices of conversational turn-taking, with a particular focus on helping students appreciate the communicative importance of "jumping into the conversation" at the right time.

Chapter 8, "Teaching Preference Organization: Learning How Not to Say 'No,'" also by Donald Carroll, introduces a phenomenon known as *preference organization*, which refers to the characteristics of different types of responses to the same action. Carroll provides a series of activities that can be used to teach, for example, how to accept an invitation, as opposed to how to reject it.

Chapter 9, "Pragmatic Competency in Telephone Conversation Openings," by Jean Wong, fills the pedagogical void related to teaching learners how to open telephone conversations. Wong begins by explaining the nature of openings in real telephone talk in English and then presents an activity that instructors can use to have ESL and EFL learners practice telephone openings, using excerpts from real telephone conversations.

In chapter 10, "Pragmatic Competency in Telephone Conversation Closings," Jean Wong goes on to introduce teachers to CA findings on closings and the preclosings that lead to closings in telephone conversations. She offers awareness-raising activities and opportunities to recognize and practice the various stages of preclosings and closings, using materials from actual interactions.

Chapter 11, "Responders: Continuers," by David Olsher, addresses an important part of spoken communication that is often ignored or oversimplified in English teaching materials—the small responses given by a listener that play important functions in showing an understanding of what a speaker is saying and that allow the speaker to continue with an extended stretch of talk. Minimal response tokens, or *responders*, include (among others) *oh, uh-huh/mm-hm,* and *yeah.* Olsher presents a set of responders that function as continuers. After an overview of continuers and their intonation, he focuses on *uh-huh/mm-hm, yeah,* and *right,* with awareness-raising, identification, and speaking activities.

In chapter 12, "Responders: Change-of-State Tokens, News Markers, and Assessments," David Olsher takes the discussion further to guide teachers in familiarizing learners with three additional types of responders (*oh, really,* and assessments such as *great, that's neat,* and *sounds good*) while developing learners' understanding of their meanings and their effect on the sequence in progress through identification and production activities.

In chapter 13, "Developing Students' Language Awareness," Maria Dantas-Whitney describes how to foster awareness of a wide range of language phenomena through learner participation in a language research project. The project entails formulating research questions, generating hypotheses, and conducting ethnographic observations of interactions in the community in order to build students' understanding about social and academic uses of language. A central component of the project is the use of Hymes's (1972) SPEAKING framework for analyzing speech events.

In sum, this volume makes new theoretical findings accessible to teachers and relevant to the language classroom. At the same time, it offers a range of pedagogical activities for teachers to put to immediate use. Taken together, *Pragmatics: Teaching Speech Acts* and *Pragmatics: Teaching Natural Conversation* offer a comprehensive basis for the theoretically sound and pedagogically effective teaching of an important, but often neglected area of language.

Noël R. Houck is associate professor in the English and Foreign Languages Department at California State Polytechnic University Pomona, in the United States. Her research centers on cross-cultural pragmatics and discourse analysis, with a focus on microanalysis of classroom discourse. She has taught and conducted research in Brazil, Mexico, and Japan.

Donna H. Tatsuki is a professor in the Graduate School for English Language Education and Research at Kobe City University of Foreign Studies, in Japan. She is currently researching multiparty talk-in-interaction of Model United Nations simulations and the representations of gender and ethnicity in government-approved language textbooks. She has taught in Canada and Japan.

CHAPTER 2

Assessing Familiarity With Pragmatic Formulas: Planning Oral/Aural Assessment

Kathleen Bardovi-Harlig

This chapter differs from other chapters in this volume in that it provides a tool to help teachers evaluate learners' familiarity with natural conventional expressions, such as those used in many English speech acts. The listening-based recognition task described here stems from work in trying to understand the root of differences between language learner and native-speaker production in pragmatics. Although production differences between second language learners and native speakers are well documented (Bardovi-Harlig, 2001; Kasper & Rose, 2002; Rose & Kasper, 2001), the cause of these differences is less well understood. Many influences on second language pragmatics have been identified, including first language and host or foreign language learning environments, but regardless of the strength of these influences, each learner brings to the task of learning second language pragmatics his or her individual interlanguage competence. The starting point for a learner (his or her individual interlanguage competence) interacts with instruction and determines, at least in part, the outcome.

In an attempt to better understand what causes production differences at the level of individual learners, my colleagues and I have investigated learners' ability to recognize pragmatic infelicities (inappropriate pragmatic acts or forms; Bardovi-Harlig & Dörnyei, 1998), learners' development of grammatical resources that are crucial to native-like production (Salsbury & Bardovi-Harlig, 2000), and, most recently, learners' recognition of conventional expressions used in speech act realization (Bardovi-Harlig, 2008, 2010).

Recognition is probably the most basic of factors that lead to a learner's trying out target-like expressions in the service of pragmatics. This is consistent with

Schmidt's (1995) formulation of noticing, a low level of awareness, as the "conscious registration of the occurrence of some event" (p. 29).

The listening task presented in this chapter offers a means of assessing learners' knowledge of *conventional expressions,* social formulas shared by a community and used in specific social or discourse contexts (Bardovi-Harlig, 2009). Conventional expressions are those phrases that native speakers actually use, as opposed to expressions that learners have been taught (e.g., the formal *thank you* as opposed to the more frequent *thanks*) or have developed on their own (e.g., *time is over* as opposed to the more idiomatic *time's up*). The task is designed to be a pre-instructional assessment to help teachers determine where to begin instruction on comprehension and production in pragmatics.

CONTEXT

The version of the listening task exemplified in this chapter was designed for university English language learners enrolled in an intensive English program. The task was conducted in the university's computer-based language lab, with each student using a computer and a headset.

Most students ranged in age from 18 to 25, but there were some older students as well. The task was used with low-intermediate-level students (Level 3 of a 7-level program) up through college-bound students in Level 7. Even though the program focuses on English for academic purposes, students want to be able to use English for conversation. The basic goal of this listening activity is to assess students' familiarity with useful pragmatic expressions before instruction on production.

The task consists of 60 expressions, of which 35 are authentic conventional expressions (e.g., *Excuse me*) and 25 are modified expressions, phrases that are grammatical, but not conventional (e.g., *You excuse me*). It took 12 minutes for students to complete the activity, including listening to the instructions and examples. Results showed the following:

- Students correctly reported that they were not familiar with most of the modified expressions.

- They often reported that they heard some full forms such as *You are welcome* as often as reduced forms such as *You're welcome.* (Learners are often more confident with full forms, but need to recognize contractions and other reductions common in connected speech.)

- Students encountered problems with two-word verbs (verb plus particles). The class recognition score for the conventional warning *Watch out!* was quite low at lower levels, and scores for the modified *Watch up!* (which is unusual, but not ungrammatical) were almost as high. The similar scores suggest that students did not distinguish between the authentic expression and the impostor. This is a pair that was identified as needing additional instruction.

- Students more easily distinguished conventional expressions from lexically modified expressions (*nice to meet you* vs. *nice to introduce you*) than from grammatically modified expressions (*no problem* vs. *no problems*). Because grammatical modifications seem to be harder for learners to recognize, these might be particularly useful in drawing learners' attention to the details of conventional expressions.

These results suggest that learners need more exposure to reduced forms and to the grammar details of conventional expressions. Also, although learners generally distinguished between conventional expressions and modified expressions, lower level learners did not differentiate between the two in some cases. This assessment was helpful in pinpointing the forms that teachers might want to focus on. As an added benefit, students reported liking the task (and the corresponding oral production task).

Conventional Expressions

As mentioned, the listening task presented here enables teachers to assess the extent to which learners are familiar with conventional expressions as opposed to grammatically correct but uncommon alternatives. Conventional expressions in pragmatics include conversational contributions such as *Nice to meet you*, as opposed to *I am very happy to meet you* in introductions; *You too* in response to *Have a nice day* in reciprocal closings, as opposed to, for instance, *You also*; and *No problem* used as a minimizer in response to expressions of gratitude, as opposed to *It is no problem*. Note that these conventional expressions are sometimes referred to as *formulas*, but because doing so makes a particular claim about how they are learned or stored, I use the neutral term *conventional expressions*. (True formulas are usually understood to be stored in and retrieved from the mental lexicon in their entirety, as a lexical whole, just as a word is stored).

For teaching, as for research, it is helpful to distinguish between the psycholinguistic and sociolinguistic characteristics of conventional speech. It is common to see the term *formula* used in two ways: acquisitional and social (Bardovi-Harlig, 2006). Acquisitional formulas are those that arise spontaneously during the early stages of acquisition and are generally not analyzable by the interlanguage grammar (thus the claim that they are stored whole). Teachers will recognize acquisitional formulas in learner language by a learner's repeated use of an expression that is generally above the level of his or her grammatical competence; these are also often nonhesitant and more fluent than the talk in which they occur. For example, Schmidt (1983) described a learner who showed no subject–verb agreement in novel questions such as *You has keys?* and *When Tim is coming?* except in repeated routine utterances such as *Are you busy?* and *Do you have time?*

On the other hand, social formulas (the subgroup or subset of formulas referred to as *conventional expressions*) may or may not be stored whole by native speakers. They are shared by a community and are used in specific social or discourse contexts. These are the expressions that may be targets of instruction in second or foreign language classrooms. Researchers report that these expressions are often learned late and that mastery may be characteristic of highly advanced learners (House, 1996; Scarcella, 1979; Yorio, 1989). For example, Scarcella reports the use of *Watch up!* for *Watch out!, Shut off!* for *Shut up!,* and *Time is off* for *Time is up.*

The social usefulness of these expressions, along with the fact that at least some of them may be learned late, suggests that classroom instruction in this area of language use might be particularly helpful to learners wishing to improve their conversational and pragmatic skills. This is the type of expression addressed in this chapter.

Assessing Students' Knowledge of Conventional Expressions

Taking an inventory of conventional expressions, whether at the individual or class level, is a basic step in planning instruction. This can be accomplished by a listening-based assessment task. Once the teacher has a profile of a learner or a class, he or she can determine whether learners need the following:

- an introduction to expressions with which they are unfamiliar

- clarification of the meaning of expressions with which they are already familiar

- examples of distribution and use of such expressions (see, e.g., Bardovi-Harlig & Mahan-Taylor, 2003)

Learners may also benefit from activities that allow them to develop easy and rapid access to expressions they recognize.

Conventional Versus Modified Expressions

The task presented in this chapter consists of conventional and modified expressions. Examples of conventional expressions and their modified counterparts include *Be quiet/Be silent, Excuse me/You excuse me,* and *I'm just looking/I'm just seeing.* Table 1 contrasts the characteristics of conventional expressions and modified expressions.

The conventional expressions were identified through observation of spontaneous conversations at the university, followed by development of discourse completion task scenarios to formally test the degree to which the expressions were used in the native-speaker community.

The remaining sections of this chapter present the task and then provide steps for developing a similar task suited to different settings and purposes.

Table 1. Characteristics of Conventional and Modified Expressions

Conventional Expressions	Modified Expressions
• Phrases that occur authentically in specific contexts • Phrases that are recognized as words that go together • Phrases used frequently and predictably in conversation, on radio, on television, or in films or interviews *Note:* All expressions are grammatical.	• Phrases that the teacher creates from conventional expressions; formed by changing the grammar or one word (using synonyms or near-synonyms if possible) of a conventional expression or by substituting full forms for more common reduced forms • Phrases that are not recognized as words that go together • Phrases that are not used predictably in conversation or media *Note:* All modified expressions are grammatical (although they may sound awkward).

CURRICULUM, TASKS, MATERIALS

This section includes directions for administering the task and instructions for teachers on how to construct a similar task to assess learners' ability to recognize conventional expressions using expressions appropriate to their own classes.

Activity 1: Assessing Learner Familiarity With Conventional Expressions

The goal of a listening assessment task of this sort is to determine which conventional expressions should be taught before students attempt other activities such as those presented in this volume. As a listening-based assessment task, it is extremely flexible in terms of content and delivery. In this activity, learners report recognition by thinking about how often they hear a string of words together and in the same order.

The full 60-item recognition task should take about 12 minutes to administer. The expressions are listed in Table 2 (on p. 13). The teacher may read these or access the audio at www.tesolmedia.com/books/pragmatics2.

A list of which expressions in Table 2 are conventional and which are modified can be found in Appendix A, which serves as an answer key.

The teacher administering this task begins by playing the audio file or reading aloud the instructions on the Student Answer Sheet (see Worksheet in Appendix B). The teacher reads each number clearly and carefully, repeating the corresponding expression twice, with 7 seconds between each. The general instructions and two examples of how to circle the answer are printed on the answer key. The audio file talks students through the sample responses. Teachers who are reading aloud may want to introduce the examples with the instructions from the audio file, reproduced here:

Let's begin.

You will hear each expression twice. Let's do two examples.

Example A: "Good morning. [7-second pause] Good morning."

You would circle "I often hear this."

Example B: "Bad morning. [7-second pause] Bad morning."

You would circle "I never hear this."

The teacher can then collect the answer sheets to see which terms are problematic. Note that there are no right or wrong answers. All of the expressions are grammatical, but some are much more natural and idiomatic (i.e., conventional) than others. However, even among conventional expressions, not all are heard as frequently as others. For native-speaker ratings of conventional expressions, see Appendix C. For guidelines on how to assess the students' performance, see Appendix D.

Activity 2: Customizing the Conventional Expression Task

Many teachers may want to use only a subset of the expressions in Table 2. Or they may eventually decide to create their own tasks with expressions that are common in their communities or that the students in their classes misuse or have difficulty forming. This is a relatively easy assessment task to construct and an especially easy one to deliver.

This section includes guidelines for teachers to use in setting up their own tasks. Even teachers who wish to add only a few expressions can profit from the steps listed here.

Step 1: Identify the Instructional Goal

To start, the teacher needs to identify the instructional goal. The 60-item task shown previously was designed as a broad survey. It could certainly be shorter, and it could easily be aimed at particular speech acts or other conversational functions such as expressions of gratitude, responses, rejections, greetings, and offers of or requests for advice. (See the functions in the list in Appendix A.)

Step 2: Select the Conventional Expressions

The teacher then composes a list of conventional expressions taken from real spoken language use, including conversation, films, videos, interviews, news broadcasts, or any other source of spoken language that is relevant to the students. Expressions should be authentic for the teacher's particular setting. These can be collected by listening in on conversations, by recording, or by having native speakers participate in role-plays. The expressions used should be those produced by speakers close to the age of the students. Native-speaker teachers and peers often behave differently from each other in recognition and production tasks, so age seems to be important (Bardovi-Harlig, 2010; Bardovi-Harlig et al., 2010).

Table 2. Expressions Used in the Listening Task

Recording	Formula	Recording	Formula
1	No, thanks	31	Watch up!
2	Shut up	32	I'm looking for
3	That works for me	33	Nice to see you
4	Sure thing	34	Could you like to?
5	Could you mind?	35	No problem
6	I thank you for your time	36	Would you mind?
7	I'd love to	37	I'm just looking
8	Excuse the mess	38	Excuse me
9	I gotta go	39	Can I get a drive?
10	Can I get a ride?	40	Thank you
11	My pad	41	Would you like to?
12	Keep it down	42	Be careful!
13	That'd be great	43	Other activities
14	Nice to meet you	44	Be quiet!
15	You also	45	I'm late
16	Want a ride?	46	Do you have a minute?
17	You are welcome	47	Be cautious!
18	Want a drive?	48	I'm tardy
19	I'm just seeing	49	The place is messy
20	Nice to look at you	50	You too
21	I was wondering	51	Thank you for having me
22	Make it down	52	The place is untidy
23	Thanks for your time	53	Other plans
24	I gotta leave	54	Nice to introduce you
25	My place	55	No problems
26	Quiet up	56	Certain thing
27	Can I leave a message?	57	You excuse me
28	You're welcome	58	Be silent
29	Do you have an hour?	59	Excuse the dirt
30	I'm sorry	60	Watch out!

Note: Phonetically reduced forms were used by the native speakers and reproduced in the listening activity. Written forms are not presented to the learners. The nonstandard spelling in items 9 and 24 indicates pronunciation.

Step 3: Create the Modified Expressions

It is important to include modified items in order to encourage learners to pay careful attention to the expressions, to give learners an opportunity to reflect on how often they hear specific expressions, and to provide a means of interpreting learners' responses. Perhaps the easiest approach is to start with the list of conventional expressions and change one word or grammatical feature. All of the "nonconventional" expressions need to be grammatical. For example, a common request to talk to a teacher is *Do you have a minute?* This can be changed to *Do you have an hour? Minute* and *hour* are both common words, but the latter expression is not conventional. Another option is to use full and reduced pairs. On a related production task, learners shied away from reduced forms such as *Thanks,* using *Thank you* instead (Bardovi-Harlig et al., 2010). Learners also favored literal expressions such as *I'll call you later* in the same situation in which native speakers favored *I'll call you back.* Such pairs can help assess learners' familiarity with the less transparent, but conventional, expressions.

One American English expression that means "Don't worry about it" is *No problem.* This can be changed grammatically to *No problems,* which is not the conventional expression. (In contrast, consider *No worries,* which can be modified to *No worry,* which is not the conventional expression.) The right-hand column of the table in Appendix A gives the modified version of the conventional expression in the middle column. Note that despite the fact that expressions such as *Do you have an hour?* and *No problems* are not conventional, they are grammatical.

Ideally, learners should be able to identify the conventional expressions and reject the modified ones. Learners who report that they recognize all the expressions are not discriminating among the items. Without the modified items, it would appear that such learners were genuinely familiar with all the expressions.

Step 4: Record the Expressions

Once the list of conventional and modified expressions has been collected, they can be recorded. It is important to use the best recording equipment available. If the teacher is concerned about pronunciation, a colleague or other native speaker may help with the recording. On the recording, each expression should be said twice, with 7 seconds between each. In the recording, each expression is preceded by a number that is read clearly and carefully so that students can mark the correct item on the answer sheet.

Step 5: Prepare an Answer Sheet

The teacher can modify the model answer sheet in Appendix B to accommodate the number of items on the listening task.

In addition to giving teachers an idea of which expressions learners need to work on, this listening assessment also provides learners with an assessment of how much of the language around them they have been paying attention to and may encourage them to listen to language used outside of the classroom.

A numeric score for the group's reported recognition of conventional and modified expressions in the listening task, or for that of an individual, can be calculated using the steps in Appendix D.

REFLECTIONS

The two most important characteristics of this listening-based assessment task are the construction of the list of expressions, discussed here, and its aural delivery. This task can easily be adapted to other settings. In fact, it is necessary to modify the list of expressions to reflect the speech patterns of the relevant discourse communities. Regionally preferred greetings or leave-takings might be included, for example; similarly, expressions might be modified for age or setting. Young children will want different expressions than college students, who in turn want expressions different from those suited to older adults in a community-based program. For example, when my college-student daughters like a suggestion that I have made, they say, "Good call." Although this expression is current among a certain group of college students in speech to classmates, friends, and apparently family members (although I admit I still find it odd), this would not be appropriate for the business world. Expressions for children might include those related to play and turn-taking, such as *Can I have a turn?*, *It's my turn,* or *I want a turn.* Or they may need to respond to classroom management instructions or questions. Older adults may prefer more conservative expressions than college students would. For example, older native speakers I have taught reported hearing *Excuse the mess* or *The place is a mess,* and they used it in a production task to comment on an untidy apartment when an unexpected visitor shows up. College students, however, reported low scores for hearing these expressions and showed few uses of them. Similarly, *Can I leave a message?* was more popular among older native speakers than younger ones who most likely have cell phones and do not leave messages with other people, but leave them directly on voicemail. In response to an offer for more food, younger and older native speakers alike used *No, thanks, I'm full,* but they also used *No, thanks, I'm stuffed* with equal or greater frequency. I should point out that *I'm stuffed* is perfectly acceptable in American English and is not off-color, the way it is in Australian and British English. (This illustrates the importance of locally relevant expressions!)

Language taught for specific purposes such as medical settings, the travel industry, or science would all suggest different expressions. Instructors might want to consider that some forms should be in the learners' recognized inventories, which might be broader than their productive knowledge. For example, this assessment includes *Be quiet, Shut up,* and *Keep it down.* If *Be quiet* were used productively, *Keep it down* and *Shut up* might be candidates for recognition and comprehension.

If a teacher knows that his or her students typically use a variant of an authentic expression, both the variation and the target expression should be included on the task to provide an opportunity to compare and discuss both.

The format of this task can be modified for different settings in multiple ways. The original listening task was recorded digitally and delivered in a language lab via individual headsets connected to computers. In settings with good technical support, the MP3 files can be made downloadable to students' own computers or MP3 players for self-study. In settings with less technical support, the expressions may be recorded on a cassette or CD and played to the whole class. For greatest spontaneity, and in teaching situations without access to recording equipment, teachers can read the expressions aloud, thus varying the assessment as needed prior to a new instructional unit. The response sheet, as described earlier, is a paper-and-pencil format.

Two caveats to task development of this type based on my experience with previous task designs need to be taken into account: The identification task must be delivered orally and a binary judgment task (with only two, rather than three, responses to circle) is not sufficient (Bardovi-Harlig, 2008). When a previous task was presented in written form, students reported much higher recognition scores than when they listened to the expressions. This may be due to the fact that written words are easier to recognize; it may also be that the binary choice (which asked learners to circle all the expressions they knew or recognized) did not promote reflection. Because the expressions used in this task are all part of conversation, and their presence in input would be aural, it is important that the assessment be in the same mode. By the same token, expressions used for letter writing, applications, or email correspondence should be investigated in writing.

ACKNOWLEDGMENTS

Thanks to Tara Zahler, Suzanne Valade, Daniel Thoms, Alexandra Harlig, and Levi King for recording the audio files for this chapter. Also thanks to Lucinda Miller, at the Center for Language Technology and Instructional Enrichment, Indiana University, for audio editing.

Kathleen Bardovi-Harlig is professor of second language studies at Indiana University, in the United States, where she teaches and does research on second language pragmatics. Her work on the teaching and learning of pragmatics has appeared in TESOL Quarterly, ELT Journal, Pragmatics and Language Learning, *and* Language Learning.

APPENDIX A: LIST OF CONVENTIONAL AND MODIFIED EXPRESSIONS

Pragmatic Function	Conventional Expression	Modified Expression
Introduction	Nice to meet you	Nice to introduce you
Agreement (to perform an act)	Sure thing	Certain thing
Agreement (to perform an act) Response to thanks	No problem	No problems
Request	Would you mind?	Could you mind?
Apology	Excuse the mess	Excuse the dirt
Leave-taking	I gotta go	I gotta leave
Request	Can I get a ride?	Can I get a drive?
Greeting	Nice to see you	Nice to look at you
Warning	Be careful!	Be cautious!
Directive	Keep it down	Make it down
Account	I'm just looking	I'm just seeing
Alerter or apology	Excuse me	You excuse me
Directive	Be quiet!	Be silent!
Account	The place is a mess	The place is untidy
Thanks	Thanks for your time	I thank you for your time
Refusal (of an invitation)	Other plans	Other activities
Invitation	My place	My pad
Warning	Watch out!	Watch up!
Refusal of offer	No, thanks	No, please
Response to thanks	You're welcome	You are welcome
Explanation (apology)	I'm late	I'm tardy
Invitation, offer	Would you like to?	Could you like to?
Prerequest	Do you have a minute?	Do you have an hour?
Request	Can I leave a message?	Can I leave a note?
Response (farewell)	You too	You also

Note: The functions listed here are not exhaustive; the expressions can be used for other purposes.

APPENDIX B: WORKSHEET: STUDENT ANSWER SHEET

Conventional Expressions: Listening Exercise

You will hear some English words and phrases. We want to know how often you hear them. There is no right answer. If you hear these words together and always in the same order, and you hear them often, circle "I often hear this." If you hear a phrase less often, circle "I sometimes hear this." If you never hear these words together or in this order, circle "I never hear this."

Example A: Good morning

(I often hear this)   I sometimes hear this   I never hear this

Example B: Bad morning

I often hear this   I sometimes hear this   (I never hear this)

1. I often hear this   I sometimes hear this   I never hear this

2. I often hear this   I sometimes hear this   I never hear this

3. I often hear this   I sometimes hear this   I never hear this

4. I often hear this   I sometimes hear this   I never hear this

5. I often hear this   I sometimes hear this   I never hear this

6. I often hear this   I sometimes hear this   I never hear this

7. I often hear this   I sometimes hear this   I never hear this

8. I often hear this   I sometimes hear this   I never hear this

9. I often hear this   I sometimes hear this   I never hear this

10. I often hear this   I sometimes hear this   I never hear this

11. I often hear this   I sometimes hear this   I never hear this

12. I often hear this   I sometimes hear this   I never hear this

13. I often hear this   I sometimes hear this   I never hear this

14. I often hear this   I sometimes hear this   I never hear this

15. I often hear this   I sometimes hear this   I never hear this

APPENDIX C: SELF-REPORTED RECOGNITION OF CONVENTIONAL EXPRESSIONS BY NATIVE-ENGLISH-SPEAKING PEERS AND TEACHERS

Expression	Native-English-Speaking Peers (N = 35)	Native-English-Speaking Teachers (N = 14)
No, thanks	2.00	2.00
Thank you	2.00	2.00
You're welcome	2.00	2.00
No problem	1.97	2.00
Excuse me	1.97	2.00
I'm sorry	1.94	2.00
That'd be great	1.91	1.93
Nice to meet you	1.91	1.93
Watch out!	1.91	1.93
I gotta go	1.89	1.93
Be careful!	1.89	1.86
You too	1.88	2.00
Shut up	1.86	1.54
I'm late	1.86	1.86
I'm just looking	1.80	2.00
I'd love to	1.80	2.00
I was wondering	1.80	1.71
Be quiet!	1.80	1.71
Want a ride?	1.77	1.93
Can I get a ride?	1.77	1.64
I'm looking for	1.74	1.57
Would you like to?	1.74	1.64
Thank you for having me	1.71	2.00
Do you have a minute?	1.71	2.00
Would you mind?	1.71	1.93
Can I leave a message?	1.66	2.00

Other plans	1.65	1.07
Thanks for your time	1.60	1.93
Nice to see you	1.54	2.00
That works for me	1.43	1.77
Sure thing	1.37	1.62
Keep it down	1.31	1.50
My place	1.29	1.64
You are welcome	1.20	0.79
The place is messy	1.11	1.36

Note: Reflects average based on the following scoring system: 2 points for "I often hear this"; 1 point for "I sometimes hear this"; 0 points for "I never hear this."

APPENDIX D: SCORING THE LISTENING ACTIVITY

The first thing to remember in scoring the task is that there are no right or wrong answers (so there is no absolute answer key). In this assessment activity, students report what they think they know so that teachers can better plan what conventional expressions to teach. If everyone recognizes an expression, it is likely that the students are ready to begin activities that help them use that expression in context. If not, then they will need input and perhaps explanations for unknown expressions. To evaluate learner responses, for each individual expression (whether it is conventional or modified!), give points as follows:

> 2 points for "I often hear this"
> 1 point for "I sometimes hear this"
> 0 points for "I never hear this"

Group Scores

Teachers can work with the scores in a number of ways. First, the assessment yields clear group profiles, which can be used to determine which expressions are familiar to the class and which need to be introduced prior to activities focusing on production or interpretation.

Calculating the group score for one expression. If the scores for an individual expression are totaled across learners and divided by the number of learners, this results in a class score for an individual expression. For example, in a class of 35 students, if 31 report that they often hear the expression *No, thanks* and 4 report that they sometimes hear it, multiply 2 x 31 (2 points for each "often hear" response) and add it to 1 x 4 (1 point for each "sometimes hear" response). The class total is (31 x 2) + (4 x 1) = 66. This total is divided by the number of students, which results in a class familiarity score of 1.83 (66/35) for *No, thanks.*

If all of the students report that they often hear an expression, the class score is 2.00. For example, low-intermediate-level students in one of my classes all reported recognizing *Thank you, Excuse me, I'm sorry,* and *Nice to meet you* (resulting in scores of 2.00). The low-advanced-level students also all reported often hearing *No problem, You're welcome,* and *I'm looking for* (again resulting in scores of 2.00).

Use of group scores. Group scores can be used by instructors to determine what types of input would be warranted for the development of subsequent materials and tasks for whole-class instruction and activities (see, e.g., chapter 3 in this volume). Level does make a difference. As the learners become more advanced, they recognize progressively more authentic expressions and are able to report that they don't hear the modified ones.

Interpreting group scores. Teachers can develop their own interpretation of the class scores. The following table gives one possible interpretation of the scores described in this section.

	2.00–1.60	1.59–1.00	.99–.00
Examples	*Nice to meet you* *I'm sorry* *I gotta go*	*That'd be great* *Shut up* *I'd love to*	*Excuse the mess* *Watch out!* *Thanks for having me*
Interpretation	Most students report knowing the expression. The teacher begins to work on context and distribution.	The teacher decides whether class review is warranted. Individual scores can be assessed.	Students may need input to help them recognize the expression.

Individual scores

The assessment also yields interesting individual profiles, which can be utilized in tutoring, self-study, or strategy training.

Calculating individual scores. An individual score is obtained by adding a student's rating for each of the items on the task. For example, in a test with 60 items, if a student rates 29 expressions as "often heard" (29 x 2 = 58), 22 expressions as "sometimes heard" (22 x 1 = 22), and 9 expressions as "never heard" (9 x 0 = 0), he or she has a total score of 80 points (58 + 22 + 0). Students will have a range of scores.

Interpreting individual scores. The original task also tested native speakers of American English to ascertain what typical scores might be. The majority of the student scores fell between 52 and 91, and the majority of the native-speaker peer scores fell between 55 and 86. Native-speaker teachers had a narrower range, between 59 and 76. For individual scores, teachers will want to concentrate on students reporting very high scores and those reporting very low scores.

Very high scores, 90–120 (on a 60-item test), suggest that students are not discriminating among conventional and modified expressions. (Remember that some modified expressions will receive a score of 1, whereas others will receive a score of 0.) In other words, students who accept everything seem less aware than other students about how often they encounter expressions. They might need more guidance than students who recognize patterns in input on their own.

Students with very low scores, 0–45 (on a 60-item test), report that they recognize very few expressions. They may have poor general listening skills, but they might also be particularly low risk takers. Individually, they might be coached to be more courageous. These students could be given expressions in class and then asked to listen for them, first in prerecorded materials and then subsequently in spontaneous conversation.

CHAPTER 3

No, Thanks. I'm Full! Raising Awareness of Expressions of Gratitude and Conventional Expressions

Kathleen Bardovi-Harlig and Edelmira L. Nickels

This chapter presents a series of activities geared toward helping students increase their comfort and facility with thanking expressions. Recent research into the use of conventional expressions by learners of English as a second language has shown noticeable differences between them and native speakers even in such simple expressions as *Thank you* and *Thanks* (Bardovi-Harlig et al., 2010). Although even advanced-level nonnative speakers can benefit from a unit on expressions of gratitude, the simplicity of the *Thank you* construction, along with its utility, makes this act a particularly good one to introduce to relatively low-level learners because little grammatical development is needed for comprehension or production of the basic expressions.

CONTEXT

Both the research guiding the present lesson and the lesson itself were conducted at the Intensive English Program at Indiana University, in the United States. The program focuses on academic language skills that prepare learners for undergraduate and graduate coursework at U.S. institutions of higher education and has a student body aged 18 and up from several countries and native language backgrounds.

The research was conducted with the voluntary participation of teachers and students from low-intermediate through low-advanced levels in classrooms with students of different language backgrounds. It also included the participation of native-English-speaking undergraduate students at the same university. The research instruments included a listening-based recognition task (see chapter 2 in this volume) and an oral production task (the results of which contributed to the exercises in this chapter). The oral production task consisted of an oral, computer-delivered adaptation of a discourse completion task. Participants listened to and read scenarios (presented simultaneously in oral and written form on a computer screen), followed by an exclusively aural conversational turn to which they responded by speaking into a headset with a microphone.

The instruments were adapted for pedagogical purposes, and the present lesson was created and successfully employed in low- and high-intermediate classes. The lesson was quite well received. Learners were told that the responses came from research conducted with native speakers in the area, and the answers were discussed in light of this information. Students reported feeling like they "finally got straight answers about what to say," as one student put it. At the end, we had many requests for additional lessons on other speech acts.

This type of task fills a need for easily adaptable (teacher-friendly) activities that can be incorporated into existing curricula in skill-based classes (like our program's communication classes). The activities can be adapted for instruction in other speech acts and can be used in second as well as foreign language settings.

Expressions of Gratitude

Expressions of gratitude, or thanking, are speech acts that state appreciation for an action or the result of an action that benefits the speaker (Coulmas, 1981). In so doing, they establish and maintain a polite and friendly social atmosphere (Leech, 1983; Searle, 1969) and engender feelings of warmth and solidarity (Eisenstein & Bodman, 1993). In addition, they can serve other functions, such as the following:

- complimenting—*Thanks for the great party.*

- signaling the end of a service encounter—*Thank you, and have a nice day!*

- signaling the end of a presentation—*Thank you.*

Furthermore, expressions of gratitude are frequently accompanied by phrases that fulfill additional functions for the speaker (Eisenstein & Bodman, 1986), such as the following, in which the boldfaced phrases perform the additional functions:

- complimenting—*Oh, **that's great**. Thanks a lot./**You're wonderful**. Thank you./Thanks a bunch. **You're a lifesaver**.* (usually after receiving a highly appreciated favor from the hearer)

- reassuring (on receipt of a gift)—*Thanks. **Just what I needed. And blue's my favorite color**./Oh, **you know me so well**. Thanks, I love it!*

- expressing surprise/delight—***Oh, wow!*** *Thank you so much!/Gee, thanks./**Oh great!** I really appreciate that.*

- expressing lack of necessity/obligation—*Oh, that's so sweet.* ***You didn't have to do that***. (after hearer performs a considerate act) *Thank you very much./ Thank you. It's lovely, **but you didn't have to get me anything**.* (after hearer presents an unexpected gift)

- expressing indebtedness—*You're a lifesaver. Thanks. **I'll never forget it. You really can't imagine what this means to me**.* (typically after hearer performs a service that involved some inconvenience)

- promising to repay/reciprocate—*Thanks.* ***Next time I'll treat you.***/*Thanks for the lunch.* ***I'll take you out next week***. (especially after hearer pays for a meal)

Expressions of gratitude have high social value and occur frequently among native speakers of American English in a wide range of interpersonal relations. The way native English speakers express gratitude can vary in length (from simple, phatic utterances to lengthy communicative events; cf. Eisenstein & Bodman, 1986, 1993), but native speakers have been found to draw from a finite pool of conventionalized expressions (Eisenstein & Bodman, 1993), illustrated in the first four examples in the previous list, in which the core thanking expressions are *Thanks* and *Thank you*, which may occur with modification such as *Thanks so much* or *Thank you so much*.

Conventional Expressions

Many studies of learners' production in the area of second language pragmatics have shown that learners may differ from native speakers in the same context along four lines: choice of speech act, semantic formulas, content, and form (Bardovi-Harlig, 2001). This chapter addresses three of those areas:

- speech acts in a specific context (some learners use apologies where native speakers of English use thanking)

- semantic formulas that accompany the thanking components (what else we say after we say *Thanks*)

- linguistic forms (learners invariably seem to prefer full forms such as *Thank you*, whereas native speakers show more variety)

In initial work on teaching pragmatics, the focus was on providing learners with information that would enable them to make their own decisions about how target-like to be (Bardovi-Harlig, Hartford, Mahan-Taylor, Morgan, & Reynolds, 1991). More recently, however, we have studied learner production of conventional expressions (Bardovi-Harlig et al., 2010), formulas that are shared by a community and are used in specific discourse contexts (see chapter 1 in this volume for a discussion of conventional expressions). This study and other reports show that conventional expressions are often not mastered by learners until they are at quite advanced levels (Eisenstein & Bodman, 1993). Thus, our emphasis has shifted to include the forms that a speech act takes. Previously, if a student said "Thank you" in a thanking context, it was considered adequate. However, our research suggests that instruction in conventional expressions may be warranted. This conclusion was influenced by specific findings related to thanking expressions, including the following:

- Learners prefer full forms such as *Thank you*, but native speakers show variety in their thanking expressions (Bardovi-Harlig et al., 2010).

- Learners frequently do not use the short form *Thanks* (Bardovi-Harlig et al., 2010).

- Learners use intensifiers less often than native speakers do, and when they do, they often use different ones; where a native speaker might say, "Thank you so much," learners may say, "Thank you very much" (Bardovi-Harlig et al., 2010).

- Textbooks do not provide examples of *Thank you for* constructions (Schauer & Adolphs, 2006).

More general findings on the learning of expressions, including the following, support the need to focus on conventional expressions (Bardovi-Harlig et al., 2010):

- Mastery of target-language conventional expressions takes time and is not automatic.

- Practice with production is necessary because learners may report that they recognize an expression, but do not demonstrate production of that very expression when given the opportunity.

- Teachers and university students (native-speaker peers to our English language learners) do not always use the same conventional expressions as each other in the same situations, so observation of target groups is important.

Although learners have a demonstrated need to focus on the form of these conventional expressions, giving learners a list of formulas alone reduces instruction to handing out vocabulary lists. On the other hand, giving them the opportunity to observe, analyze, recognize, and then produce contextually appropriate language fosters awareness of the subtleties that can be communicated through conventional expressions and encourages learners to pay closer attention to how language is used around them. Even when input containing expressions of gratitude is readily available, learners may not be aware of the wide array of contexts in which these expressions can be used (e.g., in conjunction with other speech acts, such as refusing).

The set of activities included in this chapter can be used at two levels. The activities will help develop better recognition and comprehension of a range of thanking expressions while also providing models for production of thanking expressions for students who are interested in sounding more native-like.

CURRICULUM, TASKS, MATERIALS

This section presents a three-part lesson that, taken as a whole, is designed to help students achieve the overarching goals of identifying thanking scenarios; increasing their own ranges of thanking expressions, including reduced forms; and increasing the use of thanking expressions in appropriate contexts. Each activity states specific objectives and has three phases: presentation, recognition, and production, with one main activity for each. This lesson can take one or two class meetings, depending on the level of proficiency of the class.

Activity 1: Raising Awareness of Expressions of Gratitude and Conventional Expressions

This activity introduces the topic of expressions of gratitude and the conventional expressions associated with them. Learners listen to examples that use expressions of gratitude in different situations (e.g., *Thanks for having me; No thanks, I'm stuffed*) and answer the questions on Worksheet 1 (see Appendix A) to promote discussion on different ways to express gratitude. Audio files are available at www.tesolmedia.com/books/pragmatics2. However, if access to the audio file or a teacher-prepared prerecording of the exchanges is not possible, the teacher can either read the exchanges aloud to the class or have two students enact the exchanges for their peers (see Appendix B for transcripts).

The excerpts in Part 1 of Activity 1 seem to suffice as an introduction to expressions of gratitude with learners at the low-intermediate level. However, more examples may be necessary or helpful (see Part 2), and the teacher may want to spend more time discussing Excerpts 3 and 4.

Activity 2: Recognizing Contexts for Expressions of Gratitude

This recognition activity allows learners to explore other scenarios that employ expressions of gratitude. Worksheet 2 (see Appendix A) is a matching activity in which learners complete a chart by matching each situation to an expression of gratitude and by explaining the reasons for their choices (e.g., adding adverbs, intensifiers, or other contextually appropriate phrases such as *The reception was lovely* in #5, or *You're the best!* in #2, but not a simple *No* in #7). The teacher may want to ask for volunteers to read each situation in Column A aloud to the class. Then the class can repeat after the teacher the expressions in Column B. Students should have the opportunity to clarify any unfamiliar words or phrases.

Activity 3: Producing Expressions of Gratitude in Various Contexts

Activity 3 allows learners to listen and respond to scenarios in which expressions of gratitude may be used. Learners respond in real time and demonstrate control over the use of expressions of gratitude. Practice with production is necessary because learners report that they recognize expressions, but they do not use them when given the opportunity.

Two versions of Activity 3 are provided: pair work and language lab.

Pair-Work Version

In this part of the lesson, students apply what they learned from the discussion in Activity 2 and respond to a variety of situations. Each pair of students has a copy of Worksheet 3a (see Appendix A). The teacher may want to ask for volunteers to read each situation in Columns A and B, and explain any unfamiliar words.

Language Lab Version

In this alternative version of Activity 3, students receive a copy of Worksheet 3b (see Appendix A). In the lab version, students listen to a recording of the initiating turn and immediately record a response expressing gratitude. The teacher can access the audio file at www.tesolmedia.com/books/pragmatics2. If it is not possible to access the TESOL site, the teacher may prerecord the activity or read the script aloud. (A transcript of the audio file is available for Appendix C at www.tesolmedia.com/books/pragmatics2 and may be used as a script if necessary.) In this case, the teacher plays the role of the initiating speaker, and the student responds, recording his or her answer for later review.

Although learners who have used the language lab to record their responses to Activity 3 are enthusiastic about the activity, it is a challenge for the teacher to provide feedback on all the recordings. An optional follow-up activity in which students transcribe their own recordings is a practical way to overcome this challenge. Furthermore, having learners transcribe their own speech gives them the opportunity to reflect on their growing language skills from a different perspective, while also being able to obtain feedback from others.

After recording their responses to the production activity, learners choose three scenarios, transcribe them, and write out alternative ways they could have responded or expanded the responses they used. Students can share their work with classmates, listen carefully to their feedback, and then comment on their classmates' responses.

REFLECTIONS

The use of research results in activities that incorporate an awareness of language variation, which results in a lesson that benefits learners and that they report finding valuable (cf. Schauer & Adolphs, 2006, on teaching British English expressions of gratitude; Bodman & Eisenstein, 1988; Eisenstein & Bodman, 1986).

Because English is taught in many contexts, we have suggested alternative ways of delivering the lesson in this chapter. In addition to these, more elaborate modifications for English for specific purposes, elementary school, or other contexts are also possible. The lesson can be modified by adding to the list of thanking situations presented here. Sometimes television situation comedies (sitcoms) provide examples of what not to do, which students could then correct. New situations can be taken from sitcoms or movies with characters that resemble the target student population. For instance, in a context where English is taught for medical purposes, the sitcom *Scrubs* can be used as a source, because thanking expressions (among other speech acts) abound (the show is available on DVD; episode scripts are available on various websites). The teacher can select scenes with the target expressions and have students view and discuss them (following the format in Activity 1). These can be transcribed and used in the formats presented in Activities 2 and 3.

Teachers working in elementary school contexts will recognize that children in elementary school are often still working on learning to say "Thank you" in their first language. (Many readers remember parental or teacherly prompts of "What do you say?") Children may enjoy advising imaginary characters, helping them remember to say "Thank you" in a variety of situations. They may also enjoy working with puppets that find themselves in various situations. Everyday and special events can be included in the situations, such as going to birthday parties and receiving birthday presents or treats at school, receiving or sharing supplies, sharing toys, or getting help from a teacher or another student. Television shows that focus on children can be used as sources of examples or settings. Students can view scenes with target expressions, and teachers can lead a discussion of the scenes at a level that is appropriate for the students.

The instructional techniques suggested here could also be used with other speech acts or language functions.

Although the formulaic language presented in these exercises was chosen because it dominated in the responses we collected from native speakers, the native speakers who participated in the research were from the midwestern United States, and responses may very well vary in other dialectal regions. Learners need to be reminded that, even though conventional expressions abound, they also vary. The benefit of raising awareness of conventional expressions is that these expressions can help learners convey and comprehend ways of being that are succinct and appropriate in certain situations.

ACKNOWLEDGMENTS

Thanks to Tara Zahler, Suzanne Valade, Daniel Thoms, Alexandra Harlig, and Levi King for recording the audio files for this chapter. Also thanks to Lucinda Miller, at the Center for Language Technology and Instructional Enrichment, Indiana University, for audio editing.

Kathleen Bardovi-Harlig is professor of second language studies at Indiana University, in the United States, where she teaches and does research on second language pragmatics. Her work on the teaching and learning of pragmatics has appeared in TESOL Quarterly, ELT Journal, Pragmatics and Language Learning, *and* Language Learning.

Edelmira L. Nickels is a doctoral candidate in the Department of Second Language Studies at Indiana University, in the United States. She is currently researching conceptual metaphors of cultural and political identity in Puerto Rican political discourse in the U.S. Congress. She has taught career military and civilian learners in Puerto Rico and the United States.

APPENDIX A: WORKSHEETS AND ANSWER KEYS

Worksheet 1: Becoming Familiar With Thanking Expressions

Part 1

In this part of the lesson you will listen to two excerpts (Excerpt 1 and 2) of situations that require an expression of gratitude (or thanking). Sometimes the expression of gratitude is all that is needed for an appropriate response. This is not always the case.

1. Listen carefully to each situation and its response.

2. Discuss the following questions in small groups:

   a. How were the examples similar or different? (Hint: Consider things like the relationships between the speakers, why the expression of gratitude is used, and where the speakers are.)

   b. Notice the use of the short form *Thanks*.

   c. Why do you think that a simple *Thanks* was all that was needed in Excerpt 1? Consider who the speakers are, what they are talking about, and where they are speaking.

   d. Why do you think that the speaker said more than a simple *Thanks* in Excerpt 2? Consider who the speakers are and what they are doing.

3. Compare your group's answers with those of the rest of the class. Did everyone notice the same things about the two excerpts? Does the class agree on the reasons why Excerpt 2 is longer?

Part 2

You will hear two additional excerpts (Excerpt 3 and 4) of situations that require expressions of gratitude. Listen carefully to each situation and its response, and take notes. Then answer the following questions:

    a.   How are the situations different/similar?

    b.   How are the responses different/similar?

    c.   Why did the speaker say more in Excerpt 3?

    d.   Why didn't the speaker in Excerpt 4 have to say more?

Worksheet 1: Sample Answers

Part 1

    a.   Similarities: The speakers are friends. The examples involve offers. They are everyday happenings.

    b.   Differences: The offer in Excerpt 1 is accepted, but the offer in Excerpt 2 is refused. Excerpt 1 takes place in class, but Excerpt 2 takes place at the friend's house.

    c.   *Thanks* is enough because the speakers are friends, and what was offered was just a pen (something of little value). Also, the students are supposed to be taking a test and talking is not allowed, so they needed to be brief. The speakers are friends, and they don't need to give a long explanation.

    d.   Even though they are friends, the speaker said more because he or she didn't want the friend (the host) to think that he or she didn't like the food; despite their friendship he or she still needs to give some reason for refusing the offer. The speaker likes his or her friend and doesn't want the friend to feel bad.

Part 2

    a.   Similarities: The speakers in both examples have the same relationship: teacher–student. In both examples, the student is the one thanking the teacher. They are everyday happenings.

    b.   Differences: Excerpt 3 involves a request, but Excerpt 4 is part of the leave-taking. In Excerpt 3, the speaker also included a promise, but in Excerpt 4 there was no promise.

    c.   The speaker offered a promise never to do it again because he understands that he was breaking the rules and wanted to reassure the teacher that it would not be his normal behavior.

    d.   The speaker understood that the professor was very busy and did not want to take up more of her time than was necessary.

Worksheet 2: Producing Appropriate Thanking Expressions in Context

Ask the teacher about any unfamiliar words or spellings. Then work in small groups (or pairs).

1. Match each situation in Column A with one or more of the responses from Column B. Add anything you think is necessary.

2. Write the group's response in the space after YOU SAY (in Column A).

3. In Column C, explain why each of your responses is appropriate.

Column A	Column B	Column C
1. You're in your apartment talking with your roommate. You mention that you need to pick up a book at the bookstore, but you don't have any free time today. Roommate: *I can pick it up for you.* YOU SAY:	a. Thanks b. Thank you	
2. It's raining really hard and you don't want to walk. A friend pulls his car over to offer you a ride. Friend: *Hey, want a ride?* YOU SAY:	c. Thanks so much	
3. You need to go to a store all the way on the other side of town. Friend: *I can take you.* YOU SAY:	d. Thank you so much	
4. Yesterday, you were sick and didn't go to classes. This morning you asked a friend for her or his class notes. Friend: *Sure thing. Here they are.* YOU SAY:	e. Thanks a lot f. That'd be great	
5. There is a reception on campus. The organizer invited you and a few other students. It is getting late, and you decide to leave. You go over to the organizer. Organizer: *Thanks for coming!* YOU SAY:	g. …for having us! h. You too	
6. You are in the supermarket. After paying, you pick up your bags, and you are ready to leave the cashier's counter. Cashier: *Have a nice day!* YOU SAY:	i. I'm just looking	
7. You go to a clothing store to find a new shirt. A salesperson approaches you. You don't want the salesperson's assistance. Salesperson: *Can I help you?* YOU SAY:	j. Sure k. No	

Worksheet 2: Answer Key

The following are common, accepted responses. Other thanking responses are possible.

1. Three possible answers: a + f (Thanks. That'd be great.), a (Thanks.), or f (That'd be great.)

   Explanation: This would be a good response because it is a nice offer that will save the speaker time, but it is not a big imposition because the roommate is already going to the bookstore (even if she or he doesn't pick up the book for the speaker).

2. Four possible answers: f (That'd be great), j + a (Sure, thanks!), c (Thanks so much.), or d (Thank you so much.)

   (In native-speaker peer responses, *so much* is preferred to *very much*.)

   Explanation: This would be a good response because it wasn't a request by the speaker; it was an offer from the friend. Also, it is raining really hard and immediate action is preferable to a long expression of gratitude.

3. Three possible answers: f + a (That'd be great! Thanks.), a (Thanks.), or b (Thank you.)

   Explanation: This would be a good response because it wasn't a request by the speaker; it was an offer from the friend. Also, it sounds like they are very good friends, and the emphasis placed on the response can communicate great gratitude.

4. Two possible answers: a (Thanks.) or c (Thanks so much.)

   Explanation: This would be a good response because getting sick is a common happening in school and getting notes from a classmate would be the responsible thing to do. The speaker is talking to a friend who would easily understand the situation.

5. One possible answer: a + g (Thanks for having us!)

   (Native speakers also use *Thanks for inviting us!*)

   Explanation: This would be a good response because it shows gratitude for the invitation. It is also fairly brief, which would make it appropriate for leave-taking. (It is the preferred formulaic response for the situation.)

6. Two possible answers: a + h (Thanks! You too!) or e (Thanks a lot!)

   (Native speakers also use *Have a good day!*)

   Explanation: This would be a good response because it is a brief expression of gratitude adequate for the short exchange. It is really meant as a leave-taking move. (It is the preferred formulaic response for the situation.)

7. Three possible answers k + a + i (No, thanks. I'm just looking.), k + a (No, thanks.), or i (I'm just looking.)

   Explanation: This would be a good response because it is a brief expression of gratitude that works as a polite rejection of the offer for help. (It is the preferred formulaic response for the situation.)

Worksheet 3a: Producing Appropriate Thanking Expressions (Pair-Work Version)

Ask the teacher about any unfamiliar words or spellings. Work in pairs to complete this task.

1. Student A: Fold the worksheet so that you can only see the column marked *Student A.*

   Student B: Fold the worksheet so that you can only see the column marked *Student B.*

2. Student A: Read the first situation and initiation in the Student A column to your partner. Then, listen to his or her responses. Give him or her feedback: Do you agree with the responses? Is there anything you would have said differently?

   Student B: Imagine that you are talking to your friend and he or she speaks first. Listen carefully to Student A. When Student A finishes, respond to him or her. Say the first thing you think of. You have 10 seconds to respond.

   The sequence will proceed as follows: (1) A reads the situation; (2) B responds with an expression of gratitude for 10 seconds; (3) A gives B feedback on his or her performance.

3. Then B takes a turn and follows the same steps that A followed.

The first response is provided as an example.

Student A	Student B
Example A. Old Friend Situation (Student A reads): I see my old friend B at a party. I walk over to B and say: Friend (Student A): *Hi. How are you?* **Student B: _Fine, and you?_**	**Example B. Heavy Desk** Situation (Student B reads): I need some help moving a heavy old desk out of my dorm room. A is a friend of mine. I say: Friend (Student B): *Could you help me move this desk?* **Student A: _I'd be happy to!_**
1. Class Notes Situation: Yesterday, B was sick and didn't go to classes. This morning B asks me for my class notes and I say: Friend (Student A): *Sure thing. Here they are.* **Student B:**	**1. Rainy Day** Situation: It's raining really hard, and A doesn't want to walk. I pull my car over to offer A a ride. I say: Friend (Student B): *Hey, want a ride?* **Student A:**
2. Campus Reception Situation: There is a reception on campus, and I am the organizer. I invited B and a few other students as well. It is getting late, and B decides to leave. B comes over to me. I say: Organizer (Student A): *Thanks for coming!* **Student B:**	**2. Shopping Help** Situation: A goes to a clothing store and needs to find a new shirt. A doesn't want any assistance. I am a salesperson. I approach A and say: Salesperson (Student B): *Can I help you?* **Student A:**
3. More Food Situation: B and I are friends. B is having dinner at my house. B couldn't possibly eat another bite. I say: Friend (Student A): *Would you like some more?* **Student B:**	**3. Pen** Situation: Right before the final exam begins, A notices that she or he doesn't have anything to write with. I hand A a pen and say: Friend (Student B): *Here, use this.* **Student A:**
4. Makeup Test Situation: B has been studying very hard for a grammar test, but on the morning of the test B's alarm doesn't go off, and B oversleeps. I am B's teacher. B asks me for a makeup test. I say: Teacher (Student A): *OK, I'll give you a break this time, but don't let it happen again.* **Student B:**	**4. Friendly Cashier** Situation: A is in the supermarket. After paying, A picks up his or her bags and is ready to leave the counter. I am the cashier. I say: Cashier (Student B): *Have a nice day!* **Student A:**
5. Nice Apartment Situation: I am visiting B's apartment for the first time and I say: Friend (Student A): *Nice place!* **Student B:**	**5. Store Trip** Situation: A needs to go to a store all the way on the other side of town. I am A's friend. I say: Friend (Student B): *I can take you.* **Student A:**
6. Book Pickup Situation: B is in her or his apartment talking with me (I am B's roommate). B mentions that she or he needs to pick up a book at the bookstore, but B doesn't have any free time today. I say: Roommate (Student A): *I can pick it up for you.* **Student B:**	**6. Busy Professor** Situation: A stops by his or her professor's office to ask a question about an assignment. I am A's professor. A knows I am very busy, but I answer A's question in detail. When I finish, I say: Professor (Student B): *…and that's all you have to do.* **Student A:**

Worksheet 3a: Answer Key

The following are common acceptable responses. Other thanking expressions are possible.

Student A	Student B

1. Class Notes
    Thanks.
    Thanks so much.
    Thanks a lot.
	1. Rainy Day
	    Thanks/Thank you so much.
	    That'd be great/wonderful.
	    That would be great/wonderful.
	    Sure, thanks!

2. Campus Reception
    Thanks for having us!
    Thanks for inviting us!
	2. Shopping Help
	    No, thanks. I'm just looking.
	    No, thanks.
	    I'm just looking.

3. More Food
    No, thanks.
    No, thanks. I'm full/stuffed [U.S. only].
    Thank you, but I'm full/stuffed [U.S. only].
    I'm (adverb) full. (e.g., I'm so full)
	3. Pen
	    Thanks!

4. Makeup Test
    Thank you (adverb). + optional comment.
    (e.g., *I really appreciate it*; *It won't*)
	4. Friendly Cashier
	    (Thanks!) You too!
	    Thanks a lot!
	    Have a good day!

5. Nice Apartment
    Thanks! + optional comment (e.g., *We like it*;
    It's close to school)
	5. Store Trip
	    Thanks.
	    Thank you.

6. Book Pickup
    Thanks. That'd be great.
    Thanks.
    That'd be great.
	6. Busy Professor
	    Thanks for your time.

Worksheet 3b: Producing Appropriate Thanking Expressions (Language Lab Version)

Imagine that you are talking to your friend or teacher, and this person speaks first. Listen carefully. When the speaker finishes, respond to him or her. Say the first thing you think of. You have 10 seconds to respond.

Student Notes (with prompt)	Student Notes (without prompt)
1. Class Notes YOU SAY:	1. Rainy Day
2. Campus Reception YOU SAY:	2. Shopping Help
3. More Food YOU SAY:	3. Pen
4. Makeup Test YOU SAY:	4. Friendly Cashier
5. Nice Apartment YOU SAY:	5. Store Trip
6. Book Pickup YOU SAY:	6. Busy Professor

APPENDIX B: TRANSCRIPT FOR WORKSHEET 1 LISTENING EXERCISE

Excerpt 1: Accepting an Offer

Right before the final exam begins, you notice that you don't have anything to write with. A friend hands you a pen and says:

> Friend: *Here, use this.*
>
> You say: *Thanks!*

Excerpt 2: Refusing an Offer

You are having dinner at a friend's house. Your friend offers you more food, but you couldn't possibly eat another bite.

> Friend: *Would you like some more?*
>
> You say: *No, thanks. I'm full.*

Let's listen to this conversation again. In the United States, students also said *No, thanks. I'm stuffed*. This is not used in Australia and Britain.

Friend: *Would you like some more?*

You say: *No thanks. I'm stuffed.*

Excerpt 3: Request Granted

You have been studying very hard for your grammar test, but on the morning of the test your alarm doesn't go off, and you oversleep. You ask your teacher for a makeup test.

Teacher: *OK, I'll give you a break this time, but don't let it happen again.*

You say: *OK, thank you so much. I promise it won't happen again.*

Excerpt 4: Saying Goodbye With a Thank-You

You stop by your professor's office to ask a question about an assignment. You know she is very busy, but she answers your question in detail.

Professor: *. . . and that's all you have to do.*

You say: *Thank you (so much) for your time. (I really appreciate it.)*

APPENDIX C: TRANSCRIPT FOR WORKSHEET 3b (LANGUAGE LAB VERSION)

The teacher reads the following text, pausing for 10 seconds after each YOU SAY:

Imagine that you are talking to your friend or teacher, and he or she speaks first. Follow along with me. When I finish speaking and you hear "YOU SAY," you respond. Say the first thing you think of. Please speak clearly. Here are two examples.

Example A. Old Friend

You see your old friend at a party. He walks over to you.

Friend (Student A): *Hi. How are you?*

YOU SAY: *Fine, and you?*

Example B. Heavy Desk

Your friend needs some help moving a heavy old desk out of her dorm room.

Friend (Student B): *Could you help me move this desk?*

YOU SAY: *I'd be happy to!*

Now, let's begin with the situations under the column marked *Student Notes With Prompt*.

1. Class Notes

   Yesterday, you were sick and didn't go to classes. This morning you asked a friend for her or his class notes.

   Friend: *Sure thing. Here they are.*

   YOU SAY:

2. Campus Reception

   There is a reception on campus. The organizer invited you and a few other students. It is getting late, and you decide to leave. You go over to the organizer.

   Organizer: *Thanks for coming!*

   YOU SAY:

3. More Food

   You are having dinner at a friend's house. Your friend offers you more food, but you couldn't possibly eat another bite.

   Friend: *Would you like some more?*

   YOU SAY:

4. Makeup Test

   You have been studying very hard for your grammar test, but on the morning of the test your alarm doesn't go off, and you oversleep. You ask your teacher for a makeup test.

   Teacher: *OK, I'll give you a break this time, but don't let it happen again.*

   YOU SAY:

5. Nice Apartment

   Your friend is visiting your apartment for the first time.

   Friend: *Nice place!*

   YOU SAY:

6. Book Pickup

   You're in your apartment talking with your roommate. You mention that you need to pick up a book at the bookstore, but you don't have any free time today.

   Roommate: *I can pick it up for you.*

   YOU SAY:

Now, let's continue with the situations under the column marked *Student Notes Without Prompt.*

7. Rainy Day

    It's raining really hard, and you don't want to walk. A friend pulls his car over to offer you a ride.

    Friend: *Hey, want a ride?*

8. Shopping Help

    You go to a clothing store and you need to find a new shirt. A salesperson approaches you. You don't want the salesperson's assistance.

    Salesperson: *Can I help you?*

9. Pen

    Right before the final exam begins, you notice that you don't have anything to write with. A friend hands you a pen.

    Friend: *Here, use this.*

10. Friendly Cashier

    You are in the supermarket. After paying, you pick up your bags, and you are ready to leave the cashier's counter.

    Cashier: *Have a nice day!*

11. Store Trip

    You need to go to a store all the way on the other side of town.

    Friend: *I can take you.*

12. Busy Professor

    You stop by your professor's office to ask a question about an assignment. You know she or he is very busy, but she or he answers your question in detail.

    Professor: *. . . and that's all you have to do.*

CHAPTER 4

Oh, I'm So Sorry! Are You All Right? Teaching Apologies

Carmella Lieske

Although acts that employ simple formulas are usually considered relatively straightforward (and thus unnecessary to teach), the potential for misinterpretation exists even in these formulaic exchanges. When acts that are potentially face threatening, such as apologies, are involved, the potential is even greater. Apologies are by their nature face threatening. By apologizing, the speaker assumes responsibility and seeks to "reestablish social harmony" (Bergman & Kasper, 1993, p. 82) after an offense or perceived offense was committed by the speaker (or by a person or institution that the speaker represents). The hearer, in turn, can choose whether to accept the apology.

As with other speech acts, cultural differences can affect the assessment of the severity of an offense, the offender's perceived obligation to apologize, and the language used to perform the apology. When nonnative speakers apologize, cultural and linguistic differences can cause their apologies to vary from native-speaker (NS) norms, compounding an already difficult situation. On the other hand, because basic apologies are relatively formulaic, the linguistic aspect is fairly easy for learners to master. Consequently, teachers can concentrate on teaching students when to apologize and how elaborate an apology is required in the target language.

This chapter focuses on apologies in response to a common experience that requires an apology in U.S. contexts: bumping into someone. Because of the potential for miscommunication, particularly for learners in multiethnic countries such as Australia, Great Britain, and the United States, the study of this speech event is not just theoretical but highly practical.

After providing a brief overview of the most widely used strategies for performing apologies in general, the discussion concentrates on the particular strategies typically produced in the United States by native speakers who bump into someone.

CONTEXT

The materials in this chapter were designed for students in a conversation class at a 3-year nursing college in Japan (i.e., an English as a foreign language setting). All of the students were Japanese, with the majority entering college immediately after high school. Overall, their English was at a low-intermediate level. Most had not been overseas before taking the English conversation course that incorporated these materials. However, the students had positive attitudes toward English and actively participated in class.

Apologies after bumping into someone were selected because Japanese students had observed that some Japanese did not apologize when they bumped into someone (Lieske, 2010). As a result of incorporating the activities described in this chapter into the second language (L2) classroom, students' awareness of the apology when bumping into someone in the United States increased. For one thing, they realized that an apology is expected; as a result, after completing the activities, one student noted, "Japanese may often be seen as rude" (for not always apologizing when they bump into others). In addition, classroom discussions demonstrated students' increased awareness of the perceived force of different apologies and variations in the linguistic and strategy choices of apologies in their first language (L1) and L2. (See Lieske, 2010, for a detailed discussion of the research that generated these materials and the classroom learning that resulted from utilizing them.)

Since this material was first developed, it has also been used with adults with low-level English skills, English majors at a 2-year college, and non-English majors at a university (all of whom were native Japanese speakers studying in Japan). The results have been similar, but the material is particularly effective when some or all of the students visit an English-speaking country and return before the end of the course. In this respect, students already living in a target-language culture have the advantage of being able to easily observe naturally occurring situations.

Apology Strategies

Olshtain (1989) categorizes apology strategies into five types: two general strategies that can be used in all situations requiring an apology and three situation-specific strategies (see also Blum-Kulka, House, & Kasper, 1989a, 1989b):

General Strategies (generally formulaic, routinized forms)

1. Explicit apology, also referred to as illocutionary force indicating devices (IFIDs):
   a. expression of regret (e.g., *I'm sorry*)
   b. offer of apology (e.g., *I apologize*)
   c. request for forgiveness (e.g., *Excuse me, Forgive me, Pardon me*)

2. Taking on responsibility (e.g., *I didn't mean to do it*)

Situation-Specific Strategies (nonconventional; require information specific to the situation)

1. Explanation or account for the offense (e.g., *I missed the train*)

2. Offer of repair for the offense (e.g., *I'll buy you a new one*)

3. Promise of forbearance from similar offenses in the future (e.g., *I won't be late next time*)

Apology Sequence: Bumping Into Someone

Even though bumping into someone is a common occurrence, few textbooks for English language learners deal with this speech event. This omission may be the result of an assumption that the speech act is universally similar, but as Suszczynska (1999) has demonstrated, there are culture-specific differences. In its basic form, when someone bumps into another person, the event includes the following:

1. nonlinguistic opening (i.e., speaker [S] bumping into hearer [H])

2. S's apology

3. H's acceptance

4. departure of S and H (nonlinguistic)

In cultures in which an utterance is expected, the apology is instantaneous, suggesting that it is fairly routine and scripted, with explicit apologies often used independently or in combination with other strategies.

Using a discourse completion test (DCT) to collect apologies from native speakers of American English, Hungarian, and Polish, Suszczynska (1999) studied a number of situations requiring an apology, including bumping into an elderly woman who drops her packages. She coded the responses using Olshtain's (1989) five verbal strategies, adding *concern for the hearer* as a sixth strategy. Suszczynska's study illustrates how culture affects even a "simple" speech act such as the apology offered after bumping into another person. For example, Suszczynska found that in the situation with the elderly woman, not only differences in the frequency of strategy use occurred, but also important differences in linguistic choices. For example, all of the informants regularly used explicit apologies, but whereas 85% of the Americans used a form of *I'm sorry* and the Polish most often used *I apologize*, the Hungarian apologies were more evenly divided among four IFIDs, with a preference for *Don't be angry*. This type of explicit apology would be inappropriate in American English. Similarly, 24% of the Polish informants offered to help pick up the packages and drive H home or to another location. However, in the United States this would quickly raise H's suspicions, and H might conclude that S had deliberately bumped into H with some ulterior motive. Other cultural and linguistic differences in the characteristics of the apologies in Suszczynska's study include the results found in Table 1. Modifications "upgrade" apologies by expressing emotion and making the apologies more sincere and substantive (Bergman & Kasper, 1993, p. 96); functions are not expressed.

Suszczynska's (1999) research demonstrates an ordered set of strategies, with the American English prototypical form being "Oh, I'm so sorry! Are you all right? Let me help you with your things" (p. 1061). In spite of the fact that Suszczynska found prototypical Hungarian and Polish apologies more difficult to formulate than those in English, one similarity among the three cultural groups was that the apology usually consisted of more than just an explicit apology.

CURRICULUM, TASKS, MATERIALS

When first studying speech acts, students find it easier to examine events that have "well-defined boundaries" (Saville-Troike, 1997, p. 141). Consequently, the material discussed in this chapter is limited to apologies associated with bumping into someone. Not only is this situation comparatively independent of social factors such as status and profession (Suszczynska, 1999), but actual damage is usually not inflicted. These characteristics further limit the scope of the speech event. In addition, bumping into someone is especially relevant to students because it is an experience that students from all cultures have had, and it is an event that warrants an apology in many cultures.

The purpose of the following activities is to

- increase students' awareness of the speech act and the unconscious cultural norms associated with it,

- help students discover differences between their L1 and the L2 that could lead to miscommunication,

- provide students with appropriate L2 language for the specific speech event.

Table 1. Apology Strategies and Modifications by Speakers of Three Languages

Strategy or Modification Employed	American	Hungarian	Polish
Strategy: Offer of repair (e.g., *Let me help you*)	100%	80%	80%
Strategy: Expression of concern for Hearer (e.g., *Are you OK?*)	71%	40%	24%
Modification: Emotional exclamation (e.g., *Oh!*)	64%	30%	20%
Modification: Intensification (e.g., *so* sorry)	100%	80%	69%

Source: Suszczynska, 1999.

The activities included here were generally presented during 6 nonconsecutive class periods, but by tackling several activities on the same day, the teacher could cover the material in fewer classes.

Activity 1: Raising Awareness

Students are first asked to complete a questionnaire about utterances when bumping into people. Before distributing Worksheet 1 (see Appendix A), the teacher can explain or demonstrate the act of bumping into someone, noting that it is usually not deliberate. It can help for the teacher to demonstrate various degrees of offense (e.g., lightly brushing a person as you pass by, bumping into a person with more force, bumping into a person hard enough that something is dropped). When demonstrating bumping into someone, it is important not to utter anything that could influence students' questionnaire responses. (Before class the teacher may want to practice bumping into someone without saying anything—even "Ah!"—because it is surprisingly difficult to do so.)

When students seem to understand the basic concept, the teacher can elicit from them examples of places where people often bump into each other. Students' answers generally focus on either a small space or an area that is full of people, such as crowded trains, airplanes as people board and stow luggage, narrow hallways filled with people waiting to enter a room, and department stores, particularly during big sales.

At this point, students are ready to complete Worksheet 1, which instructs them to report what they think they usually do when they bump into someone in their own culture or in the United States. Students should write their responses on their own. To assist them in discovering their cultural assumptions, the teacher might encourage students to think about why they answered the way they did.

After students have finished writing and thinking about their answers, the teacher collects the questionnaires. Several students can then give general opinions about what would happen in their country or countries. The teacher may need to emphasize that because cultures cannot be judged as right or wrong but only as different, no answer is incorrect. In classrooms with students from various countries, it is important to call on students from different parts of the world.

The teacher can then ask students why they believe an apology is or is not needed in their cultures, sharing any pertinent experiences. Then in pairs or small groups, students can reflect on how foreigners who do not comply with NS norms are viewed. For example, students may say that they have a negative feeling about the foreigner, that the foreigner seems rude, or that they believe the foreigner's L2 ability is low.

Despite evidence to the contrary, in many cases students will believe that people in their country always apologize when they bump into someone. If students are going to be collecting data in their own country, the teacher should refrain from mentioning any experiences he or she may have had. If, however, students will not be collecting data in their L1 (see Activity 2), the teacher may want to discuss his or her experiences. Because neither language nor culture can be more or less polite, but rather will have different rules or norms of courtesy, this discussion should be factual and avoid passing judgment on the students or their cultures. During this class, students' L2 responses on the questionnaire are not discussed.

To enable learners to use appropriate strategies, it is helpful to have them provide literal translations of their L1 utterances (on Part I of Worksheet 1) in their L2. In multicultural classrooms, this not only demonstrates how culture is reflected in language but also enables students to learn about the L2 and other languages.

At some time before conducting Activity 4, the teacher will compile students' responses to Part II of Worksheet 1. Some version of the blank Teacher Worksheet (see Appendix A) can be used to record students' responses. The Sample Compilation Sheet in Appendix A can be used as a guide. Completing the Teacher Worksheet involves a few simple steps:

1. Write in all student responses.

2. Count the number of students who gave each response (e.g., with check marks).

3. Calculate percentages. (These help the teacher understand how students answered.) Percentages can be calculated by adding the total number of students and then using the following formula:

    (Number of students for each answer) / (Total number of students)

4. Notice how many times the same utterances were given.

5. Determine the proportion of the utterances that vary from the NS norm (e.g., only two students, most of the class).

6. Analyze the types of mistakes students are making (e.g., literally translating an apology from their L1, omitting an apology).

Activity 2: Collecting Natural L1 Speech

In this activity, students collect samples of actual spoken apologies. If students have access to natural speech in their L1, they should collect spontaneous data. Even if not all students have access to natural speech, the class can learn from the answers of the students who complete the activity.

Students who do not live in the L1 culture can collect data by watching movies or TV shows or accessing examples of natural speech on the Internet. The teacher may want to provide a focus for these students by asking them to first look for scenes from crowded trains or subways or shows that might have people getting on and off airplanes. After this, they can begin a broader search for other situations.

Students will collect data by going to public places and observing situations in which two people accidentally bump into each other. They must then record data in their L1 on Worksheet 2 (see Appendix A) immediately after witnessing the event. They should not try to remember the situations and fill in the sheet later. The teacher assigns a date for submission of Worksheet 2.

After the homework has been collected, the teacher calculates the number of times no apology or response was given on the students' worksheets and, if possible, the languages/cultures in which nothing was said. In the next class, students are asked to talk about anything that surprised them when they collected their L1 data (e.g., *I thought all people would apologize, but some people didn't; When a little girl ran into someone, the parents didn't tell her to apologize so she just went skipping away. It's bad manners.*). The teacher can then report how often an apology was not given and invite students who observed these encounters to tell the class the following:

- how the person who was bumped reacted

- the impression the speaker created

- what, if any, of the students' previous impressions or beliefs they revised

Activity 3: Practicing Apologies for Different Levels of Offense

This activity is designed to make students aware that there is more than one form (*I'm sorry*) that can be used as an apology and that the form of the apology is affected by the situation (e.g., perceived level of offense, relationship of bumper and bumpee). The teacher begins the session by explaining the following about English apologies:

- American English speakers almost always apologize when bumping into someone.

- The American English apology is fairly formulaic.

- Because there is no time to think, this type of apology is a spontaneous reaction to the situation.

- The apology needs to be practiced until it becomes automatic.

- *I'm sorry* by itself may not be adequate.

Students then receive Worksheet 3 (see Appendix A). Students may help the teacher demonstrate several of the conversations in Part A. After completing Part A with the teacher, students practice the short interactions in Part B. Students and their partners then create their own conversations.

After students have practiced their own apology interactions in pairs, they can perform role-plays in small groups and then take turns performing them in front of the class. The teacher continues with Parts II and III of Worksheet 3 to reinforce and expand learning in a future class.

Activity 4: Identifying Native-Like Apologies

In this activity, the teacher reports the results of students' responses to the questions in Worksheet 1 Part II ("In the United States") and guides students in recognizing appropriate (i.e., native-sounding) and inappropriate (i.e., nonnative-sounding) responses.

The teacher begins by discussing the students' English responses to Worksheet 1 Part II, letting them know which utterances were most frequent and how often the class as a whole gave NS-like responses. (The teacher can refer to the information recorded on the Teacher Worksheet for this activity.) This is an excellent time to reinforce native-like apologies; the Sample Compilation Sheet (see Appendix A) has examples of apologies and responses that would be appropriate (left side) and inappropriate (right side) in the United States when bumping into someone. Using the Sample Compilation Sheet and Worksheet 3 as references, the teacher can write some examples of native-like apologies and responses on the board. The teacher may want to remind students that the apology is fairly formulaic.

Students then form pairs or small groups. The teacher reads aloud NS-like and non-NS-like apologies from the lists in the Compilation Sheet and from students' own responses. The teacher can also create apologies by combining strategies from Worksheet 3 (e.g., exclamation + taking on responsibility + concern for hearer). In their groups, students then determine whether each of the apologies is native-like. Students can be instructed to correct unnatural utterances. For example, if the teacher says, "Oh! I'm so sorry. Please don't be angry," students could provide a more natural American apology, such as "Oh! I'm sorry." Students can also be asked to identify the following:

- portions of the utterances, referencing their handout from Activity 3 (e.g., show surprise, show you're sorry)

- elements that make them stronger (e.g., exclamations, intensification)

More advanced students can be challenged to give reasons for their choices.

Activity 5: Collecting Natural L2 Speech

This activity is appropriate for students who live in or will be traveling to a target-language country. If they do not have direct access to situations in which L2 speakers might bump into each other, they can watch English-language TV and movies, noting any apologies and responses when people bump into each other.

In this activity, students again use Worksheet 2, but this time to collect data from L2 speakers. The teacher explains the task and gives students a deadline for completing the homework. On the assigned day, students bring their data collection sheets to class. As students look at their L2 data collection sheets, they should be encouraged to reflect on and discuss their observations and draw conclusions. The teacher may need to encourage and prompt students to make these discoveries by asking questions such as these:

- Were there words in the apologies and responses other than those we studied (e.g., *Oops!*) in class?

- Were any forms of the apology (e.g., *Sorry!*) used more often than others?

- Were some apologies longer than others? If necessary, the teacher may ask more specific questions such as the following:

  —Did one person say, "Sorry!" while another person said, "Oh! I'm so sorry. Are you all right?"

  —Did one person say, "Oh!" but another say, "Oh. Excuse me"?

  —Why do you think some apologies were longer (e.g., severity of offense, who H was)?

- Did everyone apologize? If no, who didn't (e.g., men or women, people of a certain age)? Did this surprise you?

Activity 6: Role-Playing

Communication cards can be used for additional role-play practice or to assess learning. These are small cards that have pictures or simple explanations of various situations. In pairs, students select a set of cards and role-play the situations presented on the cards. For example, two cards might have a picture of two people (marked Student A and Student B) bumping into each other and B dropping something, with "What do you do?" on the Student A card and "Respond to A" on the Student B card. By adjusting the linguistic difficulty and situations, communication cards can be used with students of any level. A simple set of communication cards can be found in Appendix B. Teachers might want to add pictures.

REFLECTIONS

From a linguistic point of view, the apologies in this chapter are easy enough for students of any age and level and are appropriate for students in a variety of learning situations. However, teachers in various contexts may find some of the activities and worksheets more appropriate than others, depending on students' proficiency, class time constraints, and access to native speakers of both the students' L1s and English. Additional activities, such as those in Activities 5 and 6, can be used to supplement the core material presented in this chapter. Teachers with more advanced students may want to introduce Activity 4 before Activity 3, leading students to discover characteristics of appropriate apologies in English.

To simplify Activity 1, a modified DCT, that is, a scene with a blank for the student to write in a response, can be used rather than the questionnaire on Worksheet 1 (see sample in Appendix C). Because the DCT does not require students to give reasons why the conversation changes if the person drops something or to consider how the social characteristics of the interlocutor can affect the apology, it allows learners to focus on the language of the speech act. Students are not asked to directly consider their cultural assumptions. This makes the DCT less complex and more appropriate for younger students or those with lower L2 proficiency.

Carmella Lieske has been teaching EFL in Japan since 1993. She has taught students of all ages, ranging from preschool to adult. Her research interests include pragmatics, English as an international language, and materials development. She has conducted research in Japan, South Korea, Thailand, and the United States.

APPENDIX A: WORKSHEETS AND ANSWER KEYS

Worksheet 1: Apology Questionnaire

Name _____ Class _____

Answer the questions in Part I in your native language; write your answers to Part II in English.

Part I: In Your Country

1. You are in a store. You accidentally bump into someone.

    Would you say anything? (Circle one.)   YES   NO   SOMETIMES

    Why or why not? _____

    YES or SOMETIMES => What would you say in your own language?

    _____

    Would the other person say anything after you said that?   YES   NO

    YES => What? (In your own language) _____

2. If you bumped into someone and the person dropped what he or she was holding, would that change your answer? (Circle one.)   YES   NO

    YES => Why? How? _____

3. When you answered Questions 1 and 2, what kind of person did you imagine bumping into? (Example: Man or woman? Someone you know or a stranger? Young or old?) _____

Part II: In the United States

4. You are in a store. You accidentally bump into someone.

   Would you say anything? (Circle one.)   YES   NO   SOMETIMES

   YES or SOMETIMES => What would you say? _____

   What would the other person say? _____

5. Would your answer change if the person dropped something?
   (Circle one.)   YES   NO

6. Does your answer change depending on who you bumped into? (see Question 3)
   (Circle one.)   YES   NO

   Why or why not? _____

Worksheet 1: Sample Answers

Answers will vary, particularly for Questions 1, 2, and 3, which are based on various L1 cultures and languages. Japanese will be used to give one example.

Part I: In Your Country

1. Yes. Japanese students believe everyone says something <u>because it is rude not to say anything</u>. Other possible answers include:
   - I should apologize because it is expected of me.
   - I should apologize because that's what I was taught when I was a child.
   - I should apologize because I've invaded the other person's personal space.
   - I should apologize because it's bad to bump into someone.
   - I should apologize because I want the other person to know I didn't do it deliberately.

   Yes, the other person would respond. In Japanese the conversation might be:

   A: *Sumimasen.* (I'm sorry.)

   B: *Douitashimashite.* (It's OK.)

2. Yes, the dialogue would probably change <u>because the person would express more concern for the listener</u>. For example:

   A: *Sumimasen. Daijoubudesuka?* (I'm sorry. Are you all right?)

   B: *Daijoubudesu.* (I'm all right.)

3. Students who imagine an older male who is a stranger may produce a more formal apology than students who imagine bumping into a younger sister. An example of the latter might include:

   A: *Gomen.* (Sorry.)

   B: *Iie.* (OK.)

Part II: In the United States

4. Yes, most Americans would say something. In its most basic form, the conversation might be:

    A: *Sorry.*

    B: *Sorry.*

5. Yes. The apology might be strengthened, an expression of surprise added, and/or an offer of help extended. For example:

    A: *Oh, I'm so sorry. Let me help you.* (as you bend down to help)

    B: *Thanks.*

6. Yes. The answer might change if the speaker wished to strengthen the apology or express surprise to emphasize it was not deliberate (e.g., if the other person looked angry).

    A: *Oh! Excuse me.*

    B: *It's OK.*

Teacher Worksheet: Compilation Sheet for Students' Responses to Worksheet 1 Part II, 4

Appropriate When Bumping Into Someone	Number of Students	Inappropriate When Bumping Into Someone	Number of Students
Apologies		*Apologies*	
IFIDs—Expression of Regret		Explanation	
IFIDs—Request for Forgiveness		Taking on Responsibility	
IFID + Intensification			
Concern for Hearer			
Exclamations		Promise of Forbearance	
Combinations			
Responses		*Responses*	

Note: IFID = illocutionary force indicating devices (also known as explicit apology).

Teacher Worksheet: Sample Compilation of Students' Responses to Worksheet I, Part II, 4

In an American Store			
Appropriate When Bumping Into Someone	**Number of Students**	**Inappropriate When Bumping Into Someone**	**Number of Students**
Apologies		*Apologies*	
IFIDs—Expression of Regret		**Explanation**	
I'm sorry.	8	I didn't see for shopping.	1
Sorry.	3		
IFIDs—Request for Forgiveness		**Taking on Responsibility**	
Excuse me.	2	I never did it on purpose.	1
IFID + Intensification		It's my fault.	1
I'm so sorry.	1	It's not my fault.	1
Concern for Hearer		My mistake.	1
Are you OK?	2	It's your own fault.	1
Are you all right?	1		
Exclamations		**Promise of Forbearance**	
Oops!	1	I won't do it again.	2
Oh.	1		
Ah.	1		
Combinations			
Oh, I'm sorry. Are you OK?	5		
Ah. Excuse me.	1		
Oops! I'm so sorry. Are you all right?	1		
Responses		*Responses*	
That's all right.	1	You are welcome.	3
That's OK.	1	Don't mind.	2
It's OK.	2	Never mind.	2
It's all right.	2	Not at all.	2
Sorry.	1		
No problem.	1		

Worksheet 2: Data Collection Sheet

Name _____ Class _____

Go to a public place. Observe people accidentally bumping into each other.

Answer the questions. Circle **Y** or **N** for each situation. Circle **M** or **F** for each person.

Use these codes to guess the people's ages:

1: younger than elementary school   5: 25–40 years old

2: elementary school   6: 41–60 years old

3: junior or senior high school   7: over 60 years old

4: college student

1. Where? _____ Was anything dropped? **Y**   **N**

   Person doing the bumping   **M**   **F**   Age ____   Said something? **Y**   **N**

       If said something What? _____

   Person being bumped   **M**   **F**   Age ____   Said something? **Y**   **N**

       If said something What? _____

   Any other important information? _____

2. Where? _____ Was anything dropped? **Y**   **N**

   Person doing the bumping   **M**   **F**   Age ____   Said something? **Y**   **N**

       If said something What? _____

   Person being bumped   **M**   **F**   Age ____   Said something? **Y**   **N**

       If said something What? _____

   Any other important information? _____

3. Where? _____ Was anything dropped? **Y**   **N**

   Person doing the bumping   **M**   **F**   Age ____   Said something? **Y**   **N**

       If said something What? _____

   Person being bumped   **M**   **F**   Age ____   Said something? **Y**   **N**

       If said something What? _____

   Any other important information? _____

4. Where? _____ Was anything dropped? **Y**   **N**

   Person doing the bumping   **M**   **F**   Age ____   Said something? **Y**   **N**

       If said something What? _____

   Person being bumped   **M**   **F**   Age ____   Said something? **Y**   **N**

       If said something What? _____

   Any other important information? _____

5. Where? _____ Was anything dropped? **Y** **N**

   Person doing the bumping   **M**   **F**   Age ____   Said something?   **Y**   **N**

      If said something What? _____

   Person being bumped   **M**   **F**   Age ____   Said something?   **Y**   **N**

      If said something What? _____

   Any other important information? _____

6. Where? _____ Was anything dropped? **Y** **N**

   Person doing the bumping   **M**   **F**   Age ____   Said something?   **Y**   **N**

      If said something What? _____

   Person being bumped   **M**   **F**   Age ____   Said something?   **Y**   **N**

      If said something What? _____

   Any other important information? _____

7. Where? _____ Was anything dropped? **Y** **N**

   Person doing the bumping   **M**   **F**   Age ____   Said something?   **Y**   **N**

      If said something What? _____

   Person being bumped   **M**   **F**   Age ____   Said something?   **Y**   **N**

      If said something What? _____

   Any other important information? _____

Worksheet 2: Sample Answers

When complete, students' answers may look like this. Answers will vary.

Example of answers that would be in student's L1:

1. Where? *mise* ("store")   Was anything dropped?   **Y**   <u>**N**</u>

   Person doing the bumping   **M**   <u>**F**</u>   Age <u>5</u>   Said something?   <u>**Y**</u>   **N**

      If said something What? <u>*Gomennasai* ("I'm sorry.")</u>

   Person being bumped   **M**   <u>**F**</u>   Age <u>7</u>   Said something?   <u>**Y**</u>   **N**

      If said something What? <u>*Iie* ("OK.")</u>

   Any other important information? <u>No.</u>

Example of answers in English (i.e., student's L2):

2. Where? <u>Department store</u>   Was anything dropped?   <u>**Y**</u>   **N**

   Person doing the bumping   **M**   <u>**F**</u>   Age <u>4</u>   Said something?   <u>**Y**</u>   **N**

      If said something What? <u>I'm sorry. Are you OK?</u>

   Person being bumped   <u>**M**</u>   **F**   Age <u>7</u>   Said something?   <u>**Y**</u>   **N**

      If said something What? <u>Yes, thanks.</u>

   Any other important information? <u>It sounded like something broke.</u>

Worksheet 3: Practicing Apologies With Three Levels of Offense

Name _____ Class _____

This worksheet provides practice with apologies involving at least 3 levels of offense: low, medium, and high.

I. Low Level of Offense: Even when we barely bump into someone, we apologize in English. These conversations can be short, but both people usually say something.

A. Typical Language

If you are the first person (the person who does the bumping), you

    1. can show surprise.

        (a) Oops!

        (b) Oh!

        (c) Ah!

    2. **must** show you are sorry.

        (a) I'm sorry.

        (b) Sorry.

        (c) Excuse me.

    3. can make it stronger. *So* is used most often.

        (a) I'm **so** sorry.

        (b) I'm **terribly** sorry.

        (c) I'm **very** sorry.

If you are the second person (the person who is bumped), you **should** show you are OK.

        (a) It's OK.

        (b) That's OK.

        (c) Sorry.

        (d) That's all right.

Once in a while, you may show surprise.

        (a) Oops!

        (b) Oh!

B. Practice

With your partner, practice the three conversations below.

    1. A: I'm so sorry.   Apology (show you are sorry + make stronger)

       B: That's all right.   Acceptance

    2. C: Excuse me.   Apology (show you are sorry)

       D: It's OK.   Acceptance

    3. E: Oh, sorry.   Apology (surprise + show you are sorry)

       F: Oh! Sorry.   Acceptance (surprise + show you are OK)

Now practice making your own conversations. Use ideas from above.

II. Medium Level of Offense: If you bump into someone and the person drops something that doesn't break, the conversation is usually longer.

A. Typical Language

If you are the first person, you

1. can show surprise.

2. **must** show you are sorry.

3. **should** make it stronger.

4. Many people will start to pick up whatever is dropped without saying anything **or** as they pick something up say
   (a) Let me help you.
   (b) Let me get that for you.

If you are the second person **and** the person helps you, say

1. Thanks.

2. Sorry.

3. If A says *Let me get that for you,* you can say *That's OK.*

B. Practice

Use the conversations below to practice bumping into someone when the other person drops something. Then make your own conversations.

1. A: Oh, I'm so sorry. Let me help you. (as you bend down to help)

   B: Thanks.

2. C: Oh, sorry.

   D: (as C bends down to help) That's OK.

III. High Level of Offense: If you bump into the person hard; the person spills food or a drink, especially something hot; or something breaks.

A. Typical Language

If you are the first person, you

1. will probably make the surprise stronger. (*Oh my gosh!*)

2. **must** show you are sorry.

3. will probably make it stronger.

4. **should** add concern (for example: *Are you OK? Are you all right?*).

<u>If you are the second person</u>, you can respond

1. *Yes, thanks.*

2. *Yeah, I guess so.*

3. *Yes, I think so.*

4. *Could you . . . ?* (for example: *Could you get me a wet towel to wipe off this spaghetti?*)

B. Practice

With your partner, practice the conversations below. Then make your own.

1. A: Oh my gosh! I'm so sorry. Are you all right?

   B: Yeah, thanks.

2. C: (spills coffee on D's pants) Oh! I'm so very sorry. Are you OK?

   D: Yeah, I think so, but I'm not too sure about these pants.

APPENDIX B: SAMPLE COMMUNICATION CARDS

Situation A

Student A	Student B
Place: airplane	Place: airplane
You are walking down the aisle and bump into Student B.	Respond to Student A.
What do you do and/or say?	

Situation B

Student A	Student B
Place: train station	Place: train station
Respond to Student B.	You are in a train and bump into Student A, who drops his or her bag.
	What do you do and/or say?

APPENDIX C: WORKSHEET 1A
(ALTERNATIVE TO WORKSHEET 1)

Name _____ Class _____

Discourse Completion Test to Elicit Apologetic Responses

Part I. You are shopping in a store in <u>your country</u>. You accidentally bump into someone.

   A. Do you say anything? (Circle one.) YES   NO   SOMETIMES

       NO => Go to Part II.

       SOMETIMES => <u>When</u> would you say something? _____

       YES or SOMETIMES => Complete the following conversation.

       I would say (in your language) _____

       The person would respond (in your language) _____

   B. You accidentally bump into someone, and the person drops something.

       Is the conversation different than in Part I A (above)? (Circle one.) YES   NO

       NO => Go to Part II.

       YES => Complete the following conversation.

       I would say (in your language) _____

       The person would respond (in your language) _____

Part II. You are shopping in a store in <u>the United States.</u> You accidentally bump into someone.

   A. Do you say anything? (Circle one.) YES   NO   SOMETIMES

       NO => Why not? _____

       SOMETIMES => <u>When</u> would you say something? _____

       YES or SOMETIMES => Complete the following conversation.

       I would say (in English) _____

       The person would respond (in English) _____

   B. When you accidentally bump into someone, the person drops something. Is the conversation different than in Part IIA (above)?

       (Circle one.) YES   NO

       NO => You are finished.

       YES => Complete the following conversation.

       I would say (in English) _____

       The person would respond (in English) _____

CHAPTER 5

Have You Paid Someone a Compliment Today?

Jessie Carduner

This chapter (as well as chapter 6) introduces the act of complimenting, another act that can be considered formulaic in English in that it is typically expressed using a limited number of syntactic patterns and lexical items. Despite its formulaic nature, however, complimenting is a particularly important act because it plays a number of key social and discourse roles in American English (Manes & Wolfson, 1981).

A substantial body of research is available on the teaching of compliments (e.g., Billmyer, 1990; Holmes & Brown, 1987; Rose & Ng Kwai-fun, 2001), but few classroom resources have been developed to introduce explicit complimenting behavior and strategies for responding to compliments (c.f. Regents of the University of Minnesota, 2010). This chapter provides a sequenced set of activities for teaching compliments that diagnose learners' current ability to produce compliments in English, instructing learners on the conventional nature of most English compliments, and offering opportunities to recognize different compliment and compliment response forms as well as to practice producing and responding to compliments.

CONTEXT

The activities described in this chapter were developed for an elective pragmatics course in an MA TESOL program at a large midwestern U.S. public university. The class typically includes roughly 50% international students who have met admission requirements, with a minimum Test of English as a Foreign Language score of 525 on the written exam or 197 on the computer exam. However, these international students often lack speaking confidence and sociopragmatic competence.

Instructional goals for the pragmatics course include raising international students' level of pragmatic competence in English and providing all enrollees with theoretical and practical tools for teaching pragmatic skills to their future English as a second language (ESL) students. The compliment set is introduced shortly after a general discussion of speech acts. Usually, one full class and approximately 30 minutes of the following class are allocated. Although it takes more than a single lesson for international students to use the formulas automatically and naturally, during the lesson they readily grasp the motivations behind English compliments and often seem relieved to learn how to respond to compliments modestly but appropriately with deflection strategies. This chapter focuses primarily on the practical aspects of teaching compliments and is easily adaptable to other audiences.

Linguistic Form

Compliments are expressions of positive evaluation (Manes & Wolfson, 1981; Wolfson, 1981) or admiration concerning a possession, accomplishment, or personal quality of the hearer or someone closely related to the hearer (Herbert, 1991). Compliments in English have been described in terms of their linguistic form, appropriate topics, social characteristics of speaker and hearer, social and discourse functions, and responses that they generally elicit.

Explicit compliments, utterances that express appreciation or admiration with a word or phrase that carries a positive meaning, tend to be formulaic in English. For example, 85% of the 686 compliments collected by Manes and Wolfson (1981) were rendered using one of only three basic structures. In addition to structural regularity, American English compliments tend to use a limited set of semantically positive adjectives, verbs, and adverbs. Although 72 distinct adjectives were found in Manes and Wolfson's sample, nearly 70% were 1 of just 5 adjectives: *nice, good, pretty, beautiful,* or *great.* Similarly, positive verbs were generally limited to *like, love, admire, enjoy,* and *be impressed by.*

Compliment Topics

Although some subjects of compliments, such as appearance, personal traits, work and study behaviors, and skills and tastes, may be appropriate universally, their frequency may vary across cultures. For example, Barnlund and Araki (1985) found that their Japanese and American subjects complimented on the same topics, but with different distributions. Other compliment topics are culture specific. For instance, in U.S. culture, it is appropriate to compliment another person's baby; Egyptians, however, may interpret compliments on children's health and growth as a sign of envy (Mursy & Wilson, 2001). Instruction on compliments must therefore include attention to what may be complimented.

Compliments and Speaker Characteristics

Speaker characteristics also affect the decision to offer a compliment. In English, compliments tend to occur more frequently between friends, coworkers, and acquaintances of equal status than between strangers or very close friends

(Wolfson, 1989; Yu, 2005). Evidence suggests that compliments between status unequals tend to flow downward (Holmes & Brown, 1987), with the person of higher status being the one with sufficient rights and responsibilities to compliment (Mackiewicz, 2006; see chapter 6 in this volume for a discussion of gender-based differences).

Compliment Functions

Compliments are proffered with high frequency in English and may occur at virtually any point in a conversation, which can be disconcerting to nonnative speakers, who may be unaccustomed to complimenting behaviors in English and may doubt the sincerity of a compliment from a native speaker. Conversely, if a nonnative speaker fails to issue a compliment when one is expected, a native speaker may see this as a sign of disapproval (Billmyer, 1990). Thus, understanding the functions of compliments is as important as understanding how to form them.

Manes and Wolfson (1981) conclude that a basic function of compliments in U.S. society is to create or reinforce solidarity or commonalities among the speaker and listener. A compliment about a hearer's possession, for instance, can establish that the speaker and hearer have similar tastes. In addition to their primary function of expressing admiration or approval, compliments in English may perform the following functions: greet or open a conversation, express gratitude, close a conversation, preface a request, positively reinforce desired behaviors, and soften criticism.

Compliment Responses

Data are mixed as to whether acceptance or deflection (changing the direction or force of the compliment) is the preferred strategy for responding to compliments in American English. However, researchers tend to agree that rejection or nonacceptance is the least preferred strategy (Herbert, 1989; Yu, 2004). In responding to compliments, Americans seek to balance two politeness maxims: agreement and modesty (Leech, 1983). A simple appreciation token like *thanks* or an unqualified expression of agreement may make the speaker appear immodest, and an outright rejection of the compliment might make the speaker appear disagreeable.

Cross-Cultural Differences in Compliment and Compliment Response Behaviors

Although the act of giving and receiving compliments may be universal, cross-cultural differences have been well documented (e.g., Barnlund & Araki, 1985; Nelson, El Bakary, & Al Batal, 1996; Saito & Beecken, 1997; Wolfson, 1981). Wolfson notes that nonnative speakers of English are often confounded by the frequency of American compliments. Barnlund and Araki's study was prompted by one of the researchers' experience of "being overwhelmed with unaccustomed expressions of praise for her appearance, intelligence [and] personality" (p. 10). Nonnative speakers often ignore or reject compliments or accept compliments with a token agreement when a deflection leading to extended conversation on the topic is expected (Billmyer, 1990; Wolfson, 1989) as in Example 1:

Example 1 (Billmyer, 1990, p. 43)

Native speaker (NS):	*Oh, this is a really nice picture.*
Nonnative speaker (NNS):	*Thank you.*
NS:	*I like it. I like it.*
NNS:	*(silence)*
NS:	*That's nice.*
NNS:	*(silence)*
NS:	*So you keep these in your room?*
NNS:	*Yes.*

In Billmyer's (1990) example, the native speaker issues three compliments, each an attempt to engage the nonnative speaker in a conversation about the picture. The nonnative speaker appears to be unaware of the native speaker's intention, resulting in an awkward communication breakdown or pragmatic failure. The materials presented in the next section have been designed to provide English language learners with sociopragmatic information about American compliments and to equip them with strategies for handling different compliment sets in English.

CURRICULUM, TASKS, MATERIALS

The lesson begins with an assessment of students' current knowledge of compliment and compliment response behaviors in English and then moves on to discussions of various social and cultural factors that affect decisions about how to compliment and respond. Students are then introduced to formulas for expressing compliments and responses as well as the social functions of compliments. Next, learners concentrate on recognizing and producing appropriate compliments and responses, and finally on selecting appropriate topics for compliments.

Activity 1: Assessing Students' Current Knowledge

Activity 1 involves an assessment (Worksheet 1, see Appendix A) to gauge students' prior knowledge of compliment behavior and to generate sample data for Activity 3, in which students will examine common linguistic patterns for performing compliments and responses in English.

For patterns to emerge, approximately 25–30 compliments and compliment responses should be collected from students. More situations can be added to Worksheet 1 as needed to generate enough student samples for exploration of potential patterns in compliment structures and word choices. Before discussing the results and compliment formulas, teachers should complete Activity 2.

Activity 2: Raising Awareness of Appropriate Compliments

The purpose of this activity is twofold. First, it serves as a warm-up to introduce students to cultural differences in compliment behaviors and helps them identify sources of discomfort in situations that require a compliment or compliment response in English. Second, it calls attention to the situational variability of complimenting behavior.

Students complete Worksheet 2 (see Appendix A) on their own, after which their responses may be used as a basis for discussion. Then the instructor may want to summarize important social variables—how well speakers know each other, age, gender, power differentials—that affect complimenting behaviors.

Activity 3: Presenting Conventional Formulas and Social Functions of Compliments

Handouts 1 and 2 (see Appendix A) show students common patterns for giving and receiving compliments. Students can practice reproducing the formulas by complimenting each other and responding using the sample sentences as models.

For learners at lower proficiency levels, instructors may want to abbreviate Handout 1 by presenting select compliment formulas a few at a time over several lessons.

Handout 2 presents options for responding to compliments (refer to Section 2 of Handout 2 for acceptable strategies to use when not accepting a compliment). Students should be informed that rejecting outright compliments may be perceived as a snub.

For learners at lower proficiency levels, instructors may present just a few of the compliment responses from Handout 2. Learners at more advanced levels can be provided with additional information to illustrate how formulas vary according to the social function for which the compliment is used (e.g., greeting, thanking, ending a conversation; see Appendix B).

Activity 4: Comparing Students' Compliments and Responses to Conventional Formulas

After students have reviewed the information about compliments and compliment responses, they are ready to analyze their own compliments from the initial assessment task (Worksheet 1). Selected students' responses from Worksheet 1 should be reproduced as exemplified by the top half of Worksheet 3 that is included in Appendix C (the blank worksheet is in Appendix A). Responses with multiple grammatical errors should be removed or edited so as to not distract from the pragmatic focus. For learners at lower proficiency levels, the teacher may want to select only those responses that approximate the top three or four sentence patterns.

Question 1 in the Discussion and Analysis section of Worksheet 3 is intended to help students discover which adjectives are commonly used to make compliments. Students' responses can be compared to Manes and Wolfson's (1981) finding that *good, great, pretty, nice,* and *beautiful* tend to predominate in English compliments. The teacher can note that *great* and *beautiful* are more strongly positive than *good, pretty,* and *nice.*

Questions 2 and 3 require students to compare the sentence patterns in their own data to the findings by Manes and Wolfson (1981) provided in Handout 1. If students opted not to compliment in any of the situations, they should be asked to explain why. It is important to reinforce to students that complimenting is not considered a superficial, meaningless act in English, but rather in many circumstances it is expected and is part of a social norm.

Question 4 is an invitation to identify inappropriate compliments. This discussion can be enriched by inviting native speakers to attend the class and share their reactions to inappropriate decisions to opt out and utterances that deviate from expected patterns. Additional analysis by advanced-level learners might include guessing the gender of the person issuing the compliments and looking for patterned differences between the car and haircut compliments. For example, the car compliments are typically shorter and use the formula *adjective + noun phrase* more frequently.

Question 5 focuses on compliment responses. Again, using the preassessment responses from Worksheet 1 (copied onto Worksheet 3 for analysis), students identify the general response types (accept, deflect, reject) and specific strategies (e.g., token appreciation, agreement, comment, downgrade). Students then assess whether their responses correspond to any of the common compliment response types. The class can consider the impact of cultural and personal value systems on their language choices and the potential for misunderstanding when two or more speakers from diverse cultural backgrounds are interacting. Instructors may want to emphasize that deflection, acceptance, or acceptance-plus-deflection normally are the preferred responses and that responses like "Oh, not so much" in the essay situation are very inappropriate.

Activity 5: Producing Compliments and Compliment Responses

Up to this point, students have engaged primarily in receptive activities. For productive practice in giving and receiving compliments, students can engage in role-play scenarios similar to those in Worksheet 4 (see Appendix A), in which one student gives a compliment and the other responds. Students may be asked to complete each scenario in pairs, or each pair may choose one scenario to practice and present in front of the class.

After each performance (or selected performances) of the role-plays, the class should discuss which compliment formulas and which types of responses (accept, deflect, reject) were used. If the compliments resulted in an extended exchange, students can explain how the compliments and responses led to a longer conversation. If students are comfortable with being recorded, the teacher can record the students' conversations. The recordings can be used for more accurate analysis, either as a whole-class activity or for individual feedback to students.

Activity 6: Practicing Compliment Responses

In Activity 6, the Musical Compliment Response Game (see materials in Appendix D) gives students focused practice in using the various compliment response strategies. To prepare for the game, the teacher cuts the compliment response strategies in Part I of the Teacher Worksheet in Appendix D into strips or prints them on index cards. One strategy is distributed to each student. For a large class, blank cards may be mixed in or the same strategies may be reproduced on more than one student card. Because the cards are passed around during the activity, all students have a chance to participate regardless of which card they receive initially.

For the game itself, the teacher uses the teacher's script in Part II of the Teacher Worksheet. Students stand in a circle. The teacher explains to the students that she or he (the teacher) is going to play music. The teacher hands a response card to each student. As the music plays, students pass the response cards around the circle. When the music stops, the teacher reads a compliment. Any student with an appropriate response card to the compliment that the teacher reads (from the script) should give a reply. As responses are produced, students should assess their appropriateness.

After the activity is completed, the instructor may want to give students the list of 10 compliment response strategies from the Teacher Worksheet as a summary or to prompt further discussion (Handout 3, see Appendix A). Students may be asked to supply a few examples of each.

For less proficient learners, instead of writing generic strategies such as "Express appreciation" on the cards, the teacher can write actual responses such as *Thanks, Thank you, Nice of you to say so,* and so forth. The situations for the teacher's script may be modified or adapted as needed.

Activity 7: Raising Awareness of Appropriate Compliment Topics

Through the handouts and practice tasks, students will already have been exposed to numerous examples of compliments. Students can recall the content of some of the compliments they have seen in previous exercises and brainstorm additional compliment topics. Taboo or sensitive subjects for compliments, such as change in weight, reference to money, or compliments that imply unwanted flirtation, can be noted or discussed. With prompting, students should be able to generate a general list of potential subjects open for compliment. To enhance the discussion, instructors may show students scripted video clips of compliment sets from movies (see Rose, 2001, for more on using film to teach compliments sets), TV shows, and commercials, as well as more spontaneous tokens from recorded interviews and talk shows. These media can be used not only to analyze compliment topics, but to review formulas and compliment functions.

REFLECTIONS

The lessons introduced in this chapter are limited in that their focus is on explicit compliments. Follow-up lessons might include nonformulaic and indirect compliments as well as instruction on how compliments can serve secondary functions such as greetings, closings, prerequests, and precriticisms. Students must also have opportunities to observe and use compliments in real-life settings.

The unit presented in this chapter has been employed with graduate students in an MA TESOL program. For younger learners who may not have the vocabulary or cognitive sophistication to analyze and discuss language abstractly, the tasks and activities are easily adaptable by adjusting the length of the activities, reducing grammatical terminology, and selecting compliment topics and situations that appeal to the group of learners and reflect their immediate surroundings. For instance, when working with younger learners, the teacher can change the compliment topics in the assessment to items (e.g., electronic gadgets, fashion items) that are popular among children and young adults. In Activity 2, which explores social variables and attitudes toward compliments, "coworkers" can be replaced with people with whom younger learners are likely to exchange compliments and compliment responses, such as peers, extended family members, and important adults in their lives, including teachers, babysitters, and friends' parents.

It is essential that learners acquire the structural patterns for compliments and compliment responses. However, for younger learners and learners unfamiliar with grammar terminology, the use of technical terms should be minimized and replaced with examples of sentences containing the patterns. These younger students can look for answers they gave during the assessment phase that contain positive words such as *love, like, admire, pretty, good*, and so forth, without using terms like *noun phrase* and *intensifier*. Younger learners can be provided with examples of two or three compliment patterns such as *cool phone* and *I like your T-shirt* and then instructed to compliment fellow classmates using these same patterns in a drill-like but also communicative fashion. A similar approach can be used with compliment responses, selecting just a few acceptance and deflection patterns at a time. Role-plays and the musical compliments game should again be adapted to learners' ages and proficiency levels. The teacher can select compliment topics and situations that relate to students' lives and surroundings. For learners at very low proficiency levels, partially completed compliments and compliment responses can be provided for the role-play activity. Regardless of learners' level, the concepts should be reintroduced and reinforced over the course of the term or academic year. This should occur naturally and spontaneously because compliments are so much a part of everyday interactions among speakers of English.

Jessie Carduner is an assistant professor of Spanish and foreign language pedagogy in the Department of Modern and Classical Language Studies at Kent State University, in the United States. Her research interests are the acquisition of speaking and writing proficiency in a second language, interlanguage pragmatics, and career advising for foreign language majors.

APPENDIX A: WORKSHEETS, ANSWER KEYS, AND HANDOUTS

Worksheet 1: Giving and Receiving Compliments

A. Compliments. Give a compliment for each of the following situations. Put an X in the space if you would not say anything.

1. You and your classmate Dave have just walked out to the school parking area when you notice his car (or bicycle or motorbike) is brand-new.

   You say: _____

2. Your friend Lisa has just arrived at work (or school). You notice she has a new haircut.

   You say: _____

B. Compliment Responses. How would you respond to the following situations (adapted from Yu, 2004)? Put an X in the space if you would not say anything.

1. A male professor with whom you are studying returns your essay (or homework) to you and says, "You did a terrific job on this!"

   You say: _____

2. You gave a presentation in class today. After class your female professor says, "Your presentation was great."

   You say: _____

3. You are playing tennis (or another game, such as badminton) with a male friend. He says, "Wow, you're such a good player."

   You say: _____

4. After you present your final project in class, a classmate says, "Great job!"

   You say: _____

Worksheet 1: Sample Responses

A1: *Nice car.*

A2: *I like your haircut.*

Your hair(cut) looks great.

Wow! I love your haircut!

B1: *Thank you. I worked really hard on it.*

Thank you. I put a lot of work into it.

B2: *Thank you. I'm glad you liked it.*

Thank you. I put a lot of time into it.

B3: *Ha! So are you!*

Thanks. Beginner's luck, I guess.

B4: *Thank you. I was really nervous.*

Thank you. I liked your project too.

Thanks. I spent a long time on it.

Worksheet 2: Exploring Social Variables and Attitudes Toward Compliments

Think about compliments you have given and received. Then answer the following questions.

1. Whom do you tend to compliment?
   a. Your parents
   b. Close friends
   c. Coworkers
   d. Classmates
   e. Your professors
   f. Your brother and sister
   g. Your boyfriend or girlfriend

2. I like receiving compliments from _____ (people from #1), and I like to be complimented on _____.

3. I do not like receiving compliments from _____ (people from #1), and I am uncomfortable when complimented on/for _____ _____.

Worksheet 2: Sample Responses

1. I sometimes compliment my close friends or classmates. I rarely compliment my professors.

2. I sometimes like receiving compliments from my teachers and boss. I like to be complimented on my hard work or effort.

3. I do not like to be complimented too much by my friends. I do not like to be complimented on my appearance.

Handout 1: Compliment Formulas

Frequency	Formula
1 (53.6%)	Noun phrase + *is/looks* + (*really*) + adjective Your hair looks (really) great.
2 (16.1%)	*I* + (*really*) + *like/love* + noun phrase I (really) like that necklace.
3 (14.9%)	Pronoun + *is* + (*really*) + *a/an* + adjective + noun phrase That is (really) a great idea.
4 (3.3%)	*You* + verb + *a/an* + (*really*) + adjective + noun phrase You did a (really) good job.
5 (2.7%)	*You* + verb + (noun phrase) + (*really*) + adverb You play the piano (really) well.
6 (2.4%)	*You* + *have* + *a/an* + (*really*) + adjective + noun phrase You have a (really) great sense of humor.
7 (1.6%)	*What* + *a/an* + adjective + noun phrase What a lovely dress!
8 (1.6%)	Adjective + noun phrase Nice car!
9 (1.0%)	*Isn't* + noun phrase + adjective Isn't that necklace precious!
10 (2.8%)	All other patterns

Source: Adapted from Manes & Wolfson, 1981.

Handout 2: Compliment Response Strategies

1	Accept the compliment
	    With an appreciation token
	    With agreement
		
		Thanks.
		I like it too.

2	Deflect the compliment
	    With a comment
	    With a shift in credit
	    With a return compliment
	    With a downgrade
	    With a question
		
		I got it for my birthday.
		I had a great coach.
		I like your earrings too.
		It looks harder to do than it was.
		You really think so?

3	Reject the compliment
	    With a denial
	    By disagreeing
	    By ignoring it (silence or topic change)
		
		It's nothing special.
		I don't like it very much.

Source: Adapted from Billmyer, 1990.

Worksheet 3: Examining Your Own Compliments and Responses (see Appendix C for answers)

Compliments

Situation 1: Car   Situation 2: Haircut

   a.   a.

   b.   b.

   c.   c.

   d.   d.

   e.   e.

   f.   f.

Compliment Responses

Situation 1: Essay   Situation 2: Tennis

   a.   a.

   b.   b.

   c.   c.

   d.   d.

   e.   e.

   f.   f.

Discussion and Analysis

1. Highlight the adjectives used in the compliment situations. Which are used most frequently?

   _____

2. For complimenting a new car, it is very common to use the simple formula adjective + noun (e.g., *Great car!*). Which compliments in Situation 1 use this formula?

   _____

3. For complimenting a haircut, one common formula is *I* + (*really*) + *like/love* + *your* + noun. (e.g., *I really like your haircut!*). Which compliments in Situation 2 use this formula?

   _____

4. Do any of the compliments for either situation seem inappropriate? If so, why?

   _____

   _____

5. Look at the compliment responses, and indicate for each whether the speaker

    a.   accepts the compliment.

    b.   acknowledges the compliment but lessens it, gives credit to someone else, or gives an explanation of the item or topic that was complimented (deflects).

    c.   rejects or ignores the compliment.

Responses to the essay compliment				Responses to the tennis compliment		
a.	☐ accepts	☐ deflects	☐ rejects	a. ☐ accepts	☐ deflects	☐ rejects
b.	☐ accepts	☐ deflects	☐ rejects	b. ☐ accepts	☐ deflects	☐ rejects
c.	☐ accepts	☐ deflects	☐ rejects	c. ☐ accepts	☐ deflects	☐ rejects
d.	☐ accepts	☐ deflects	☐ rejects	d. ☐ accepts	☐ deflects	☐ rejects
e.	☐ accepts	☐ deflects	☐ rejects	e. ☐ accepts	☐ deflects	☐ rejects
f.	☐ accepts	☐ deflects	☐ rejects	f. ☐ accepts	☐ deflects	☐ rejects

Worksheet 3: Sample Responses

1. Car situation: All of the responses except *d* use one of the five most common adjectives for paying compliments.

   Haircut situation: All of the adjectives except *better* are among the top five adjectives identified by Manes and Wolfson (1981; and *better* is an inflected form of *good*).

2. Utterances *a*, *b*, and *e* use the formula adjective + noun phrase.

3. Utterance *a*, *b*, *d*, and *e* use the formula *I* + (*really*) + *like/love* + noun phrase.

4. Car situation: *d* does not contain one of the five typical adjectives; the adjective *shining* has a neutral, not positive meaning; *c* seems oddly impersonal because it is not clear whose car is being complimented; and possibly a stronger adjective such as *great* or *beautiful* might be used.

   Haircut situation: *c* implies that the hearer did not look good enough before the haircut. In *e*, *good job* is used to compliment performance and would be appropriate only if the listener cut his or her own hair.

5. For the essay situation:

       a = acceptance
       b = inappropriately ambiguous because it might be taken as a rejection or nonresponse by a native speaker
       c = rejection
       d = two deflections
       e = an acceptance with deflection
       f = acceptance

For the tennis situation:

    a = might be considered a deflection but potentially might be interpreted by the person issuing the compliment as a rejection

    b = deflection

    c = deflection

    d = deflection

    e = deflection

    f = acceptance

Worksheet 4: Role-Play Scenarios

Create a dialogue with your partner that contains a compliment and response for each of the following situations.

1. You notice an article of clothing or accessory (e.g., watch, jewelry, baseball cap, T-shirt).

2. You have just gone over to your friend's new apartment (or house).

3. It is the last day of class and students have brought home-cooked dishes from their native countries. Compliment a classmate on a dish he or she prepared or brought.

4. Your friend is in a musical group. You have just heard him or her play at a café or bar.

Worksheet 4: Sample Responses

Situation 1

    Speaker A: Hey, cool T-shirt.

    Speaker B: My brother got it for me when he was in California.

    Speaker A: Well, it's really neat.

Situation 2

    Speaker A: Great apartment. It's nice and big.

    Speaker B: Well, you know for the rent they're charging . . . but I like it too.

Situation 3

    Speaker A: These dumplings are delicious! Did you make them?

    Speaker B: Yes. My mother gave me the recipe.

    Speaker A: Wow! Do you like to cook?

    Speaker B: Sometimes, if I have time. But I don't cook as well as my mom.

Situation 4

    Speaker A: I can't believe it! That was incredible.

    Speaker B: Thanks. I've been playing for a long time.

    Speaker A: Really? How long?

    Speaker B: Well, I started lessons when I was 9. And then I played in school, and then I joined this band.

Handout 3: Compliment Response Strategies

This handout includes the 10 compliment response strategies used by your teacher in the Musical Compliment Response Game.

Express appreciation	Agree with the complimenter	Return the compliment	Agree with the compliment modestly	Express surprise at the compliment
Ignore the compliment politely	Give a history or explanation of the object that was complimented	Downgrade or minimize the compliment without being disagreeable	Shift the credit to something or someone else	Deny or reject the compliment

Handout 3: Sample Answers

1. *Hey, I like your haircut!* Possible responses from students:

   Shift credit: *I have a great hair dresser.*

   Ignore politely: *Not to change the subject, but did you finish the assignment?*

   Agree: *Yeah, I like it too, I think.*

   Deny: *God, they never cut the way I want them to.*

2. *Good job on your presentation today!* Possible responses from students:

   Express appreciation: *Thank you. I really value your opinion.*

   Give history: *Really? I must have changed my topic a hundred times.*

   Downgrade: *Well, it wasn't the best I could have done, but thank you.*

   Express surprise: *You mean it?*

3. *Nice place you got here.* Possible responses from students:

   Shift credit: *Thank you, but my friends helped me pick it out.*

   Downgrade: *Yes, it's not bad for something on a student's budget.*

   Accept modestly: *Thanks, I was lucky to find it.*

APPENDIX B: SUPPLEMENTARY HANDOUT FOR ADVANCED-LEVEL STUDENTS

Some Functions of English Compliments
(adapted from Manes & Wolfson, 1981)

1. Greet or open a conversation (sometimes even setting the topic for an entire exchange)

   Speaker A: Hey, <u>I like your shirt</u>.

   Speaker B: Really? Thanks. I got it at X (store). They're having a sale this week.

   Speaker A: I love X (store). They always have such cool things.

   Speaker B: I know. They have a huge buy-two-get-one-free sale going on. I'm gonna* go back on Friday after I get paid. Wanna go?*

   Speaker A: Sure.

   Speaker B: OK. I'll call you. See ya later.

   Speaker A: Bye.

2. Express gratitude

   Thanks for dinner. <u>I really enjoyed it</u>.

3. Close a conversation

   <u>It was nice talking to you</u>. I hope I run into you again.

4. Preface a request

   <u>Hey, you seem really good with computers</u>. I can't figure out how to post the assignment. Do you think you could help me?

5. Positively reinforce desired behaviors

   <u>Good job</u>! (mother to a child who tied his or her own shoes)

6. Soften criticism

   Overall, <u>you did a really good job on the paper</u>, but the conclusion is a little weak.

---

*Gonna and *wanna* are common ways of pronouncing *going to* and *want to* in informal speech.

APPENDIX C: WORKSHEET 3— MODEL WITH RESPONSES FROM A CLASS

Examining Your Own Compliments and Responses

Compliments

Situation 1: Car	Situation 2: Haircut
a. ⎡Nice⎤ car. When d'you get it?	a. Wow, I really like your new haircut. You look great!
b. Wow! ⎡Great⎤ car!	b. I love your hair!
c. What a good car over there.	c. Nice haircut. You look better.
d. Wow, look at the shining car. Did you just buy it?	d. I really like your hair. Did you get it cut?
e. Nice car.	e. Good job. I like your hair.
f. You have a nice car.	f. Did you get your hair cut? It looks good.

Compliment Responses

Situation 1: Essay	Situation 2: Tennis
a. Thank you.	a. Really?
b. (Smile)	b. I just bat the ball around. Got lucky, I guess.
c. (Say nothing)	c. You're a great player too.
d. I'm glad you liked it. I worked hard on it.	d. I had a great coach in high school.
e. Thanks. I enjoyed writing it.	e. I used to play every day.
f. Oh, not so much.	f. Thanks.

APPENDIX D: MATERIALS FOR
MUSICAL COMPLIMENT RESPONSE GAME

Teacher Worksheet

Part I: Responses (to be cut up and distributed by the teacher)

Express appreciation	Agree with the compliment	Return the compliment	Agree with the compliment, but be modest too
Express surprise at the compliment	Ignore the compliment politely	Give a history or explanation of the object or quality that was complimented	Downgrade or minimize the compliment without being disagreeable
Shift the credit to something or someone else	Deny or reject the compliment		

Part II: Situations and Compliments

(to be read by the teacher; students do not see these)

Situation	Compliment
1. Friend to friend:	*Hey, I like your haircut!*
2. Teacher to student:	*Good job on your presentation today.*
3. Friend to friend:	*Nice place you got here.*
4. Husband to wife:	*You look beautiful tonight.*
5. One mother to another:	*Oh, he's so cute.*
6. Friend to friend:	*This dinner is delicious.*

CHAPTER 6

Male and Female Complimenting Behavior

Anne McLellan Howard

Students from cultures with clear gender-related differences in speech (such as Japan) are frequently surprised to find that such differences occur in English as well. One of the best ways to illustrate these differences is by having students examine complimenting behavior (see chapter 5 in this volume for definitions and more discussion). This chapter provides students with an opportunity to compare their ideas about complimenting with characteristics of English compliment formulas revealed in research studies. In particular, students will replicate a simplified form of a study originally carried out by Knapp, Hopper, and Bell (1984), the methodology of which provides students with an opportunity to conduct an experiment and contrast their results with those from other studies on English compliments.

In Knapp et al.'s (1984) research, subjects were asked to recall the last compliments that they had given or received, some characteristics of the person with whom they exchanged compliments, the subject of the compliment, and their opinion as to whether the compliment was sincere. For the activities in this chapter, students examine compliments that they have given and received, analyze their characteristics, and compare their results with the results of research on English compliments. They focus particularly on differences in frequency according to the gender of the speaker and of the recipient.

CONTEXT

The series of activities in this chapter was created for a linguistics class at an English-medium liberal arts college in Japan. Students had completed 2 years at the college and 1 semester of study abroad, and their level of English was comparatively high. Most of the students were highly motivated English education majors preparing to become high school English teachers. Classes generally consisted of fewer than 20 students. The entire lesson took two 90-minute class periods.

The topic of gender differences generated a high level of interest, and the ensuing discussions were among the liveliest of the semester, with many students writing journal entries about the topic and some pursuing it further as a semester project.

Compliments in English

Research indicates that English speakers use a limited number of sentence structures to perform compliments, with 85% of compliments employing one of three structures: (1) [noun phrase] *is/looks really* [adjective], (2) *I really like/love* [noun phrase], and (3) [pronoun] *is* (*really*) (*a/an*) [adjective] [noun phrase]. This led Manes and Wolfson (1981) to refer to such limited structures as *compliment formulas* (see Handout 1 in chapter 5 for more details). Compliments are limited in word choice as well, with *nice* and *good* making up a majority of the adjectives used (Manes & Wolfson, 1981), and certain topics predominate (see chapter 5 for a discussion).

Compliment giving is also affected by social factors such as gender. Although the research is not unequivocal (c.f. Tatsuki & Nishizawa, 2005), differences have been observed in the frequency with which men and women give and receive compliments (Wieland, 1995), topics selected (Nelson, El Bakary, & Al Batal, 1996), and the forms used to express them (Parisi & Wogan, 2006). Holmes (1988) found that women are more likely to give and receive compliments. On the other hand, Knapp and colleagues' (1984) research suggests that compliments are more likely to be exchanged by members of the same sex, whether men or women. And according to Herbert (1990), women's compliments tend to be more personal, using expressions such as *I think*.

CURRICULUM, TASKS, MATERIALS

In this project, students first are introduced to compliments and then practice distinguishing between compliments and other positive statements. Once students have a clear idea about this distinction, they recall the last compliments they gave and received, and discuss this in their group. When data have been collected for the entire class, students analyze their own compliments and compare them with the research on compliments produced by native English speakers. They also compare complimenting behaviors of men and women, and discuss why these might be different.

Activity 1: Identifying Compliments

Occasionally, students are unclear as to what type of positive statement constitutes a compliment. The purpose of Worksheet 1 (see Appendix A), which students go over individually or in pairs, is to ensure that they understand what a compliment is before completing the rest of the project.

Some discussion may be necessary to clarify the compliments in Worksheet 1.

Students sometimes interpret compliments to mean any positive statement, not necessarily one directed at the hearer. The teacher may want to follow up this worksheet by asking students, "In a compliment, who is the speaker making a positive statement about?" (Students should answer "the hearer," not another person.)

Once the notion of compliment is clear, additional questions for discussion could include the following: Have you noticed any difference in the way that men and women speak in English? Why do you think women might tend to give and receive more compliments? What are common situations in which you found that people give and receive compliments?

Activity 2: Recalling Compliments

In this activity, students recall compliments they have given and received. Students' responses on Worksheet 2 (see Appendix A) form the basis for the analysis and discussion of subsequent worksheets. On Worksheet 2, students write the last compliment they received (translated into English if necessary), the person who gave it, and the circumstances. Then they recall the last compliment they gave and the recipient, and they write what they said and the circumstances.

After students have completed Worksheet 2, they share their answers in small groups. First, each student tells his or her two compliments to the group members. This reminds students of what a compliment is and helps some students remember compliments they have forgotten. While students are working in groups, the teacher listens in on the groups to be sure that all of the students understand the meaning of *compliment*.

Once students have shared their compliments with their small group, they begin comparing their compliments to typical English compliments. The teacher distributes Handout 1 (see Appendix A) and informs students that they will be analyzing how similar the compliments they recalled are to compliments in English.

Activity 3: Analyzing Compliment Patterns: Topics and Formulas

In Activity 3, students begin classifying their data according to the topics identified by Knapp et al. (1984) and three of the most common formulas. The topics and strategies, as well as examples, are included in Handout 1.

After students are familiar with the topics and formulas, they are ready to start working on classifying the data in small groups, starting with the topic of the compliment. The topics outlined by Knapp et al. (1984) are listed in Worksheet 3 (see Appendix A). True compliments generally fit into one of these categories (note that accomplishments are subsumed under *skills* by many authors). Those that don't are usually not true compliments.

Next, students analyze the compliments they wrote on Worksheet 2 in terms of their linguistic form. After everyone understands the categories in Part II of Handout 1, students classify each of the compliments collected in their group (the ones they gave and the ones they received) according to grammatical pattern using Worksheet 4 (see Appendix A).

Activity 4: Analyzing Compliment Patterns: Gender

Students calculate how many of the total number of compliments in their group were given by women and how many were given by men. They then count the total number given to women and to men and record the results on Worksheet 5 (see Appendix A).

After students complete Worksheet 5, the teacher might also ask whether they have noticed any difference, in general, in the way that males and females give compliments.

Activity 5: Comparing Learner and American English Compliment Patterns

After students have analyzed their own compliments and those of their group members, they are ready to compare these with native-speaker compliments. For this activity, the teacher assigns students to new groups, each of which has at least one member of each original group. Students share the data from their original group with their new group. At this point, everyone has data from the entire class. In the new groups, students compare the data with claims about compliments in English from studies by Herbert (1990), Holmes (1988), Knapp et al. (1984), and Manes and Wolfson (1981), and they complete Worksheet 6 (see Appendix A). (Refer to the discussion in the Context section for details.)

Students usually find that women receive more compliments than men do and that these compliments tend to be about appearance. If the results do not correspond to those in the research literature, the teacher can elicit possible explanations. In an English as a foreign language context, a disproportionate number of compliments may not fit any of the patterns. This may be because students are translating the compliments from their first language (L1), and they may not be translating them in a native-like way. For instance, they could look at their compliments, compare them with the native-speaker compliment formula, and then try to translate them to correspond more closely with the patterns (e.g., *That's a nice sweater* rather than *You're wearing a good sweater*). Of course, if students are translating compliments, it may be the case that compliments in the students' L1 may not follow the same pattern. The teacher can elicit students' opinions about this. Another possible explanation is that students might remember certain compliments more than others and thus skew the data. The teacher can mention that this is a pitfall of research that depends on memory. A class that is overwhelmingly male or female will, of course, also skew the results.

Activity 6: Discussing Differences in Compliment-Giving by Gender

In this activity, learners reflect on the use of compliments in English according to gender. As a first step, students can discuss what the data on the gender of givers and recipients of compliments mean in terms of differences between the way men and women use language.

First, they might think about what compliments are used for. Students usually say that compliments are used to make someone feel happy. The teacher can remind them that compliments can also be used to break the ice or start a conversation in English.

Students can also discuss complimenting in their L1 and in English—when and to whom is it appropriate to give a compliment or what kinds of compliments are inappropriate. For example, some compliments specifically dealing with appearance might not be appropriate to a member of the opposite sex. *Your shirt is nice* is usually acceptable, but *You are really attractive* might not be because general evaluations of a hearer's physical attributes are often considered too personal.

From these discussions, students can get a good idea of the social uses of compliments. Students can then be introduced to two theories of gender differences and reflect on these using Worksheet 7 (see Appendix A).

REFLECTIONS

The activities presented in this chapter are designed to teach students about doing research while drawing attention to specific sociolinguistic aspects of complimenting. In an English class, the teacher may want to limit the discussion of the research method. For a lower level class, the teacher could focus more on form and appropriateness (see Worksheet 8 in Appendix B).

Because the most common forms of complimenting are syntactically quite simple, students can benefit from additional information on how compliments are used for social purposes, especially in an English as a second language situation. In classrooms in which students do not share the same L1, they can discuss the different customs related to compliment giving in their cultures (see Worksheet 9 in Appendix B): What are common times to give compliments? What kinds of compliments are inappropriate (e.g., about the skill of someone older or of higher status than the speaker)?

To follow up on this project, students can discuss or write about the kinds of compliments they find most meaningful. Knapp et al. (1984) found that comments on personality tend to mean the most to the listener. Students might also discuss the types of compliments that bother or annoy them.

Anne McLellan Howard is an assistant professor of English at Miyazaki International College, in Japan. She is currently doing research on the role of praise in university-level discussion sections and on the pragmatics of advice giving. She has taught in the United States and Japan.

APPENDIX A: WORKSHEETS, ANSWER KEYS, AND HANDOUTS

Worksheet 1: Recognizing Compliments

When someone tells you something good about you, he or she is giving you a compliment. For example, the following are compliments:

You play the trumpet really well!
I like your hat.
I like spending time with you.

Which of the following are compliments? If a sentence expresses a compliment, write Yes; if not, write No. The first one is done for you.

<u>Yes</u> 1. The curry you made yesterday was delicious!

      2. You always dress so nicely.

      3. The store at the corner has delicious coffee.

      4. You should be a professional singer.

      5. I really loved that book.

      6. My teacher is a really kind person.

      7. I wish my hair were the same color as yours.

      8. My cat is really cute.

      9. Professor, the lesson today was very interesting.

    10. I know I'll have a good time at your party.

Worksheet 1: Answer Key

Numbers 1, 2, 4, 7, 9, and 10 are compliments. They are about the person you are talking to, something that belongs to him or her, or something that he or she did.

Numbers 3, 5, 6, and 8 are not compliments. They are positive statements, but they are not about the person you are talking to. In some cases it depends on the circumstances. For example, number 5 could be a compliment if you are talking to the author of the book.

It is difficult to say whether something is a compliment unless you know the person who made the statement and the person who received it. For example, some people would think *You've lost weight!* is a compliment; others definitely would not. *Your daughter is so quiet!* might be a compliment to the parents of a very little girl, because it implies that they are good parents with a well-behaved child; to the parents of a grown woman, though, it is just a statement.

Worksheet 2: Compliments You Have Given and Received

Write down compliments that you have given and received. Then use them in your discussion.

Answer the following questions. Write two compliments—the one that you received and the one that you gave.

A. Think of the last time someone gave you a compliment in your native language.

1. Who gave you the compliment?

2. What was the situation?

3. What was the compliment? (Translate it into English and write it out.)

B. Now think of the last time you gave someone a compliment.

1. Who did you give the compliment to?

2. What was the situation?

3. What was the compliment? (Translate it into English and write it out.)

Handout 1: Compliment Patterns

I. Compliment Topics

Compliments in English usually are on one of the following topics:

Appearance: *You look great. / Your hair is so pretty!*

Skills: *You can run very fast! / I like the way you dance.*

Possessions: *Nice car! / Your apartment is pretty.*

Personality: *I like being with you. / You are so kind.*

II. Compliment Formulas/Patterns

Most compliments in English have one of the following patterns.

Pattern 1: [Noun phrase] *is/looks really* [adjective]
Your dress is really nice. / This cake you made is really good.

Pattern 2: *I really like/love* [noun phrase]
I really love your necklace.

Pattern 3: [Pronoun] *is* (*really*) *a/an* [adjective] [noun phrase].
This is really a nice house.

Worksheet 3: Analyzing Your Compliments: Topics

Look at the data that you wrote on Worksheet 2. What characteristic of the hearer did you compliment? In your group, calculate the number of compliments that fall into each of the following categories:

Appearance: _____

Skills: _____

Possessions: _____

Personality: _____

Report your group's results to the class.

Worksheet 4: Analyzing Your Compliments: Grammatical Patterns

Classify the compliments in your group according to their grammatical pattern.

Pattern	Number of compliments
[Noun phrase] *is/looks really* [adjective]. Ex: *Your dress is really nice.*	
I really like/love [noun phrase]. Ex: *I really love your necklace.*	
[Pronoun] *is* (*really*) *a/an* [adjective] [noun phrase]. Ex: *This is really a nice house.*	
Another pattern	

Worksheet 5: Analyzing Your Compliments: Gender

Classify the compliments that you and the members of the group

   a. **received,** according to the gender of the person who gave you a compliment;

   b. **gave,** according to the gender of the person to whom you gave a compliment.

	Received by female	Received by male	Total
Given by female			Total number of compliments given by females
Given by male			Total number of compliments given by males
Total	Total number of compliments received by females	Total number of compliments received by males	

   1. How many of the compliments your group collected were given to women?

   2. How many were given to men?

   3. How many were given by women?

   4. How many were given by men?

Worksheet 6: Analyzing Your Compliments: Comparison With English Compliments

Below are some facts about compliments in English. Check to see whether the data from your class fit the pattern.

1. Research on English compliments has shown that most compliments (85%) fit the three patterns in Handout 1. The most common pattern is Number 1: [Noun phrase] *is/looks really* [adjective]. Do the class data fit this pattern?

2. Research indicates that women tend to give and receive more compliments. Do the class data fit this pattern?

3. Research indicates that women frequently receive compliments about their appearance. Do the class data fit this pattern?

Worksheet 7: Compliments and Gender: Accounting for the Facts

There are two theories of why women might exchange compliments more, and why these compliments might be about appearance:

- Theory 1 says that it is important for women to have a good appearance. So they are praised for being pretty so that they will try to be prettier.

- Theory 2 says that women give and get compliments more because they use language more for social purposes. Men tend to use language to exchange information. So women tend to give more compliments because they make other people feel good and help to keep better relations.

Which idea do you agree with, or do you have an idea of your own? Discuss your ideas with your class.

Discussion Questions

Have you noticed any difference in the way that men and women speak in English?

Why do you think women tend to give and get more compliments?

What are common situations that you found people give and get compliments in?

Worksheet 7: Sample Answers to Discussion Questions

Have you noticed any difference in the way that men and women speak in English?

Students usually say that there is no difference in men's and women's speech in English. (This chapter is designed to raise their awareness of actual differences.)

Why do you think women tend to give and get more compliments?

Many students say that women are "nicer" or more considerate of people's feelings and thus tend to give more compliments.

What are common situations that you found people give and get compliments in?

In an American context, it is quite common to give a compliment to start a conversation, or when meeting someone for the first time that day.

APPENDIX B: WORKSHEETS FOR LOWER LEVEL STUDENTS

Worksheet 8: Making Compliments in English

1. Create a sentence out of each of the following sets of words:

   like/I/room/your: _____

   shoes/really/Those/are/pretty: _____

   nice/a/That's/car: _____

   These sentences are compliments. A *compliment* is saying something positive to another person about them, something they own, something they can do, or how they look. Here are some examples:

   I like your shoes.

   You play the piano very well.

   It's fun to be with you.

   Your dress is pretty.

   You have a nice car.

2. Many compliments follow the following patterns:

   a. *I (really) like/love* _____ _____ .
                                       your/that   noun

   Examples:

   I like your hair.

   I like that picture you painted.

   I like the dinner you made.

   b. _____ *is (really) a/an* _____ _____ .
            that/this   adjective   noun phrase

   Examples:

   Those are really nice clothes.

   This is a very pretty house.

   c. _____ *is/looks (really)* _____ .
              noun   adjective

   Examples:

   Your hair looks really pretty.

   Your English is really good.

3. Now try to make some compliments with each pattern:

I like _____.

I really love _____.

That's a _____ _____.

These are really _____ _____.

Your _____ is _____.

Your _____ is really _____.

A compliment is a good way to start a conversation with someone. Remember, sometimes compliments don't make people happy. If you give a compliment about how someone looks (for example, *You're pretty, You are handsome,* or *You look cute today*), it should probably only be to someone you know very well.

4. Now move around the room and try to give three different compliments to three different classmates.

Worksheet 9: Comparing Compliments Across Cultures

Discuss compliment customs in your culture.

	My Culture	**My Partner's Culture**
When do you give a compliment?		
Is it appropriate to compliment an older person?		
Is it appropriate to compliment someone's appearance?		
Is it appropriate to compliment someone of the opposite sex?		
Is it appropriate to compliment someone's possessions?		
Is it appropriate to compliment someone's talents or abilities?		
What is another compliment-related custom that you would like to tell your partner about?		

CHAPTER 7

Taking Turns and Talking Naturally: Teaching Conversational Turn-Taking

Donald Carroll

Taking turns in conversation is usually as effortless as breathing. However, few people (and few language teachers) have given any conscious consideration to just how we manage our turn-taking in talk-in-interaction. This chapter makes a case for teaching and practicing the norms of conversational turn-taking in the English to speakers of other languages (ESOL) classroom. It debunks some common misperceptions about the way turn-taking works in conversation and provides a brief overview of a more accurate description of conversational turn-taking, as revealed by studies of conversation analysis (CA). It then offers a series of activities that have been used successfully to sensitize students to the practices of conversational turn-taking, with a particular focus on helping students appreciate the communicative importance of "jumping into" the conversation at the right time.

CONTEXT

Initially, the activities described in this chapter were created in response to the needs of first-year university students in Japan enrolled in a conversation course. Class size was around 15, and most of these learners fell into the "false beginner" category, with minimal speaking skills. But perhaps the greatest barrier was the students' passivity—a characteristic of many students from Asia. It soon became obvious that any conversational skills would need to be grounded in some basic interactional skills. These activities assume little in the way of prior English ability, and with minor modifications they are suitable for learners of most ages and any prior competence.

Popular Perceptions of Turn-Taking

Michael Agar (1994) expresses one of the most common popular perceptions of how turn-taking in conversation works: "Someone talks, and I lie back and listen and let them roll for a while. When they're done, there'll be a pause that will flash like a green light to announce that someone else can have the floor" (p. 172).

In this view, participants in a conversation wait for the person who is currently speaking to stop, and then someone else begins speaking. But there are several inadequacies with this explanation. First, it is at odds with the observable facts of most talk. Turns-at-talk are not invariably separated by pauses (or more precisely, gaps). Instead, speakers show an incredible precision in their ability to begin speaking at just the right moment, and a great many speaker transitions are achieved with no gap and no overlap (Jefferson, 1973, 1986; Sacks, Schegloff, & Jefferson, 1974). Even novice nonnative speakers are regularly able to achieve no-gap start-ups in conversation (Carroll, 2000, 2006). This doesn't mean that gaps don't occur in talk or that gaps are somehow "unnatural" (or *disfluent*). What it does mean is that when inter-turn silences do occur, they are heard as intentional, purposeful, and interactionally meaningful.

Second, the wait-for-speaker-to-stop explanation doesn't specify how a particular person in the conversation ends up with the right to speak next. This might seem obvious if there are only two people. However, even in two-party talk, it is entirely possible for one person to speak and then (often after a beat of silence) for that same person to speak again—effectively taking two back-to-back turns, as A does in lines 01 and 03 in Example 1. Thus, turns-at-talk will not necessarily be distributed in a simple ABABAB pattern.

> **Example 1** (adapted from Pomerantz, 1984, p. 77; Sacks, 1987, p. 64)
>
> 01 A: Do they have a good cook there?
>
> 02   (1.7 second pause)
>
> 03 A: Nothing special?
>
> 04 B: No. Every- everybody takes their turns.

In multiparty talk, with two or more possible next speakers, the need for a fuller explanation is even more obvious. In naturally occurring conversations with, for example, three people, turns-at-talk are not distributed in a cyclical ABCABC-ABC pattern, although this is often the pattern that language learners fall into during arranged conversations in the classroom. Instead, the turn-taking can appear random, which is the result of the participants following a more complex system. For these reasons, the overly simplistic wait-to-stop explanation of turn-taking is unsatisfactory.

The Conversation Analysis System of Conversational Turn-Taking

In a now classic paper, Sacks, Schegloff, and Jefferson (1974) propose what has turned out to be an extremely robust description of conversational turn-taking, based on recordings of naturally occurring conversations. It is a system in the sense that participants themselves display an orientation to the "rules" in managing their interaction. This system has been shown not only to hold true across a wide variety of kinds of talk in English but also to describe accurately how turn-taking works in conversations in a diverse range of other languages (see also Wilson, Wiemann, & Zimmerman, 1984, for a discussion of competing systems of turn-taking organization).

Speaker Selection

Sacks, Schegloff, and Jefferson (1974) begin by distinguishing between a turn-taking system for conversation and systems employed for other activities. For example, in bowling the order of who bowls first, second, and so on is decided in advance; it's *preallocated*. Some speech events, such as graduation ceremonies, are similarly preallocated. An impromptu system of preallocation can, and often does, develop in English as a foreign language classroom conversations, where students drop into a fixed pattern of "going around the circle."

In contrast, speaker transitions in naturally occurring conversation are *locally managed* in the moment-to-moment flow of the interaction. At the heart of the SSJ system is a simple set of three recurrent speaker selection rules, which come into play as each turn-at-talk reaches a point of possible (that is to say, "hearable") completion (more precisely defined as a *transition relevance place*, the end of a *turn construction unit*). The following, in somewhat simplified form, are the rules (Sacks et al., 1974, p. 702).

1a.   Current speaker may select next speaker. That is, current speaker may use some technique to direct his or her talk at one particular participant, thereby designating that, and only that, person as the ratified next speaker.

1b.   If current speaker does not select next speaker, next speaker may self-select. What this means is that any possible next speaker in the conversation can choose him- or herself as next speaker. Whoever begins speaking first becomes the new current speaker.

1c.   If no other participant self-selects, current speaker may, but need not, continue speaking.

Timing of Speaker Transitions

Just as important as who speaks next is when the next speaker begins speaking. As mentioned earlier, next speakers regularly time the beginning of their speaking turn to correspond with the exact moment at which the prior speaker brings the prior turn to possible completion; they do so without allowing even the briefest of gaps. This is referred to simply as a *no-gap/no-overlap* speaker transition. An orientation on the part of participants to no-gap transitions is critical to the operation of the turn-taking system (and to the organization of preference; see chapter 8 in this volume).

There are, in practice, three ways that any given speaker transition might end up being done: on time, delayed, and early. These three timings for speaker transition (illustrated in Example 2) are not merely random possibilities; rather, they represent systematic alternatives that strongly project the communicative action to be performed by the forthcoming turn. That is to say, the timing of the speaker transition is an integral part of the linguistic design of the upcoming turn.

Example 2: Timing of Speaker Transitions

On Time	Delayed	Early
A: TALK	A: TALK	A: TAL[K]
B: TALK	(gap)	B: [T]ALK
	B: TALK	

Note: Brackets indicate simultaneous talk.

Several decades of CA research based on recordings of naturally occurring interaction support the applicability of the SSJ system across a wide range of cultures and languages, including Thai, Korean, Japanese, Finnish, Spanish, Danish, German, Russian, and Arabic. The Sachs et al. (1974) system has also been shown to hold true in native speaker–nonnative speaker interactions as well as nonnative speaker–nonnative speaker interactions.

Rationale for Teaching Turn-Taking

If these patterns of turn-taking are so natural and so widespread among the world's cultures and languages, teachers may wonder why it would be necessary to teach turn-taking in the classroom. The problem is that the organization of traditional pedagogic interaction follows a highly specialized system of turn-taking (see McHoul, 1978; Seedhouse, 2004), in which the teacher largely controls who speaks and when. Students, through a lifetime of exposure to schooling, have learned to check their conversational practices at the door, so to speak. This is equally true for most language classrooms. If teachers hope to have students engage in conversational interaction in the classroom, the first step will be to reintroduce and encourage the practices of conversational turn-taking.

CURRICULUM, TASKS, MATERIALS

The following sections present a series of activities designed to introduce students to the ideas of conversational turn-taking, to sensitize them to the need for (and normative nature of) on-time speaker transitions, and to practice aspects of the Sachs et al. (1974) turn-taking system. These activities are fun, require few or no materials, are simple to manage, and can be recycled and adapted week after week. They would nicely complement any course involving conversation (or more generically, speaking) at any proficiency level from beginning to advanced.

The first activity, Jumping Into a Conversation, provides a visual illustration of the idea of *projecting turn completion* and emphasizes why this matters. The Speaking in Circles set of activities is designed to sensitize students to the normative nature of on-time speaker transitions—to train them to avoid inter-turn silences (because these are heard by proficient speakers as meaningful). The Fighting for a Turn set of activities practices Rule 1b of the Sachs et al. (1974) system (self-selection). This is necessary because the usual norms of classroom interaction strongly discourage self-selection. The final activity, Monitoring the Turn, lets students practice projecting the upcoming completion of a turn and demonstrates that multiple next speaker start-ups are a natural result of the Sachs et al. turn-taking system.

Activity 1: Jumping Into a Conversation

This activity visually illustrates to students the idea that there is just one perfect moment to jump into a conversation, that is, to begin a turn-at-talk. It illustrates the idea of projecting turn completion (in order to be able to start on time), the recurrent nature of turn completion, and the consequences of starting either too early or too late.

This activity requires a long jump rope and a clear space in the classroom or outside. The teacher selects two students to turn the rope. The two rope turners should start by getting the jump rope spinning slowly. The teacher can point out that each rotation of the rope is like one turn-at-talk. On each revolution, as the rope hits the bottom of its swing, the teacher can point out that this is like the end of a turn-at-talk and is the perfect moment to jump in and take a turn. As already mentioned, in the terminology of CA, this is the transition relevance place (TRP), and when doing this jump-rope demonstration with advanced-level students—or students in an Introduction to CA course—the teacher might say, "TRP, TRP, TRP," each time the rope hits the bottom. As everyone knows, the whole trick to jump-roping lies in projecting when this moment is going to come. A bit too early or a bit too late, and you might trip on the rope. Next, students one by one jump into (and out of) the turning rope. If this is not possible, students clap their hands at the moment they should jump in.

Activity 2: Speaking in Circles

This sequence of activities is designed to sensitize learners to the rhythm of no-gap speaker transitions. The series proceeds from a basic version and with each additional level becomes slightly more complex (and more natural). As students participate in the activities, they quickly realize that to start on time they need to closely monitor the rhythm of the talk by prior speakers in order to project when, in the immediate future, they need to start speaking.

Level 1

As suggested by the title, for this activity, students stand in a circle, with the teacher in the middle. The teacher explains that the first student will say, "One," then the next student in the circle will say, "Two," and so on up to "Ten." Then, the next student in the circle starts over with "One." Note that if there are exactly 10 students, the students count only to nine before starting over. Once they get the idea, the counting should continue, going around and around until the group sounds like one person counting quickly and smoothly to 10. The teacher can demonstrate what counting to 10 should sound like. In order to speed things up, the teacher can clap or tap out a rhythm for the counting. The goal is to get to a speed where there are no silences (gaps) between the numbers.

Level 2

Students count in rounds so that more than one person is speaking all the time. This is a great way to sensitize students to what natural conversations often sound like—and what a conversation class *should* sound like. The same student begins counting, saying, "One," as in Level 1. Then when the counting gets halfway around, the teacher points to the first student to start the counting off again (in the same direction). At first this causes some confusion, but the students soon get the idea. A group of 10 or more students can manage up to three or four simultaneous rounds. It helps to have students look at the next person as they speak.

Level 3

In this activity the numbers are replaced with words in a sentence such as "On Saturday, I went to [place name]," with each person saying just one of the words. Or if the teacher prefers, longer sentences might be parsed into chunks, for example, starting with "On Saturday," and each student says one chunk. For the purpose of this activity, however, it doesn't matter which method is used. Again, the talk should go around and around (using the same place name) until the group starts to sound like one person speaking. The teacher needs to ensure that the number of students isn't a multiple of the number of words in the sentence (e.g., 12 students, 6 words), because this results in the same student saying the same word over and over. The students continue until they can achieve a smooth joint production of this turn. Next, to make this talk more real, students can be encouraged to think about where they went, then have the final person provide a place name. It is important to make sure that each student has thought of a place beforehand (if necessary, by having students write down their ideas), because there shouldn't be any pauses in the production of the sentence.

Level 4

The process from Level 3 can now be made a bit more interactive and natural by having everyone else in the circle respond with "Oh" when the final speaker says the place name: Student: "On Saturday, I went to Tokyo." Chorus: "Oh." This also has the advantage of keeping all the students on task. There should be no gap between the place name and "Oh" because a silence in this location can be heard as disinterest or disbelief and may have negative implications for the talk.

Level 5

Once students are comfortable with previous levels, they can include the use of *um* as a temporary placeholder, for example, "On Saturday, I went to um . . . [pause] Tokyo." The same person says "um" and the place name. The English token *mm* or *um* should be used rather than the equivalent in the student's native language, because this is part of English. A further step in this activity is for one person to say, "to um . . ." and then—after a slight pause—have the next person suggest a place name with questioning intonation so that with five speakers, the talk would unfold as follows: A: "On" B: "Saturday" C: "I" D: "went" E: "to um . . ." F: "Tokyo?" Speaker E can then ratify this *co-completion* through repetition ("Yeah, Tokyo"). Actually, the variations and elaborations on this activity are virtually endless. This type of activity might be used to warm up the class for 5 minutes each day or each week, progressing to more and more natural routines.

Activity 3: Fighting for a Turn

The goal of this series of activities is to illustrate the functioning of Sachs and colleagues' (1974) Rule 1b (next speaker self-selects) and have students practice self-selection. Students are used to waiting for someone to "pick" them before they respond (Rule 1a), but this makes carrying on a conversation extremely difficult (and, in fact, turns a conversation into an interview). This series of activities encourages self-selection and demonstrates to students the need to "fight" for a turn-at-talk.

Level 1

Three students are arranged on three sides of a desk (or in a circle on the floor). A wadded-up piece of paper (or a small ball) serves as a ball for each group. One person picks up the ball, then firmly places it back in the middle of the desk. Then another person picks up the ball, and so on. The teacher emphasizes that the ball should be moving all the time (like in a game of tennis). The ball resting on the desk would be equivalent to a silence in conversation. To illustrate how the ball should be constantly moving, it's useful as an initial demonstration to have just two students quickly pick up and put down the ball.

What will initially happen is that students quickly fall into an ABCABC pattern, going around in a circle. Once they do, the teacher can point out what is happening and tell them this doesn't happen in natural conversation. To drive home this point, the teacher can have one group attempt to have a conversation in the L1 while strictly following the ABCABC pattern. Students will quickly realize how unnatural and impossible this is.

The teacher can explain that students will need to "fight" for their turn-at-talk. No one will "give" them a chance to speak because any possible next speaker may self-select. Once Sachs and colleagues' (1974) Rule 1c (current speaker may continue speaking) is included, this means that each time the ball is put down, there are potentially three people (in a group of three) who might take the next turn.

Very quickly a number of interesting situations will emerge. For example, two people will try to grab the ball at the same time (overlapping start-up; see Activity 4), and there will be some physical negotiation about who takes the turn. The students will also learn tricks for putting the ball down and then immediately snatching it up again without allowing the other participants a chance. This also occurs in natural interaction; one technique is the "rush through," when a person rushes through the end of one turn and quickly into the beginning of another before anyone else has a chance to speak.

It can be fun to organize a whole-class competition for competitive self-selection in this ball-snatching activity. The teacher picks the most competitive student (the one dominating the self-selection) in each group and moves him or her into increasingly more competitive groupings. The teacher can also join the "final battle."

Level 2

Up to now students have been reacting only physically. This time around they are required to say something when they pick up the object (i.e., take a turn-at-talk). An easy way to start is by having each group count one-turn-at-a-time from 1 to 50. That is, someone says, "One," then someone else says, "Two" (probably another speaker, under Rule 1b, or possibly the same speaker again, under Rule 1c), and so on. One nice demonstration here is for the teacher to time himself or herself counting smoothly to 50, which typically takes approximately 30 seconds. Then students can compete to see which group can come closest to this time. This activity requires that next speakers attend to both the content and the timing of the turn-in-progress in order to project when they can begin as well as which number they will need to say. The groups can race each other for the fastest time.

If students are fighting hard enough for a turn-at-talk, the teacher should hear multiple instances of overlapping talk. The teacher should assure the students that this is perfectly natural. Also, the teacher needs to make sure that they don't fall back into an ABCABC (around the circle) pattern of preallocated turn-taking.

I have experimented with removing the ball during this game and having the students take "free turns," but this almost always results in *massive* and *lengthy* overlap, which is to say, shouting matches. Also, if this self-selection counting activity is done with the whole class (as one group), there will be some students who never self-select. One solution is to begin with all the students standing up, then one by one, as they take a turn and say a number, they sit down. Only the students still standing are part of the pool of possible next speakers, so eventually everyone has to speak. Once all the students are sitting down, someone stands up to say the next number, and so on.

Level 3

Once students have grasped the idea of continuous no-gap self-selection, the teacher can give them something a bit more turn-like to say. It helps to start with something easy, such as "I like [food item]," for example, "I like apples." The teacher needs to demonstrate to students that they should be saying the first word (*I*) at the very moment that they start to pick up the ball and that they should be placing the ball back on the desk just as they complete the final word of the turn.

Another easy turn, even for beginners, is "I wanna go to [country name]." The teacher can adjust the difficulty of the turn format to suit the students' level. For example, advanced-level learners might (eventually) be constructing turns like "What I really hate(d) about high school is/was. . . ." The game is the same; it's just that the turns are longer.

After they have played this game for a while, problematic turn-taking strategies may become apparent. For example, students might begin holding their hand over the ball while thinking of what to say. The teacher can demonstrate that anyone can (legitimately) snatch the ball away from under another student's hovering hand. That is, holding a hand over the ball is not the same as officially beginning a turn-at-talk, so during this time someone else may self-select.

After pointing this out, the teacher can show students a trick that all proficient speakers of a language know: Pause *after* starting the turn—not *before*. Have them grab the ball as they begin to say the "I" in, for example, "I want to go to . . ." and only then pause to think how to finish the turn. Once a student has grabbed the ball, it is officially his or her turn until he or she puts the ball back down. If a silence (technically, an inter-turn pause) develops during the production of the turn, this silence officially belongs to the current speaker. This would be a good time to introduce the use of *um* in word searches (Carroll, 2005, 2006).

Level 4

In the lower level tasks so far in Activity 3, the students have been employing only a one-rule turn-taking system, namely Sachs and colleagues' (1974) Rule 1b (self-selection), although they may have also been occasionally following Rule 1c (taking two or more turns in a row). At this point Rule 1a (current speaker may select next speaker) can be reintroduced. To illustrate this rule, the teacher has students go back to the first silent version of the game. This time, however, the teacher explains that instead of placing the turn on the table, they can also, if they want, hand the turn (i.e., the ball) over to a specific participant. The choice is always the same at the end of each turn: Either place the turn on the table (in which case, any possible next speaker can self-select) or hand it directly to another participant.

Once students get the idea, the spoken turns, as in prior variations, can be reintroduced, for example, "I'd like to visit [place]." At the end of the turn, the current speaker can either place the ball back on the desk or hand it to a specific participant. The most common technique for selecting the next speaker is the use of eye contact, perhaps accompanied by a device such as "How about you?" (Note that in naturally occurring interaction, speakers may only employ *How about you?* after a next speaker fails to self-select or to respond when selected.) If the current speaker doesn't specifically select someone, any next speaker can self-select. At the end of each turn, the alternatives are the same: Hand the ball to someone or put it back on the table.

Note that a self-selecting next speaker may elect to use his or her entire turn to select another next speaker, as C does in the final turn of Example 3:

> **Example 3**
>
> A: I like pizza.
>
> C: I like hamburgers. How about you? (looks toward B)
>
> B: I like sushi.
>
> C: I like . . . um . . . spaghetti.
>
> B: I like chocolate cake. What about you? (looks toward A)
>
> A: I like donuts.
>
> C: What do you like? (hands the turn to B)

Level 5

At this point, the talk is still relatively artificial. Although there are many reasons for this, one obvious problem is that the participants are still occupying their turns with an extremely limited set of turn types, such as statements of likes and questions selecting a next speaker. They are also not displaying any kind of uptake of the prior speaker's turn. In naturally occurring conversations, news telling (e.g., telling one's likes or dislikes) is regularly acknowledged in the next turn with an *oh* (i.e., a change-of-state token; Heritage, 1984; see also chapter 12, in this volume, on listener response tokens). *Oh* can serve as a complete turn in its own right, but it can also make a substantial claim on the production of further talk, such that the person (or persons) who says "Oh" may well go on to produce a further turn-at-talk, as in Example 4:

> **Example 4**
>
> A: I like pepperoni pizza.
>
> B: Oh, I just had pizza last night.

One particularly common thing to do following a statement of an opinion (or in CA terms, an *assessment*) is for the next speaker to respond with an agreeing or disagreeing second assessment (Pomerantz, 1984). By adding in this third turn type, participants can now create much more natural-sounding interactions, as in Example 5 (note that B's "Oh, I love pepperoni pizza!" is actually an upgrade):

Example 5

A: I like pepperoni pizza.

B: Oh, I love pepperoni pizza!

C: I like ramen. What do you like?

B: I like octopus sushi.

C: [[Oh, me too!

A: [[Eeew! Yuck!

(Double brackets indicate that these last two speakers started speaking at the same time.)

If the participants are really paying attention and competing hard for the turn, that is, if they are actually trying to project the end of the current speaker's turn, overlapping talk may occur, as in the last two lines of Example 5. This is perfectly all right and in fact is completely natural in conversation. The idea of multiple next-speaker start-ups is also demonstrated in Activity 4.

There is obviously still a long way to go, but if students are producing similar interactions within this activity, they have already accomplished a great deal. They are monitoring the moment-by-moment development of the turn-in-progress; evaluating it for grammatical, intonational, and pragmatic completion; gearing up for on-time, no-gap, no-overlap speaker transitions; using *oh* tokens; agreeing and disagreeing; and managing overlapping talk. And if students can do all this, they are probably ready for some short free conversation. But before that, there is one more activity that teaches self-selection, which is so vital to conversational interaction.

Activity 4: Monitoring the Turn

The goal of this activity is to give students practice in monitoring the talk-in-progress for points of possible upcoming completion. It also demonstrates that one natural outcome of the Sachs et al. (1974) turn-taking system is that several speakers might, if they feel they have something relevant to say, self-select at the same time. This activity is designed to result in instances of multiple simultaneous next-speaker start-ups and to reinforce the idea of self-selection.

For this activity, the teacher needs multiple sets of 5 index cards each, with each card containing one of the following items written on one side: *three, red, Yuko, London, pizza* (or other generic responses; see this chapter's Appendix at www.tesolmedia.com/books/pragmatics2 for sample materials). There should be enough sets so that each student has one card. For example, for 30 students, six sets are required. Students stand in a circle with the teacher in the middle. There should be more than one student who has each answer (e.g., two or more students will have the *London* card) so that there will always be two or more students who have a relevant answer to any question.

The teacher asks a question for which one of the cards will be the obvious answer, taking care not to direct the question to any particular student (e.g., with eye contact) because this would defeat the purpose of the activity, which is to promote self-selection. The following questions can be used to start with and then replaced with other questions that fit the answers:

Q: What time does the party start?	A: Three
Q: What color was the car?	A: Red
Q: Who did you go with?	A: Yuko
Q: Where are they going this summer?	A: London
Q: What are we having for dinner?	A: Pizza

The students need to monitor the unfolding turn-in-progress and think about whether their card is a possible answer to the question. If they have a relevant answer, they jump in. If everything goes well, there should be two (or more) students calling out simultaneous answers, with no gap between the question and the response.

REFLECTIONS

The activities in this chapter have been designed to teach and practice the norms of conversational turn-taking, which lie at the heart of conversational interaction. In particular, these activities focus heavily on encouraging self-selection, because next-speaker self-selection, which is so common in conversation, is suppressed within the turn-taking system typical of traditional (teacher-dominated) classroom interaction.

For the most part, these activities are not specific to any culture or language and as such are as relevant to the teaching of any language as they are to teaching ESOL. The Sachs et al. (1974) turn-taking system also provides a relevant baseline for the teaching of more specialized interactional genres (e.g., discussion) and particularly the sorts of discussion skills relevant to English for academic purposes. Discussion is, in many respects, a different activity than casual conversation and can involve distinct turn-allocation systems, but the Sachs et al. (1974) system provides a baseline for comparison. Furthermore, the orientation to no-gap speaker transitions (and the organization of preference discussed in chapter 8, in this volume, which crucially depends on this orientation) is relevant to a wide range of goals related to English for specific purposes, from the teaching of medical interaction to English for tourism. Silence in interaction is heard as purposeful, and unintended inter-turn gaps can lead to significant intercultural and pragmatic failures.

The activities presented in this chapter focus on aspects of interaction that are beyond the traditional boundaries of language as commonly perceived. Few language teachers think of the orientation to no-gap speaker transitions as part of the core conversational grammar of language. Yet in many ways, it is as fundamental as any other part of grammar and plays a key role in the use of language for successful interaction. The activities in this chapter also suggest, as least in terms of teaching spoken interaction, that there needs to be a stronger emphasis on teaching the practices of interaction. Indeed, research from the field of CA suggests the need to reconceptualize language as a much broader phenomenon.

The basic environment for language development is oral interaction, and the turn-taking system is its core form of organization. Without a thorough understanding of this system, conversation could be problematic. Language teachers often talk about "getting back to basics." Well, the turn-taking system is part of the basics and belongs on every conversation teacher's syllabus.

―――――――――――――――

Donald Carroll is a professor at Shikoku Gakuin University, in Japan. His research focuses on turn construction and repair in novice second language interactions, with a focus on the embodied aspects of such interactions. Prior to coming to Japan, he taught EFL, linguistics, and second language methodology in Mexico, Oman, Kuwait, Saudi Arabia, and the United States.

CHAPTER 8

Teaching Preference Organization: Learning How Not to Say "No"

Donald Carroll

There is an indispensable feature of the structure of spoken English that the majority of the world's language teachers, as well as textbook publishers, seem unaware of. It is called *preference organization,* and it is as real as the verb system—and as immediately observable in practically any sample of naturally occurring talk-in-interaction. For example, among the basic structures in the traditional grammar-based syllabus are short answers to yes/no questions (e.g., *Do you like music?* → *No, I don't*). Yet once teachers become aware of preference organization, they will realize that there is something pragmatically wrong with this sort of reply in the sense that it is precisely how experienced English speakers display hostility or impatience (see Sacks, 1987). As such, it is a strange bit of language to teach as a default response.

To be able to appreciate and teach preference organization, it is necessary to expand the horizons of what is generally thought of as language and grammar and to move beyond a grammar of language to a *grammar of use,* which reflects the "grammatical structure of language as a set of social resources" whereby "the ground for grammatical description shifts from the structures of language to the structures of practice" (Lerner, 1996, pp. 238–239).

This chapter introduces the basic facts about preference organization and provides several sample activities that can be used to teach the structure of preference to English language learners.

CONTEXT

The classroom activities described in this chapter evolved from my own research interests in conversation analysis and within the context of several conversation-style English as a foreign language (EFL) courses at a Japanese university.

Although the students in these classes had officially gone through 6 years of preuniversity EFL, in functional terms they were mostly false-beginners with little real ability to interact in English. In this sense, the activities presented here would be suitable for even absolute beginners because the activities don't rely on any previous English abilities. However, these activities are probably more suited to young adult and adult learners who are already fully socially competent speakers of their native languages.

From a traditional perspective, the activities presented in this chapter do not involve the sorts of structures familiar to most language teachers and language students. Nevertheless, they deal with significant and socially consequential aspects of language as used in the real world.

Preference and Adjacency Pair Organization

The word *preference* generally involves a choice: Each time someone says something in a conversation, that turn-at-talk sets up conditions for what might be expected to follow. This property of discourse has been termed *conditional relevance* (Schegloff & Sacks, 1973). For example, if I say, "Hi," the expectation is that my greeting will be reciprocated. It may not be in some particular instance, but a greeting is nevertheless the relevant next action and the basis upon which I will interpret whatever is said in its place, including a nonresponse. When there is a particularly tight relationship between a first turn and its relevant second turn, the two turns are referred to as an *adjacency pair*. Other types of turns-at-talk besides greetings set up a systematic choice between two (and only two) relevant next actions, for example, invitations, requests, and assessments.

Invitation → Acceptance or Rejection

Request → Granting or Refusal

Assessment → Agreement or Disagreement

Although each of these adjacency pairs allows for two relevant next actions, the two alternatives are not treated equally. A clear, unmistakable, and systematic preference exists for accepting, granting, and agreeing. Conversely, rejecting, refusing, and disagreeing are *dispreferred* next actions.

Preference is not just a fancy way of saying that people like to accept, grant, and agree. If someone receives an invitation that she or he would definitely prefer, in a personal sense, to reject, she or he will still format the rejection with reference to the practices of preference organization (which encompasses resources for "being rude" as well as "being polite"). This is why conversation analysts talk about a *systematic/structural preference* for acceptance, granting, and agreeing (among other preferences that are operational in talk). This preference is built into the design of the talk and is independent of any personal inclination. Preference also has nothing to do with whether accepting, granting, or agreeing gets done with any greater frequency. People do not accept invitations that they would rather reject simply because there is a systematic preference for acceptance. They just design their rejections in particular ways.

The Shape of Preferred Responses

The structure of preference can be summed up quite simply: Preferred actions are done as soon as possible, and dispreferred actions are delayed. The rest is merely the various practices through which these outcomes can be achieved. Consider an invitation sequence. If invited to do something, a recipient might either accept or reject the invitation. Note that in the case of accepting, people do not normally say, "I accept." It is also rare for the acceptance to take the form of a stand-alone *yes* or a *yes* combined with the traditional short-answer format as in Example 1:

> **Example 1**
>
> A: Do you want to get some coffee?
>
> B: Yes. (I do.)

B's answer sounds a bit odd. This is not to say the *Yes, I do* is not a possible response here, only that it may be heard as a special sort of acceptance (perhaps somewhat emphatic or contrary to expectations).

Many invitations in English get accepted with *Sure* or *Yeah* (or a casual *Uh-huh*). This is often followed up with an assessment such as *That sounds great* or *I'd love to*. But whatever words are used to display acceptance, there's the matter of when to say it so that it gets heard as having been said as soon as possible. As discussed in chapter 7, on the turn-taking system, an orientation exists toward achieving no-gap/no-overlap speaker transition. This is what *as soon as possible* means. Note that in Example 2, B begins speaking as soon as A stops:

> **Example 2**
>
> A: Wanna (= Want to) get something to eat?
>
> B: Sure, that'd be great.

Any earlier and B would be talking with overlap with A; any later—even one- or two-tenths of a second later—and B's response would sound delayed to A. Not only should the acceptance of an invitation be done in the very next turn (if possible), but it should be done so that no gap occurs between the invitation and the acceptance. Both starting early and starting late do additional interactional work. For example, starting slightly early is one way to have the acceptance heard as being "eager." The timing of the speaker transition is a structural part of the language of acceptance, and language learners need explicit training in this (see the activities teaching turn-taking in chapter 7 in this volume).

The Shape of Dispreferred Responses

Turns that are occupied with doing a preferred action are produced without delay. Accepting is done immediately. Granting of requests is done immediately.

Agreeing is done immediately. And *immediately* in this context means with a no-gap speaker transition. This is not the case for dispreferred actions, such as rejecting, refusing, and disagreeing. These turns (and often sequences of turns) are generally characterized by efforts to delay, delay, delay. Ideally, the dispreferred action can be delayed so long that it ends up not being done at all.

The first opportunity for delaying a dispreferred action is the moment at which talk would be expected, that is, the moment the prior turn reaches a point of hearable completion. A lack of response at precisely this point will be heard and interpreted as "doing something." Silence is meaningful. Because next speakers regularly achieve no-gap speaker transition, a gap at this point is not perceived as merely a gap (or thinking pause); rather, it is heard as the purposeful withholding of talk. This is not a quantitative matter of a given time duration, but rather a qualitative perception (on the part of the participants) that the next turn did not start on time.

A gap (or silence) alone is often sufficient warning of a possible upcoming dispreferred action, thus prompting a preemptive effort to deal with it. However, a silence is often only the beginning. In their efforts to delay (and, with any luck, avoid completely) doing a dispreferred action, experienced English speakers employ a range of resources, including the use of conversational objects such as *um, er, well, I dunno* [*don't know*] in addition to hedges of various sorts (*I'm sorta* [*sort of*] *busy*). They also make excuses (*I have some stuff I have to do*) and may challenge some aspect of the invitation (*Today?*).

Presequences

Speakers who would like to avoid a dispreferred response often rely on *presequences*—a conversational structure that is underrepresented in English as a second language (ESL) textbooks. Introductory ESL textbooks often include a unit on likes and dislikes, in which learners exchange personal likes and dislikes on conventional topics in response to questions such as *Do you like X?* But consider a question such as *Do you like pizza?* from the perspective of someone hearing this question in an actual conversation. Proficient speakers of English would not hear this as an unmotivated query about generic likes and dislikes. Instead, the assumption by the hearer is often that this question is preliminary to some further action—very probably an invitation or offer. In real life, questions such as *Do you like X?* (as well as a range of other question types, e.g., *What are you doing tomorrow?*) frequently initiate a presequence (Schegloff, 1990), that is, a sequence of turns that has as its goal to minimize the possibility of a dispreferred response. As Schegloff explains, "one job pre-sequences are designed to do is to explore the likelihood that the utterance being prefaced, and the action(s) it will do, will not be responded to in a dispreferred way—will not for example be rejected" (p. 60).

Preinvitations suggest a possibly forthcoming invitation, *prerequests* establish an expectation for a request, and *preannouncements* (e.g., *Guess what?*) project an upcoming news telling. Next speakers respond to these hinted-at, future actions in predictable ways. Consider the example of a prerequest sequence. The first turn in such a sequence might inquire, for example, into the availability of some object (*Do you have a dictionary?*) or into the addressee's ability to provide some service (*Do you know how to change a tire?*). Analysis of naturally occurring conversations reveals that there is a systematic preference in this sequential environment for a hearer to offer (a *preemptive offer*) rather than waiting for an overt request (Schegloff, 2007; see Example 3).

Example 3

| | A: | Do you have a dictionary? | (prerequest) |
| → | B: | Sure, here you go. | (preemptive offer) |

However, a specific request is not always predictable, in which case the next speaker might display receptiveness toward a request (or class of requests) that has not yet been specified by doing a *go-ahead* type of turn as in Example 4:

Example 4

	A:	Do you have Dave's phone number?	(prerequest)
→	B:	Yeah, I do.	(go-ahead move)
	A:	Could you call to remind him about the meeting?	(request)

On the other hand, if the next speaker does not want to give a positive response to the request (or class of requests) implied by the prerequest, a *blocking* move can be produced. Obviously, the nature of the block will be fitted to the request implied by some particular *pre*, but common types of blocking moves involve claims that one lacks either the time or the ability to grant the expected request, as in Example 5:

Example 5

	A:	Do you know how to fix a computer?	(prerequest [to fix a computer])
→	B:	Um . . . I don't really know much about it.	(blocking move)
	A:	Oh.	(OK, never mind.)

Presequences are only haphazardly represented in ESL textbook dialogues and are often out of sync with normative practices (Bernsten, 2002). EFL learners usually respond to turns intended as presequences (e.g., *What are you doing tonight?*) as if they were literal information questions. They do not realize that by answering the question (e.g., *I am going to cook dinner*) they are, from their conversation partner's perspective, doing a blocking move and thereby precluding a possible invitation. Here are a couple of common examples of these sorts of presequence initiators: *What are you doing tonight? Are you busy tomorrow afternoon?* Note that these two require different sorts of go-aheads. For the first, a response might be *Nothing much*, whereas for the latter, a better tailored response would be *No, not really*. These sorts of responses are rarely explicitly taught in EFL/ESL materials.

Preference and Responses to Assessments

Like many of the actions discussed so far, assessments (e.g., *It's cold today*; *That was awful*; *It's beautiful, isn't it*) make either agreeing or disagreeing a relevant next action. In EFL materials agreement/disagreement is commonly done directly with *I agree/I disagree* or *I think so too/I don't think so*. However, Pomerantz (1984) noticed that, in naturally occurring conversations, assessments are frequently followed by second assessments, as in Example 6:

> **Example 6** (adapted from Pomerantz, 1984, pp. 59–61)
>
> J: It's a beautiful day out, isn't it?
>
> L: Yeah, it's just gorgeous.

Pomerantz (1984) also found a clear structural preference for agreement over disagreement, with agreeing second assessments being done as soon as possible and disagreements being delayed. Furthermore, turns (and often sequences of turns) occupied with disagreeing (or rather avoiding disagreeing) regularly display gaps, repair initiations, hedges, and other delaying devices. In addition, Pomerantz found three distinctive types of agreeing assessments in her data: upgrades, same evaluations, and downgrades. Although all of these appear superficially to display agreement, Pomerantz determined that upgrades show strong agreement. In contrast, same evaluations, which merely echo the intensity (or lack of intensity) of the first assessment (e.g., by saying "me too," by simply repeating the words of the first assessment), mark weak agreement and frequently preface subsequent disagreement. In this observation lies the problem with teaching *I agree* and *I think so too* as default formats for agreement: Both fall into the category of same evaluations and can be heard as prefacing disagreement. One can almost hear the *but* that is likely to come next (*I think so too, but . . .*).

Downgrades such as B's response in Example 7 work in the opposite way from upgrades and are also heard as weak agreement and a warning of possible upcoming disagreement.

> **Example 7**
>
> A: That's beautiful.
>
> B: Yeah, it's nice, but . . .

Despite the fact that all three forms of agreement employ relatively simple linguistic resources, few ESL/EFL textbooks provide explicit instruction in doing agreement.

CURRICULUM, TASKS, MATERIALS

This section presents a series of activities that introduce students to the norms of preference organization in English. The activities are designed to raise teachers' and students' awareness of these common everyday conversational phenomena, and they require few or no materials, are simple to manage, and can be adapted and recycled week after week. Just as teachers wouldn't imagine teaching the entire verb system in one lesson, they will need to come back to preference organization regularly. The activities assume small class sizes, but the creative teacher should have little problem modifying them for larger classes.

The first activity provides an opportunity for students to produce preferred responses, such as accepting an invitation, granting a request, or agreeing with an assessment. In particular, it focuses on the as-soon-as-possible design of preferred turns. The second and third activities offer an orientation to and practice in signaling and structuring dispreferred turns. They focus on what Pomerantz (1984) calls the *dispreferred turn shape*, with an emphasis on the role of gaps between turns in foreshadowing a possible upcoming dispreferred response, such as refusing a request. The fourth activity deals with presequences, sequences that are related to preference and are used to preface other sequences. The last activity provides an orientation to producing preferred and dispreferred responses to assessments (e.g., *That was a great movie*). Students are often unsure how to respond to such turns and aren't aware of the pragmatic problems with stock phrases such as *I think so too*.

Activity 1: The Preferred Turn Shape—Accepting Without Delay

This activity is designed to help students recognize the importance of accomplishing acceptances (of invitations) with no-gap speaker transitions. For this activity, the teacher has students stand (or sit) in a circle. This configuration is not crucial, so if it is not feasible, the teacher can make other arrangements. Because many students won't know what a no-gap acceptance is supposed to sound like, the first step is to go around the circle having each student repeat both the invitation and the uptake together as one utterance. Initially, the teacher will need to provide the students with a specific invitation. Ones that have a strong rhythmic pattern are good: *<u>wanna</u> play <u>tennis</u>? <u>Wanna</u> get some <u>coffee</u>? <u>Wanna</u> get <u>something</u> to <u>eat</u>?* This is followed by a simple acceptance token (*sure*), which replaces the *yes* that most students use. This yields the following compound utterance: *<u>Wanna</u> get <u>something to eat</u>? <u>Sure</u>!* Note that *wanna* represents a common pronunciation of *want to* in casual speech.

Each student will need a chance to practice rhythmically producing both the invitation and its acceptance as a single unit. When students can produce this without hitches in their speech, they can begin responding with *Sure* to an invitation by the teacher. That is, the teacher produces the invitation, and the student responds with *Sure!* at the very instant it is due. The teacher can accompany the invitation with a gesture that begins with pointing to himself or herself and ends with pointing at the student at the very moment the teacher's turn comes to completion (i.e., the moment the teacher says "eat"). Once students have the timing down, their acceptance turn can be expanded to *Sure! Sounds good/fun/ great!*

Once students can produce these turns in coordination with the teacher, the last step is to have the students practice responding to each other in a no-gap manner. This can be done by having them go around the circle a few times, with one student issuing the invitation and the next accepting. In subsequent sessions, students can produce their own invitations. Experience has shown that it is best to have students come up with specific invitations ahead of time, because if there are any production hitches in their invitations, it is very difficult for the next speaker to produce a no-gap acceptance.

Activity 2: The Dispreferred Turn Shape—Signaling a Dispreferred Turn

This activity aims to sensitize learners to the sound of a gap and to teach them that this gap is meaningful as an indication of a possible upcoming dispreferred action, such as rejecting an invitation. Students sit in a circle, if possible. Although a circle isn't strictly necessary, going around a circle speeds up the activity and facilitates both teacher–student interaction and student–student interaction. If students are seated in rows, the talk can go up and down the rows.

As in Activity 1, the teacher gives students an easy invitation (e.g., *Wanna play tennis?*). This time, however, instead of an immediate no-gap reply, students tap their foot twice (or perhaps tap their finger on the desk) before responding with *um* (see Example 8).

> **Example 8**
> T: Do you want to play tennis?
> S: (tap, tap) Um . . .

Once students become used to producing this response with the teacher, one student says the invitation to the student on his or her left. The next student taps his or her foot and says, "Um." Then that student repeats the invitation to the next student, who taps and says, "Um"—and so on around the circle. To get more students practicing at the same time, this can be done in rounds (as in Activity 2 in chapter 7 in this volume).

Activity 3: The Dispreferred Turn Shape—Building a Dispreferred Turn

This activity provides learners with the English resources they need to reject an invitation or refuse a request using typical components of the dispreferred turn shape. It can be useful to put the diagram in Figure 1 on the board.

As with Activity 2, this activity also can be done with the students in a circle and the teacher in the middle. To begin, the teacher invites one of the students

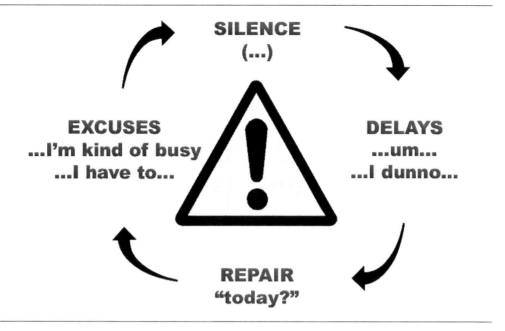

Figure 1. Some Practices for Delaying a Dispreferred Action

to do something. As in Activity 2, the student should respond first by tapping his or her foot once or twice before saying, "Um." The teacher shouldn't respond in any way (verbally or nonverbally). After this nonresponse, the student moves to another component of the dispreferred turn, for example, *I dunno*. When this also gets no response, the student moves on to the next element.

After the student has produced at least two or three warning signs of a possible upcoming dispreferred action (in this case, a possible rejection), the teacher can initiate an "escape sequence" such as in Example 9:

Example 9

T: Do you want to play tennis?

(silence)

S: Um . . . I dunno . . . I have to study.

T: Well, maybe some other time.

S: Yeah, maybe some other time.

Once students can do this routine with the teacher, they can practice it with each other walking randomly around the classroom. They can initiate a conversation with a typical opening (*Hi.* → *Hi. How's it going?* → *Fine.*) and then lead in with the invitation (possibly prefaced with *Hey*), as in Example 10:

Example 10

S1: Hi.

S2: Hi.

S1: How's it going?

S2: Fine.

S1: Hey, do you want to play tennis?

(silence)

S2: Um . . . I dunno . . . I have to study.

S1: Well, maybe some other time.

S2: Yeah, maybe some other time.

Once students have shown that they can format their rejections using the dispreferred turn shape, the teacher can let them give either a preferred response (e.g., *Yeah, sure!*) or a dispreferred one. One way for the teacher to manage this is to split the class into several groups and then privately give each group a reason to turn down certain people's invitations. For example, one group can be told to always reject an invitation by anyone wearing something blue. Another group might be told to reject invitations by anyone wearing a jacket.

Activity 4: Presequences—Go-Ahead or Blocking Moves

The goal of this activity is to teach students to hear and interpret certain types of questions as initiating presequences, therefore making relevant the production of either a go-ahead move or a blocking move rather than an answer. For this activity, students again stand in a circle with the teacher standing in the middle. The teacher goes around the circle asking, "What are you doing tonight?" to which the students should respond, "Nothing much." These go-ahead responses should be accomplished in a no-gap manner. After going around the circle once, the teacher can change to saying, "Are you busy (tomorrow afternoon)?" This time, students need to respond, "No, not really."

After all students can respond appropriately without a gap, the teacher can alternate between the two formats so that students need to vary their response based on the type of prerequest.

The next step is to add in the projected invitation sequence. It needs to be emphasized to students that a go-ahead in the presequence projects the fact that an invitation is welcome and that, therefore, an acceptance is likely. So in the practice session, students should accept invitations, as in Example 11:

Example 11

A: Hi.

B: Hi.

A: How's it going?

B: Good.

A: (Hey) what are you doing [time phrase,
e.g., "Tuesday afternoon"]?   (preinvitation)

B: Nothing much.   (go-ahead)

A: Wanna play tennis?   (invitation)

B: Sure! Sounds good.   (acceptance)

Another way to organize this practice is to put students into two rows facing each other. They run through this routine with one partner, then one line of students moves one chair over so that each person has a new conversation partner, and they repeat the conversation. This allows students to practice the routine several times with different partners. Note that this activity can also be arranged so that students need to self-select (see chapter 7 in this volume) simply by addressing the preinvitation to multiple students at one time (e.g., using sweeping eye contact).

Activity 5: Agreement (and Disagreement) With Assessments—Upgrades (and Downgrades)

This activity aims to demonstrate to learners several simple practices for making upgraded and downgraded agreements as a more natural alternative to agreement phrases such as *I think so too*. For Activity 5, it can be useful to write the following series of words on the blackboard or on flashcards.

BIG
⇓
HUGE
⇓
ENORMOUS
⇓
GIGANTIC
⇓
HUMONGOUS

Students then stand in a large circle with the teacher in the middle. The circle needs to be large enough so that all of the students can fully stretch out their arms. The teacher starts by holding his or her hands approximately 1 foot apart (as if talking about, for example, a fish or snake) and saying, "It was big." Students then make the same gesture and say, "Big." Next, the teacher repeats the gesture with hands roughly 2 feet apart and says, "Huge." The students copy this. Then, the teacher says, "Enormous," with hands about 3 feet apart. Students do the same. When saying, "Gigantic," the teacher spreads his or her arms as far as he or she can. This will cause the students to wonder how they will possibly do *humongous*. The teacher then wildly shakes his or her fully extended arms while excitedly yelling, "Humongous!" The students love this and have fun doing it themselves. The teacher runs though the series of gestures and words a couple of times until the students understand the progression.

The next step is to have students do an upgrade by giving the next "larger" word than the one used by the teacher, as in Example 12:

Example 12

A: It was big.

B: Yeah, huge!

A: It was huge.

B: Yeah, enormous!

After students have practiced this a few times, they can do downgrades by choosing a "smaller" vocabulary item. A downgrade assessment is intended to be heard as noticeably weaker than the prior assessment, so it might be worth having students go down several sizes in this activity (e.g., *gigantic* → *big*). Note that they should be doing downgrades with less enthusiasm than upgrades because this is definitely part of the performance of dispreference. Students might also add *but* to communicate the idea that downgrades often preface disagreement, as in Example 13:

Example 13

A: It was gigantic!

B: Yeah, it was big (. . . but . . .)

Another simple technique for doing upgrades that does not depend on students knowing graded series of adjectives (e.g., *pretty* → *beautiful* → *gorgeous*) is to insert *really* before the word used by the prior speaker, as in Example 14:

Example 14

A: It was expensive.

B: Yeah, really expensive!

The teacher goes around the circle doing simple assessments with a variety of vocabulary items (e.g., *tall, old, delicious, sad, long, boring, expensive, fun, easy, complicated*). The students add "Yeah, really" and repeat the prior word. Throughout this activity, it is essential that the students produce their second assessment in a no-gap manner.

As a final demonstration of how flexible this technique is, the teacher can say,

"It was really expensive." Initially, students will be stumped on how to respond. The solution is simply to say, "Yeah, really, *really* expensive!" To emphasize the point, the teacher can even go a step further and say, "It was really, really fun!" To which the students reply, "Yeah, really, really, *really* fun!" Students have a great time doing this.

REFLECTIONS

This chapter aims to convey that preference is pervasive in spoken interaction and possibly just as important in social interaction as a major grammatical category such as the tense system.

The activities presented here reflect the context in which they were developed, a university EFL course. However, the ideas about preference that underlie these activities can be introduced to students of other ages or in other contexts. My own experience is that advanced- and beginning-level learners alike are equally unaware of the organization of preference, but they are also equally capable of learning the appropriate practices. Designing turns in accordance with the empirically demonstrated practices of preference organization doesn't require extensive linguistic resources. In a sense, it is really about helping learners realize that how and when something is said is just as important as what words are used. For example, people regularly accept invitations with an energetic voice and reject them with an edge of hesitance.

The activities here assume little in the way of prior English ability and, with minor modifications, are suitable for most adult and adolescent learners at almost any level of language development. The only limitation is that this material may not be appropriate for younger children who have not yet fully learned the norms of preference in their native languages or cultures.

These activities suggest just a few of the areas in which preference organization is relevant to the teaching of spoken interaction. Furthermore, the reality of preference organization prompts speakers to use a further set of interactional practices specifically designed to deal with the possibility of a dispreferred action, namely presequences (as presented in Activity 4). The various presequences and their respective go-ahead and blocking moves are given little or no attention in the traditional language teaching curriculum—even in courses claiming to focus on conversational skills. Textbook dialogues continue to offer unnatural formatting of short answers, which continue to be taught to language learners.

The activities in this chapter are intended only as illustrative examples of possible ways to introduce learners to preference organization. There are, no doubt, many more and perhaps better ways to raise learners' awareness of preference organization and to teach the specific practices through which it is displayed in a range of sequential contexts. Most important, teaching preference should be differentiated from teaching students to speak "politely" through a focus on the vocabulary of politeness. Preference organization integrates politeness in the structure of oral interactional behaviors. An awareness of preference organization constitutes an important accomplishment of the grammar of interaction.

———————————————

Donald Carroll is a professor at Shikoku Gakuin University, in Japan. His research focuses on turn construction and repair in novice second language interactions, with a focus on the embodied aspects of such interactions. Prior to coming to Japan, he taught EFL, linguistics, and second language methodology in Mexico, Oman, Kuwait, Saudi Arabia, and the United States.

CHAPTER 9

Pragmatic Competency in Telephone Conversation Openings

Jean Wong

Telephone talk is one genre of communication with which learners of English as a second or foreign language (ESL/EFL) do not receive enough practice. Learners have stated that they avoid telephone conversations or keep them to a minimum (Wong, 1984, 2002). They may find talking on the telephone difficult also because body language is not available. Given the weaknesses or gaps in instructional materials referred to in chapter 1 of this volume, observations from conversation analysis (CA) represent a gold mine and can contribute to deepening the understanding of how language works. In this chapter, I tap into and apply some of that CA knowledge for teachers of ESL/EFL.

There is an increased interest in the role of pragmatics in ESL/EFL instruction (Bardovi-Harlig & Mahan-Taylor, 2003; eslandcateaching, 2009; Kasper, 2006; Wong & Waring, 2010). Second language pedagogy is as much about pragmatics as it is about grammar, pronunciation, and vocabulary, particularly beyond beginning levels. Along these lines, this chapter aims to raise consciousness about the nature of telephone openings and to offer a CA-inspired phone game activity, restricting the discussion to telephone openings between friends or acquaintances (see Bowles, 2006, for a discussion of telephone openings in institutional contexts).

CONTEXT

The main task described in this chapter, Wong's Phono-logical Phone Game, was piloted in courses with students who were pre- or in-service mainstream or ESL teachers, some of whom were not native English speakers. The activity was quite stimulating, generating lively discussion and hearty laughter. The students said they were unaware how structured telephone openings are in terms of interactional knowledge. During the game, some even pretended to hold a phone to their ear to figure out whose turn it was to speak. The in-service teachers remarked that ESL and EFL students would find this activity to be "ear-opening" and an enjoyable hands-on approach to learning about telephone talk.

Four Sequences in Telephone Openings

To address the first aim of increasing teachers' awareness of telephone openings in English, this section offers a cursory overview of relevant CA literature. (For discussions of CA's interface with applied linguistics see Bowles & Seedhouse, 2007; Kasper, 2006; Mori, 2007; Schegloff, Koshik, Jacoby, & Olsher, 2002; Seedhouse, 2005; Wong, 2002; Wong & Waring, 2010.) Transparent as it may seem, telephone talk is interactional and collaborative in nature. Participants *do* the opening, producing turns that unfold and build from one another. The interlocking turns form sequences, that is, first and second pair parts of adjacency pairs (for more on adjacency pairs, see chapter 8 in this volume).

In phone conversations, before speakers reach the first topic they must get through the opening segment, which usually consists of four types of sequences, in the following order, if they all occur (Schegloff, 1968):

1. Summons–answer sequence

2. Identification/recognition sequence

3. Greeting sequence

4. *How are you* sequence

These opening sequences also occur in mobile phone calls. (See Hutchby & Barnett, 2005, for a study that used a database of mobile phone calls. The authors claim there are more similarities than differences between mobile and landline openings.)

Examples 1 and 2 are from recorded and transcribed telephone conversations (C = caller; A = answerer). These and other examples mentioned throughout the chapter predate caller identification technology, the current predominance of which might strongly influence how openings are executed.

Example 1 (adapted from Schegloff, 1986, p. 115)

(1) Summons–answer sequence (turns 01–02)	01 ((ring))
	02 A: Hello.
(2) Identification sequence (turns 03–05)	03 C: Hello, Jim?
	04 A: Yeah.
	05 C: It's Bonnie.
(3) Greeting sequence (turns 06–07)	06 A: Hi.

(4) First *How are you* sequence (turns 07–08)   07 C: Hi, how are you?

    Second *How are you* sequence (turns 08–09)   08 A: Fine, how are you?

    09 C: Oh, OK I guess.

    10 A: Oh, OK.

    First topic of conversation   11 C: Um (0.2), what are you doing New Year's Eve?

Example 2 (adapted from Schegloff, 1986, p. 114)

(1) Summons–answer sequence (turns 01–02)   01 ((ring))

    02 A: Hello.

(2–3) Identification and greeting sequences (turns 03–04)   03 C: Hi.

    04 A: Hi.

(4) First *How are you* sequence (turns 05–06)   05 C: How are you?

    Second *How are you* sequence (turns 06–07)   06 A: Fine, how are you?

    07 C: OK.

    08 A: Good.

Sequence 1: Summons–Answer Sequence

All phone conversations begin with a summons–answer sequence (except on those rare occasions when someone "answers" a phone that he or she claims did not ring). The ringing (or pulsating or flashing) of the telephone is regarded as a summons (i.e., first pair part), and the answering of it is considered a response (i.e., second pair part) to this action. This sequence is sometimes absent or incomplete in ESL textbook dialogues (Tatsuki, 2005; Wong, 1984, 2002; Wong & Waring, 2010). Simplistic as it may seem, in a summons–answer sequence, the answerer speaks first, yet in some ESL textbook phone dialogues, the caller speaks first (Wong, 1984, 2002).

In American English, a speaker answers a phone summons by saying *hello, hi, hey, yeah,* or the like, and by doing so, she or he provides a minimal voice sample (Wong & Waring, 2010). Alternatively, a speaker might answer using self-identification such as *Nathan speaking* or *English Department. Hello,* the most common answer, can be used for business or personal calls (Schegloff, 1968; see also Wong & Waring, 2010, for a discussion of *signature hello*). *Yeah, hi,* or *hey* can also be used as answers, but they are more likely reserved for when there is previous knowledge of who is calling (as is the case with caller identification). That is, when someone answers the phone with *hello,* she or he does not necessarily claim to have foreknowledge of the caller. *Yeah* or *hi* are also used as answers when one party immediately calls back the other (e.g., after checking a piece of information).

Sequence 2: Identification and Recognition Sequence

In telephone openings, parties must work to identify and recognize one another. Sometimes this interactional task is taken care of by the summons–answer sequence because when the answerer (A) says, for example, "Hello" or "Hi," she or he provides a voice sample that may be used by the caller (C) for recognition purposes. C may begin an identification sequence by tentatively identifying A, as in Example 3, line 03. After establishing A's identity (line 04), C then identifies herself (line 05). (Note that Examples 3–8 are short segments excerpted from Examples 1 and 2.)

> **Example 3** (adapted from Schegloff, 1986, p. 115)
>
> (1) Summons–answer sequence (turns 01–02)   01 ((ring))
>
> 02 A: Hello.
>
> (2) Identification sequence (turns 03–05)   03 C: Hello, Jim?
>
> 04 A: Yeah.
>
> 05 C: It's Bonnie.

On the other hand, if C recognizes A from the minimal voice sample, as illustrated in Example 4, she or he can display that recognition by offering the first part of a greeting sequence, such as in line 03 of Example 4. In return, A can display that she or he recognizes who the caller is by doing a return greeting (line 04).

> **Example 4** (adapted from Schegloff, 1986, p. 114)
>
> (1) Summons–answer sequence (turns 01–02)   01 ((ring))
>
> 02 A: Hello.
>
> (2–3) Identification and greeting sequences   03 C: Hi.
>
> (turns 03–04)   04 A: Hi.

The use of *hi* rather than *hello* in line 03 of Example 4 indicates that C recognized A's voice, that is, C and A display the intimacy of their relationship at their exchange of *hi*. In fact, there are nine basic types of caller's first turns that deal with the issue of identification and recognition, but space does not allow for amplification (see Schegloff, 1979; Wong, 2003; Wong & Waring, 2010).

Sequence 3: Greeting Sequence

The greeting sequence is separate from the *hello* that is used to answer the phone. In Example 5, the greeting sequence consists of the exchange of *hi* in line 06 (first pair part) and line 07 (second pair part).

> **Example 5** (adapted from Schegloff, 1986, p. 115)
>
> (1) Summons–answer sequence (turns 01–02)   01 ((ring))
>
> 02 A: Hello.

(2) Identification sequence (turns 03–05)	03 C: Hello, Jim?
	04 A: Yeah.
	05 C: It's Bonnie.
(3) Greeting sequence (turns 06–07)	06 A: Hi.
	07 C: Hi, how are you?

Often, as mentioned earlier, an exchange of greetings between friends or acquaintances simultaneously accomplishes the interactional task of identification and recognition of the parties. For example, when speakers greet one another with a minimal voice sample (e.g., *hi* as shown in Example 6), they not only do the job of identification and recognition but they also display something of the intimacy of their relationship.

Example 6 (adapted from Schegloff, 1986, p. 114)

(1) Summons–answer sequence (turns 01–02)	01 ((ring))
	02 A: Hello.
(2–3) Identification and greeting sequences (turns 03–04)	03 C: Hi.
	04 A: Hi.

Notice that in Example 6, the identification sequence, in which C and A show their mutual recognition (through the use of *hi)*, also serves the function of a greeting sequence.

Sequence 4: **How Are You** *Sequence*

Unlike greeting sequences, which are limited to one per interactional occasion, there may be more than one *How are you* sequence in the same conversation (Schegloff, 1968). Consider Example 7:

Example 7 (modified from Schegloff, 1986, p. 115)

(1) Summons–answer sequence (turns 01–02)	01 ((ring))
	02 A: Hello.
(2) Identification sequence (turns 03–05)	03 C: Hello, Jim?
	04 A: Yeah.
	05 C: It's Bonnie.
(3) Greeting sequence (turns 06–07)	06 A: Hi.
(4) First *How are you* sequence (turns 07–08)	07 C: Hi, how are you?
Second *How are you* sequence (turns 08–09)	08 A: Fine, how are you?
	09 C: Oh, OK I guess.

In Example 7, the first *How are you* sequence consists of C's "Hi, how are you?" in line 07 and A's "Fine, how are you?" in line 08. The second begins with A's "Fine, how are you?" in line 08 and concludes with C's "Oh, OK I guess" in line 09. Now look at Example 8:

Example 8 (adapted from Schegloff, 1986, p. 114)

(1) Summons–answer sequence (turns 01–02)	01 ((ring))
	02 A: Hello?
(2) Identification and greeting sequences (turns 03–04)	03 C: Hi.
	04 A: Hi.
(4) First *How are you* sequence (turns 05–06)	05 C: How are you?
Second *How are you* sequence (turns 06–07)	06 A: Fine, how are you?
	07 C: OK.
	08 A: Good.

In Example 8, the first *How are you* sequence consists of C's "How are you?" in line 05 and A's "Fine, how are you?" in line 06. The second begins with A's "Fine, how are you?" in line 06 and concludes with C's "OK" in line 07.

Callers typically initiate a first *How are you* question in order to be the respondent of a second one because, from this sequential position, they may have the opportunity to shape or convert the response to the *How are you* into the first topic or the reason for the call (Schegloff, 1967, 1968). Relatedly, the answers given in reply to a *How are you* question are categorized as neutral, plus, or minus (Sacks, 1975). Neutral answers (e.g., *good, OK, fine*) ordinarily lead to (immediate) shutdown of the *How are you* sequence. Plus or minus answers (e.g., *great, terrific, super, terrible, awful, depressed*) more likely lead to extended talk (e.g., why a speaker is feeling unusually positive or negative). Thus, answers of the plus or minus category tend to keep the *How are you* sequence open, whereas those of the neutral category may not. Studies reveal that in ESL textbook dialogues, answers to *How are you* questions are usually of the neutral type, which does not lead to extended talk (Wong, 1984, 2002; Wong & Waring, 2010).

Overall, across other languages telephone opening sequences are mostly similar, with slight variations (for CA analyses of telephone openings in Dutch, Korean, Swedish, Cantonese, Samoan, and Persian, respectively, see Houtkoop-Steenstra, 1991; Lee, 2006; Lindstrom, 1994; Luke, 2002; So'o & Liddicoat, 2000; Taleghani-Nikazm, 2002; see also Wong & Waring, 2010, for a brief summary of telephone openings in other languages).

CURRICULUM, TASKS, MATERIALS

This section presents a series of pretask, task, and posttask activities designed to familiarize students with telephone openings in American English and to improve their ability to participate in openings as the caller or the answerer. The central task is Wong's Phono-logical Phone Game.

Activity 1: Raising Students' Awareness

Before playing the game, teachers should find out what students know about talking on the phone in English. Handout 1 (see Appendix A) provides sample discussion questions.

From discussions with students about telephone talk, teachers may discover that learners are somewhat nervous or even anxious when talking on the phone in English. In fact, language learners, especially at the beginner level, often keep telephone conversations to a minimum or may ask someone else (e.g., a more proficient speaker) to do the calling or talking for them (Wong, 2002; see Wong & Waring, 2010, for "author's stories," which reveal that ESL learners may experience special problems or concerns with telephone talk and with ESL more generally). My father, an immigrant from China who spoke Toisanese (a dialect spoken in the Toishan/Taishan area, which is in southwestern Guangzhou, in the province of Guangdong) and never really studied English formally, once handed me the phone after answering it because he said it was someone speaking Mandarin, which he did not speak but I did. I spoke with the person and then informed my father that the person wasn't speaking in Mandarin but in English!

Simply picking up the phone and saying "Hello" can be an unnerving experience because the learner may be unprepared for what she or he should say next. Even the expression *May I speak to [person's name]*, which students may learn in or outside of the classroom, is not always the correct thing to say after someone has answered the phone, and doing so can even have negative interactional consequences, which a learner may not be aware of (e.g., Why didn't you recognize me by my voice? Why are you treating me like a receptionist?).

An English language learner may answer a phone by not saying anything, expecting the caller to speak first (this goes against the *distribution rule* in CA; Schegloff, 1968). Some learners do this because they will only talk on the phone with people whom they know. (I have had experience with this with my immigrant uncle, who was originally from China. I would call him and have to be the first one to say, "Hello.") From the point of view of pragmatics, learners may also have problems selecting an appropriate closing (see chapter 10 in this volume). I once had a fairly long chat on the phone with someone who I could detect was a nonnative English speaker. He had called to discuss a business concern, and when he was ready to draw the conversation to a close, he said, "I had a *very*, very nice time with you." Fortunately, he did not ask me on a date in his next utterance, and I properly analyzed his utterance as an innocuous preclosing.

Activity 2: Identifying Moves in Telephone Openings

Handout 2 (see Appendix A) provides an opportunity for students to become familiar with the four types of sequences that typically occur in telephone openings in American English. Teachers should be prepared for a variety of responses to the discussion questions in Handout 2. For example, in Korean, someone who answers a phone sometimes produces the equivalent of a second *hello* (i.e., *yeposeyyou*) rather than offering self-identification (Lee, 2006). In Dutch and Swedish, self-identification by name appears to be more common than voice sample identification (Houtkoop-Steenstra, 1991; Lindstrom, 1994). And there are some slight variations in *How are you* sequences in Cantonese (Luke, 2002), Persian (Taleghani-Nikazm, 2002), and Samoan (So'o & Liddicoat, 2000).

Once students are comfortable with the four opening sequences, they are ready to tackle identification of a novel opening (Worksheet 1, see Appendix A). Conversation 2 is somewhat more challenging than Conversation 1.

Once they have identified the sequences and become aware of their functions, students are ready to practice manipulating these opening sequences in a hands-on game, which helps deepen their understanding of how the turns and sequences build from one another.

Activity 3: Practicing Ordering Conversational Openings

In this task, students play Wong's Phono-logical Phone Game (which first appeared in Wong & Waring, 2010). The game is played on a blank game board, which consists of cells for the first six turns of five telephone openings, labeled Conversations A–E. A miniature version of the board is reproduced in Figure 1 (see Appendix B for the actual game board and Appendix C for instructions on how to create the materials).

The object of the game is to re-create real telephone openings by placing the correct answer piece (or Post-It note) from a set of 30 on the proper blank square on the game board.

Students may work individually, in pairs, or in groups. The teacher distributes one blank game board and one set of 30 scrambled game board pieces to each student, pair, or group. The following text can be used as instructions to the students:

	A	B	C	D	E
1	phone ring	phone ring	phone ring	phone ring	phone ring
2					
3					
4					
5					
6					

Figure 1. Miniature Version of Wong's Phono-logical Phone Game Board

> You are going to play a game on a board that consists of slots (or cells) for the first six turns of five real telephone conversational openings, labeled A through E. To play the game, take your scrambled game pieces and place them on the game board to re-create five natural telephone openings. All of the pieces should be used. The first individual (or pair or group) to re-create five appropriate telephone openings wins the game.

When students are finished, the teacher can hand them a copy of the game with appropriate answers. (A set of answers is included in a template for the completed game in Appendix B). Samples of alternative appropriate answers are available at www.tesolmedia.com/books/pragmatics2.

This activity can be extended by having learners act out the telephone openings in pairs, one assuming the role of caller and the other assuming that of answerer. The students may sit back to back when acting out the openings, holding make-shift telephones or mobile phones (but turned off) up to their ear.

REFLECTIONS

The game in this chapter is geared toward adult intermediate- to advanced-level English language learners. However, it could be adapted for other age groups and competency levels. For beginning- and intermediate-level students, the instructor can begin the game by focusing on a subset of the openings. The instructor may provide clues, as needed, by filling in some of the cells before or during the game. Beginning-level learners may also work with a limited number of openings, as needed. For high-intermediate- to advanced-level learners, the teacher can extend the task by asking learners to compare the varying forms of *hello* and *how are you* found on the game board. The instructor might ask questions such as the following (see Appendix A for possible answers):

1. What is different about the variants of *hello* in turn 2?

2. Can you pronounce each of the items in turn 2, showing how they differ?

3. In which conversation(s) is the initial /*h*/ sound not pronounced?

4. In which conversation(s) is the first vowel sound (which is a schwa) omitted?

5. In which conversation(s) does the answer to the summons (the telephone ring) end in rising intonation? (Note: *Hello* need not end in rising intonation. The point is simply to call students' attention to how *hello* can be produced.)

6. In which conversation(s) does the answer to the summons end in falling intonation?

Learners can also be asked to compare the varying forms of *How are you*. This may be done after the students have played the game. For example, the instructor might ask the following questions:

7. What are the differences in pronunciation among the three forms of *How are you* found in conversations A and E?

8. What does the speaker's use of *hawar* in conversation C stand for? Are the forms *hawar* and *hawar yuh* acceptable English? If so, why? If not, why not?

The teacher can also ask students questions about the way identification and recognition are expressed in the conversational openings. For example, the instructor might ask students to identify the conversations in which participants indicate that they recognize one another by voice alone (i.e., self-identification by the caller is not necessary) and how they know this. (See Appendix A for suggested answers to these discussion questions.)

Learners of all levels can compare openings used in English with those used in their native languages. Learners at more advanced levels can also record, transcribe, and analyze real telephone openings in English, their native languages, or both. (For other ideas and suggestions regarding how to teach telephone openings, see Wong & Waring, 2010.)

The ability to engage in interaction, which includes how to open or enter into a conversation in the first place (Pillet-Shore, 2008), is crucial to a learner's interactional competence. Increasingly, everyone relies on the telephone for communication in this global society. Teachers can help smooth the path for learners by raising their awareness of the sequential structures that are regularly used and by providing a range of opportunities for practice, including the use of examples from naturally occurring conversation whenever possible.

ACKNOWLEDGMENTS

Thanks to Craig Gochanour for initial layout assistance with an earlier version of the game in Activity 3.

Jean Wong is an associate professor in the Department of Special Education, Language and Literacy at The College of New Jersey, in the United States. She teaches graduate courses in the TESL and Reading Programs. She received her doctorate in applied linguistics from the University of California at Los Angeles.

APPENDIX A: WORKSHEETS AND ANSWER KEYS

Handout 1: Raising Awareness of Telephone Talk

1. How much do you talk on the phone in English?

2. Do you avoid talking on the phone in English?

3. How does a typical telephone conversation in English begin?

4. What are some of your problems or concerns about talking on the phone in English?

Handout 2: Telephone Openings

The following example illustrates the four sequences used when opening telephone conversations in English. How are these telephone openings done in your native language? What do people say in each case?

(1) Summons–Answer Sequence (turns 01–02)	01	(ring)
	02	A: Hello.
(2) Identification Sequence (turns 03–05)	03	C: Hello, Jim?
	04	A: Yeah.
	05	C: It's Bonnie.
(3) Greeting Sequence (turns 06–07)	06	A: Hi.
(4) First *How are you* Sequence (turns 07–08)	07	C: Hi, how are you?
Second *How are you* Sequence (turns 08–09)	08	A: Fine, how are you?
	09	C: Oh, OK I guess.
	10	A: Oh, OK.
First Topic of Conversation	11	C: Umm (0.2), what are you doing New Year's Eve?

Use these questions to discuss telephone talk in your native country:

1. What does the person who is called say when she or he answers the phone (i.e., after the summons)?

2. What kinds of greetings are typical?

3. How are identification and recognition of the parties done?

Worksheet 1: Identifying Sequences in Telephone Openings

Label the sequences in the telephone opening below. The participants in the sequence are the answerer (A) and the caller (C).

Conversation 1

(1) _____ Sequence (turns 01–02)	01	((ring))
	02	A: Hello.
(2) _____ Sequence (turns 03–05)	03	C: Hi, Ida?
	04	A: Yeah.
(3) _____ Sequence (turns 05–06)	05	C: Hi, this is Carla.
	06	A: Hi, Carla.
(4a) _____ Sequence (turns 07–09)	07	C: How are you?
	08	A: OK.
	09	C: Good.
(4b) _____ Sequence (turns 10–11)	10	A: How about you?
	11	C: Fine. Don wants to know. . . .

Read each of the four sequences below (A, B, C, and D). Then put them in the proper order in the blanks that follow to re-create a typical telephone opening. Write the sequence that functions as a summons–answer sequence in the space designated, then write the identification and recognition sequence if there is one, then the greeting and first and second *How are you* sequences (the relevant utterances in each sequence are boldfaced). The participants in the sequence are the answerer (A) and the caller (C).

Conversation 2

Sequence A

A: Fine, **how are you?**

C: **OK.**

A: **Good.**

Sequence B

((**ring**))

A: **Hello.**

Sequence C

C: **How are you?**

A: **Fine**, how are you?

Sequence D

C: **Hi.**

A: **Hi.**

Summons–Answer Sequence _____

_____

Identification and Recognition Sequence _____

_____

Greeting Sequence _____

_____

First *How are You* Sequence   _____

    _____

Second *How are You* Sequence   _____

    _____

    _____

Worksheet 1: Answer Key

Conversation 1

1. Summons–answer
2. Identification and recognition
3. Greeting plus self-identification
4a. *How are you* (first *How are you* and response)
4b. *How are you* (reciprocal *How are you* and response)

Conversation 2

Summons–answer sequence:	Sequence B
Identification and recognition sequence:	Sequence D
Greeting sequence:	Sequence D
First *How are you* sequence:	Sequence C
Second *How are you* sequence:	Sequence A

Suggested Answers to Discussion Questions in the Reflections Section

1. There are differing forms: *hello, 'ello, hallo,* and *h'llo.*

2. If we take *hello* as the standard, most correct form, in *'ello* the initial /h/ sound is omitted; in *hallo,* the first vowel has an /a/ sound (as in *father*) rather than an /ɛ/ sound (as in *pet*); finally, in *h'llo,* the first vowel is run together or even omitted altogether.

3. B

4. E

5. A

6. B–E

7. In A, we find the most standard, correct form in which each of the words in the utterance is clearly and audibly pronounced: how–are–you? In the first *how are you* (*hawar yuh*) in C, the first two words are run together as if they were one word, i.e., howare (*hawar*). And *you* is pronounced more colloquially as *yuh.* In the second *how are you* in D, the word *are* is reduced to a single sound /r/. But here, the word *you* is pronounced as it is in standard English (in contrast with the *yuh* in the just prior *how are you* sequence).

8. This has been responded to, in part, in answer to #7. *Hawar* (for *how are*) and *hawar yuh* (for *how are you*) are acceptable in everyday spoken English; they are reflective of dialectal forms. However, in more formal written or academic

English, these utterances should not be used unless the writer is mimicking the dialogue or language of everyday speech; nor should learners write or spell these expressions in written or academic English in these "deviant" ways.

Answer to discussion questions on identification and recognition:

In A, the speakers recognize one another by voice sample alone.

In B, the caller recognizes Monica, the answerer, at her saying of *'ello* in answering the phone (turn 02). The caller does not self-identify himself, but Monica displays that she knows who he is when he answers his question ("Your company there?") at line 06 ("Yeah").

In C, the caller is not entirely sure that the answerer is Nate and so utters "Um, Nate?" with rising intonation. Nate's answer ("Yeh") does not necessarily display that he knows who the caller is; that notwithstanding, the caller continues by asking to speak with Laura ("Is Laura there?").

In D, the caller displays some recognition of the answerer as evident in his question with rising intonation ("Hello, Joan?"), but when Joan responds with "Yeah," she does not necessarily display that she knows who the caller is. In the next turn (line 05), the caller self-identifies ("It's Craig"), and after he does so, Joan recognizes who it is, as displayed by her greeting ("Hi").

In E, the speakers recognize one another by voice sample alone. When the answerer picks up the phone and says "H'llo," the caller recognizes the answerer and produces a greeting ("Hi"). The answerer also recognizes the caller by his minimal voice sample ("Hi") and returns the greeting ("Hi").

APPENDIX B: WONG'S PHONO-LOGICAL PHONE GAME (VERSION A)

(For additional versions of this game, visit www.tesolmedia.com/books/pragmatics2.)

	A	B	C	D	E
1	phone ring	phone ring	phone ring	phone ring	phone ring
2	Hello.	Hello?	'ello.	H'llo.	Hallo.
3	Hello, Joan?	Um, Nate?	It's Craig.	Hi, how are you?	Hi, Monica.
4	Hi.	Yeah.	Hawar yuh?	Fine, how'r you?	Hi.
5	Hi.	Is Laura there?	OK, what's new?	--------	--------
6	Your company there?	No, she went to the concert.	Oh nothin'.	--------	--------

APPENDIX C: CREATING THE MATERIALS

Prepare copies of the blank game board and copies of the 30 answers from one of the versions of the completed game board in Appendix A (i.e., each of the six turns in the five telephone openings, A–E, as needed). Teachers should create as many copies as there are students working individually or pairs/groups sharing game boards.

A larger game board can be created and placed in the front of the classroom for demonstration at the end of the game-playing session.

CHAPTER 10

Pragmatic Competency in Telephone Conversation Closings

Jean Wong

An understanding of pragmatics is vital to language learners' development of the interactional practices of conversation (Wong & Waring, 2010). Interactional practices, however, are sometimes given short shrift or overlooked in English as a second or foreign language (ESL/EFL) instruction. This is supported by the fact that textbook dialogues are not sufficiently in sync with the sequential structures of real interaction (Bernsten, 2002; Grant & Starks, 2001; Wong, 2002, 2007). Grant and Starks found that interactional closings of television soap operas were more natural than those found in ESL textbook dialogues. Similarly, Wong (2007) reports that the kinds of preclosing sequences contained in textbook dialogues are restricted, and in her corpus the speakers never moved out of a closing. Yet the importance of openings (Pillet-Shore, 2008; also see chapter 9 in this volume) and closings cannot be overstated; they are the on-ramps and off-ramps to social interaction (Wong, 2002, 2007; Wong & Waring, 2010). Teachers and students alike need a navigation system of sorts, and that is what is provided here.

Being able to talk on the telephone in one's native language, which includes getting through interactional rituals (Schegloff, 1986), does not necessarily mean one can do the same in another language. Even in the speech of advanced-level English language learners, there is often an absence of "high frequency, often idiomatic routines, or typical expressions" (Thornbury & Slade, 2006, p. 223) such as closings. Closing a conversation is easier said than done. It consists of more than merely saying "Bye" or "Goodbye." And saying "Bye" too soon, too late, or not at all possibly bears negative interactional consequences (e.g., the person is seen as impatient, impolite, or aloof). My goals here are to raise teachers' awareness of what it takes to *do* conversational closure, or not, and to present tasks that will help ESL/EFL students navigate telephone closings. In addressing these goals, I rely on insights and findings from conversation analysis (CA).

CONTEXT

The main task in this chapter, Recognizing Preclosing Moves (Activity 2), was piloted in a graduate course for pre- or in-service mainstream or ESL teachers. The students, some of whom were nonnative English speakers, noted that figuring out types of preclosing sequences on a turn-by-turn basis was not as easy as they had thought.

The Structure of Telephone Closings

Telephone closings are composed of preclosing signals, preclosing sequences, and terminal exchanges. A basic telephone closing consists of four turns, that is, two adjacency pairs. An *adjacency pair* is a set of two turns, usually consecutive, that are related to one another (see chapter 8 in this volume for a discussion of preference and adjacency pair organization). The first turn, the *first pair part*, strongly conditions what can occur in the next turn, the *second pair part*. Example 1 illustrates two sets of adjacency pairs, the first of which is a preclosing sequence and the second of which is a terminal exchange. The two pairs form a basic telephone closing.

> **Example 1** (Schegloff & Sacks, 1973)
>
> | | |
> |---|---|
> | Preclosing (first pair part; turn 01) | A: OK. |
> | Preclosing (second pair part; turn 02) | B: OK. |
> | Terminal exchange (first pair part; turn 03) | A: Bye bye. |
> | Terminal exchange (second pair part; turn 04) | B: Bye. |

Terminal Exchanges

In a two-party telephone conversation, a terminal exchange sequence is a set of two turns, one uttered by each speaker, which ends the conversation. Aside from the closing in Example 1, speakers may use other utterances in terminal exchanges (e.g., *OK, see you, thank you, you're welcome*), as in Example 2. (The second exchange in Example 2, *OK/See you*, is actually part of an arrangement sequence that simultaneously ends the conversation, whereas in the third exchange, an appreciation preclosing sequence ends the conversation. More about preclosing sequence types is included later in the chapter.)

> **Example 2** (Schegloff & Sacks, 1973)
>
> | | |
> |---|---|
> | A: Bye. | (first pair part) |
> | B: Bye. | (second pair part) |
> | A: OK. | (first pair part) |
> | B: See you. | (second pair part) |
> | A: Thank you. | (first pair part) |
> | B: You're welcome. | (second pair part) |

A: OK.	(first pair part)
B: OK.	(second pair part)

If a first speaker does not leave interactional space for a next speaker to produce a reciprocal *goodbye* (i.e., a second pair part), that action possibly bears interactional consequences. Conversely, if a next speaker does not reciprocate a first speaker's saying of *goodbye*, there may be interactional consequences as well. These actions speak to the normative character of interaction, that is, something that speakers do and orient to in emergent talk. But interestingly, research reveals that an exchange of *goodbye* is not a regular component of telephone closings in all languages (e.g., it is not necessarily done in Kiswahili and Ecuadorian Spanish, although space does not allow for discussion here; see Omar, 1993; Placencia, 1997; Wong & Waring, 2010).

Preclosing Signals

In an "author's story," Wong and Waring (2010) relate the experience of one nonnative English speaker who initially had difficulty at her job catching on to the different functions of the word *OK* (e.g., to signal conversational closure). Indeed, without direct, explicit instruction, some English language learners may not pick up on these interactional cues or respond to them quickly enough or appropriately (Griswold, 2003). For example, *OK* can function as a preclosing device in addition to a terminal, closing utterance (i.e., equivalent to *goodbye* as illustrated in Example 2). Example 3 shows *OK* and *all right* used as preclosing signals in an adjacency pair as a preclosing sequence.

Example 3 (Schegloff & Sacks, 1973)

A: OK.	(first pair part)
B: OK.	(second pair part)
A: OK?	(first pair part)
B: All right.	(second pair part)

In Example 3 the first pair parts of the preclosing sequences serve as an invitation to close; the second pair parts serve as an acceptance of the offer. By responding with a minimal, reciprocal token such as *OK, all right*, or the like, the second speaker neither continues talking on the current topic nor raises a new one. These are cues that display an orientation toward closure. Also note that in Example 3 the intonational contour of *OK* can be falling or rising (see the Transcription Conventions List at the beginning of this volume).

Aside from *OK* and *all right*, other preclosing signals in English include *OK then, all right then, well, so, anyway, yes* (Wright, 2004), or the like:

- OK

- OK then

- All right

- OK all right

- All right then

- Well

- Well all right

- Well then

- So

- Anyway

- Yes (yeah, yep), OK

- Yes (yeah, yep), OK then

- Yes (yeah, yep), all right

- Yes (yeah, yep), all right then (Wong & Waring, 2010, pp. 190–191)

Also, for a comparison across languages, see Table 1 for other preclosing signals.

Juxtaposing the preclosing signals from the CA literature and from ESL textbook phone dialogues, Wong (2007) inspected 81 dialogues and found one case of *well*, one case of *Oh + thanks*, seven cases of *all right*, and ten cases of *OK + thank you*. There were no cases of stand-alone *OK*, the most common way of "doing" preclosing in American English.

Table 1. Preclosing Signals in Languages Other Than English

Language	Preclosing Signal	English Translation
Ecuadorian Spanish	*ya okay* *muy bien*	*okay okay* *excellent*
German	*also* *gut* *bis dann*	*so then* *good* *til then*
Greek	*lipon* *ejine* *orea* *kala*	*well, so then* *done* *nicely* *good*
Russian	*vse* *jasna* *ponjatno* *tak shto takie dela* *vot*	*that's that* *I see* *I see* *that's how things are* *(boundary particle)*

Source: Wong & Waring, 2010, p. 190.

Preclosing Sequences

Aside from the preclosing signals mentioned in the previous section, speakers also jointly navigate conversational closure using various preclosing sequences (Button, 1987, 1990, 1991; Schegloff & Sacks, 1973; Wong, 2007; Wong & Waring, 2010). Table 2 exemplifies the various preclosing sequence types discussed in the CA literature. Of the types shown in this table, arrangements, solicitude, appreciation, reason for call, and announced closing are preclosings that generally, although not invariably, lead to minimal movements out of closings (Button, 1987, 1990). Types such as back-reference, in-conversation object, and topic initial elicitor generally, although not invariably, lead to development or expansion of talk, that is, drastic movement out of closing (Button, 1987, 1990).

Teachers should be familiar with the range of preclosing sequence types; however, as previously mentioned, this chapter deals only with the making of arrangements and expressions of solicitude. These two types are quite common in telephone talk. (For more on preclosing sequences in general, see Button, 1987, 1990, 1991; for their connection to second language pedagogy, see Wong, 2007; Wong & Waring, 2010).

Making arrangements. In a preclosing sequence involving the making of arrangements, participants make or restate plans to get together or to contact one another (Wong & Waring, 2010). Arrangement sequences have a special status as the last topic of the conversation in that they emphasize the relationship between

Table 2. Preclosing Sequence Types

Preclosing Sequences	Examples
Minimal movement out of closing	
Arrangements	*I'll see you in the morning.*
Solicitude	*Thank you.*
Appreciation	*Take care.*
Reason for call	*I just called to find out if you're going.*
Announced closing	*OK, let me get back to work.* *OK, I'll let you go.*
Maximal movement out of closing	
Back-reference	*So what are you doing for Thanksgiving?*
In-conversation object	*Mm-hmm?*
Topic-initial elicitor	*Anything else to report?*
Moral or lesson	*Yeah well, things always work out for the best.*

Source: Adapted from Wong & Waring, 2010, p. 201.

participants and thus make it easier to close the conversation quickly (Schegloff & Sacks, 1973). Example 4 illustrates minimal movement out of closing. The conversation shuts down at the terminal exchange sequence.

> **Example 4** (adapted from Button, 1990, pp. 97–98)
>
> PCL   01 Emma: Um, sleep good tonight, sweetie.
>
> PCL →   02 Lottie: **OK, OK. Well, I'll see you in the morning.**
>
> PCL →   03 Emma: All right.
>
> PCL   04 Lottie: All right.
>
> TER   05 Emma: Bye bye, dear.
>
> TER   06 Lottie: Bye bye.
>
> ((end call))
>
> Note: PCL = preclosing; TER = terminal exchange.

In contrast to Example 4, in Example 5 the arrangements discussed by Wilbur touch off another topic, which leads to drastic movement out of closing where Lila starts to tell a story about an experience that she had. The story was triggered by Wilbur's saying that he and Lila should get together (Button, 1990). Button does not provide the next lines after Lila says "the fog," but it seems plausible that Lila's opening up of the closing is linked to Wilbur's saying that they will get together as soon as she can get down to see him.

> **Example 5** (adapted from Button, 1990, p. 99)
>
> PCL   01 Wilbur: OK.
>
> PCL →   02 Wilbur: **Well, well, maybe we will see each other, uh, maybe not Thursday but as soon as you can get down.**
>
> PCL →   03 Lila: Yes.
>
>   ⇒   04 Wilbur: I'm free in the evenings.
>
>   ⇒   05 Lila: Yeah, I'll call you an' bec—I'll ( ) something I've experienced that I must tell you, I tried to get home before five o'clock since the fog . . .
>
> Note: PCL = preclosing; → indicates arrangement turns; ⇒ indicates the beginnings of a drastic movement out of closing.

Solicitude. In a solicitude preclosing, one or both parties express concern, well wishes, (holiday) greetings, or the like (Wong & Waring, 2010). Example 6 shows a case of minimal movement out of closing, that is, the turns that follow the solicitude lead to termination of the conversation. (The bolded utterance indicates the solicitude or first pair part of the adjacency pair. Single arrows indicate the entire solicitude adjacency pair.)

Example 6 (adapted from Button, 1990, p. 101)

PCL →   01 Marge: **Uh, tell your little girlfriend or other little girlfriend hello an' everything like that.**

PCL →   02 Sam: **I will, dear.**

PCL   03 Marge: OK.

PCL   04 Sam: Thank you.

TER   05 Marge: Bye bye.

TER   06 Sam: B'bye.

         ((end call))

Note: PCL = preclosing; TER = terminal exchange.

Notice that in Example 7, however, a solicitude provides an opportunity for drastic movement out of closing.

Example 7 (adapted from Button, 1990, p. 103)

PCL →   01 Mark: **a happy Thanksgiving and, uh, may all your dreams come true.**

PCL →   02 Bob: **Well, thank you. Thank you.**

         (.)

⇒   03 Mark: Ah,

⇒   04 Bob: What are you doing tomorrow night, anything?

         05 Mark: hhhhhhhhhhhh Oh uh, well uh . . .

((continues))

Note: PCL = preclosing; → indicates solicitude turns; ⇒ indicates the beginnings of a drastic movement out of closing.

In Example 7, Mark offers a solicitude in line 01, which Bob responds to in line 02. Notice, however, that Bob's utterance "What are you doing tomorrow night, anything?" (line 04) begins movement out of the preclosing. This utterance orients to Mark's desire to continue the conversation, as signaled by his "Ah," which is preceded by a micropause (Button, 1990). Mark then continues the conversation with "Oh uh, well uh" (line 05).

ESL textbook phone dialogues and their attendant activities do not necessarily offer guidance or instruction for learners in how to negotiate a move out of a closing, which is a regular, systematic practice—an action of everyday conversation—both on the telephone and in face-to-face interaction (Wong, 2007). English language learners need to know how to open up closings, on some occasions, and how to abort others' attempts to do so as well.

CURRICULUM, TASKS, MATERIALS

The activities presented here offer students an opportunity to familiarize themselves with typical preclosings and closings. The activities aim to do the following:

- raise learners' awareness about the pragmatics of closings

- guide students to think about current- and next-turn relationships in closing sequences

- give students hands-on practice with movements from closings (i.e., in minimal and drastic ways)

Activity 1: Raising Learner Awareness

The teacher begins by generating a discussion with students about preclosing and closing sequences in telephone talk (referring to the introductory sections of this chapter if necessary). Worksheet 1 (see the Appendix) is a guide for this activity.

The range of responses that a teacher may receive to the questions on Worksheet 1 will offer clues as to how to go about instruction. In answering those questions, learners may say that in English, we end with *goodbye*, which is different from the way phone calls are closed in their native languages (e.g., *hasta luego, adios, ciao, auf wiedersehen, zaijian*). Learners may also reveal that they are not aware of the ways in which preclosing signals (e.g., *OK, well, so*) are used in English. And they may not know that there are different preclosing sequences (e.g., announced closing, making of arrangements, reason for the call). Students' responses may also reveal that they have not learned how to open up a conversation that is about to close, especially because ESL/EFL textbook dialogues do not direct attention to this area (Wong, 2007). Finally, learners may express fear, anxiety, or nervousness about talking on the phone in English. The teacher will need to provide validation and to help learners become interactionally competent by focusing on the various interactional practices of closings (Wong & Waring, 2010).

Activity 2: Recognizing Preclosing Moves

To aid students in recognizing some of the variations in closing sequences, the teacher might begin by focusing on two types of preclosing: making arrangements and expressing concern or solicitude. These types of preclosings can lead to another round of preclosings or a terminal exchange, thus ending the conversation. Or they can result in a drastic movement out of the preclosing, in which the closing is abandoned and conversation continues.

Students who often have great difficulty in getting off the phone in English can familiarize themselves with what can occur by studying Handout 1 (see the Appendix). (Examples are adapted from Schegloff & Sacks, 1973, p. 317; Button, 1987, pp. 101, 102, 105.) The teacher may wish to explain that punctuation represents intonation (period = falling pitch; question mark = rising pitch; comma = semi-rising pitch).

After the teacher has discussed Handout 1 with students, they are ready to practice identifying preclosings and terminal exchanges on their own (see Worksheet 2 in the Appendix). (The example is adapted from Liddicoat, 2007; the conversations are adapted from Button, 1987, pp. 104, 269, 120, 101.) When students have completed Worksheet 2, the teacher can go over the answers with the class.

Activity 3: Practicing Preclosings

At this point, the teacher might ask if students can think of other possible arrangement-making phrases and expressions of concern or solicitude (see Worksheet 3 in Appendix).

The teacher can write students' responses on the board, making a separate column for each preclosing type. Alternatively, the teacher can pair students and ask them to jointly create a list of arrangement-making and solicitude preclosings, which subsequently may be shared with the whole class. Under the arrangement column in Worksheet 3, possible expressions include *I'll give you a call next week; OK, I'll see you next week; I'll see you tomorrow; Let me know how it goes;* and *I'll talk with you another time.* For solicitudes, possible utterances include *Take care; Take it easy; Get some rest; Don't work/study too hard; Give my love to the family;* and *Hang in there.*

Activity 4: Constructing Closings

This activity affords an opportunity for students to think through how actual sequences of closings work. Students can work alone or in groups on Part I of Worksheet 4 (see Appendix).

After students have finished Part I, the teacher passes out an answer sheet containing the proper sequencing of the closing turns or puts the answers on a PowerPoint slide or an overhead transparency for everyone to view. After students have checked their answers, the teacher discusses with the students their various responses. Students can then role-play the closings.

Activity 5: Reconstructing Closings

This activity, which is especially appropriate for learners at more advanced levels, involves students receiving a set of scrambled telephone closings. Before conducting this activity, the teacher needs to prepare for distribution strips of paper with turns from one or more of the telephone closings in the Teacher Worksheet (see Appendix).

In Closing 1, there is a drastic movement out of an arrangement preclosing sequence (i.e., the conversation continues). However, in Closing 2, there is a solicitude preclosing sequence, leading to a shutting down of the conversation. In

Closing 3, an arrangement preclosing sequence is immediately followed up with one that involves a solicitude, but that, in turn, leads to movement out of closing. In other words, the recipient of the solicitude, Bob, starts (i.e., latches on to) a new topic in saying, "What are you doing tomorrow night? Anything?" (Compare this preclosing with the one in Worksheet 4, which is a simple solicitude and arrangement closing.)

Once the teacher has determined which closings to use in the game, he or she scrambles the turns and places them in a pile or in an envelope, keeping separate each set of turns comprising each sample closing.

If more than one set of closings is going to be used, only one set should be distributed at a time. When students finish working with one set, they may move on to another one. If students work individually, each student gets one set of sentence strips. If students work in groups, each group gets one set of sentence strips per conversational closure. Having students work with a partner or in groups will generate interaction and discussion. Students need to be reminded that some sequences do not include a terminal exchange (but rather continue with the conversation).

For students at more advanced levels, the teacher may extend the activity by scrambling all the turns together in both sets of arrangements. The students' task is to unscramble the turns, the outcome of which should be to have two separate arrangement closings, one that closes drastically and the other minimally. The same activity may be done with the two sets of solicitude closings. Advanced-level students may be asked to role-play the drastic movement examples and engage in a closing (or not) tug of war. Finally, when students are comfortable with arrangements and solicitude, the instructor can teach other preclosing sequence types to provide learners with the full range of interactional resources used by proficient speakers of English (see Wong & Waring, 2010).

When students have completed all the activities, the teacher can ask: What did you learn about how to close telephone conversations in English? Was there anything that was surprising or unexpected? How is closing a phone conversation in English different from doing so in your native language, if at all?

REFLECTIONS

Because the activities described here involve various types of preclosings (e.g., making arrangements, expressing concern or solicitude) typical of everyday phone conversation, they are relevant for all learners. However, depending on students' proficiency levels, variations may be introduced. Beginning-level students may be asked to list utterances that could be used to express concern or solicitude or simply to predict the vocabulary that one might find in expressions of concern (e.g., *take care, good talking with you, say hi to X, tell mom I said hello*).

Students who participated in the activities described in this chapter enjoyed them, claiming that doing so got them to think about telephone closings in ways that they had not thought about before. Most of the students stated that it had not occurred to them how important the teaching of telephone closings and the related skills actually was. Pragmatic competence does not necessarily transfer from native language to second language readily or easily. Thus, a teacher's efforts in helping to raise learners' awareness of closings and to provide them with ample opportunities for direct practice will go a long way in augmenting learners' pragmatic competency skills despite the fact that learners may already know how to engage in closings in their native or dominant languages.

ACKNOWLEDGMENTS

I owe gratitude to the students in my graduate courses at The College of New Jersey, who have helped in the piloting of some of the ideas discussed here.

———

Jean Wong is an associate professor in the Department of Special Education, Language and Literacy at The College of New Jersey, in the United States. She teaches graduate courses in the TESL and Reading Programs. She received her doctorate in applied linguistics from the University of California at Los Angeles.

APPENDIX: WORKSHEETS, HANDOUTS, AND ANSWER KEYS

Worksheet 1: Discussion About Closing Telephone Conversations

1. What utterances typically occur in telephone closings in your native language(s)?

2. What utterances typically occur in telephone closings in English?

3. How do you move out of a closing?

4. How do you cut off or cut short a phone conversation?

5. What other questions, problems, or concerns do you have regarding telephone closings?

Handout 1: Examples of Closings and Preclosings

English telephone closings consist of preclosings (PRE) and terminal exchanges (TER):

PRE 01 A: OK.

PRE 02 B: OK.

TER 03 A: Bye Bye.

TER 04 B: Bye.

Sometimes a speaker will insert an additional preclosing sequence involving matters such as making arrangements or final expressions of concern or solicitude. Examples 1 and 3 provide relatively simple instances, and Examples 2 and 4 involve more complex negotiations, which move out of closing and back into conversation.

1. Preclosing with arrangements (minimal movement out of preclosing)

	01 Heather: Let me know what the doctor has to say.
PRE (Arr 1)	02 Maggie: **Yeah, OK. Well, I'll call you later, then.**
PRE (Arr 2)	03 Heather: OK.
PRE	04 Maggie: OK, sweetie.
PRE	05 Heather: OK.
TER	06 Maggie: Bye bye.
TER	07 Heather: Bye.
((end call))	

2. Preclosing with arrangements (⇒ indicates beginning of movement out of preclosing)

PRE (Arr 1)	01 Pete: **I'll see you Tuesday.**
PRE (Arr 2)	02 Marvin: Right.
PRE	03 Pete: OK, Marvin.
⇒	04 Marvin: You—you're all right? You can get there?
((continues))	

3. Preclosing with expression of concern or solicitude

PRE (Sol 1)	01 Marge: **Uh, tell, uh, your little girlfriend or other little girlfriend hello an' everything like that.**
PRE (Sol 2)	02 Sam: I will, dear.
PRE	03 Marge: OK.
PRE	04 Sam: Thank you.
TER	05 Marge: Bye bye.
TER	06 Sam: Bye.

4. Preclosing with expression of concern or solicitude (⇒ indicates beginning of movement out of preclosing)

	01 Char: I'll remind her Wednesday.
	02 Jo: Yeah.
	03 Char: That we need it Friday.
	04 Jo: Yeah.
PRE (Sol 1)	05 Jo: **OK, take care of yourself.**
PRE (Sol 2)	06 Char: Oh, I will. I've had it several days an' I'm go[nna be all right.
	07 Jo: [Hmm.
⇒	08 Char: We got our new kid in class.
	09 Jo: Oh, did you get that boy?
	((continues))

Worksheet 2: Identifying Preclosings and Closings

In the following conversations, locate the preclosing sequences that involve arrangements and solicitude and the terminal exchanges, wherever they are found. Label the sequences according to the key given below.

- Pre (FPP and SPP) = Preclosing signals and sequences
- Pre Arr (FPP and SPP) = Preclosing: Arrangements
- Pre Sol (FPP and SPP) = Preclosing: Concern/solicitude
- Ter (FPP and SPP) = Final closing

Example

Pre Sol FPP	01 K: So have a safe trip.
Pre Sol SPP	02 N: Yeah.
Pre Sol FPP	03 K: And a good time.
Pre Sol SPP	04 N: Sure will.
Pre FPP	05 K: All right.
Pre SPP	06 N: All right.
Ter FPP	07 K: Bye bye, dear.
Ter SPP	08 N: Bye bye.

1. Conversation 1

	01 H: Let me know what the doctor has to say.
_____	02 M: Yeah, OK. Well, I'll call you later, then.
_____	03 H: OK.
_____	04 M: OK, sweetie.
_____	05 H: OK.
_____	06 M: Bye bye.
_____	07 H: Bye.

2. Conversation 2

_____ 01 E: Oh we::ll, I'll no doubt bump into you next week.

_____ 02 H: Yeah. I'll see you sometime.

_____ 03 E: All righ::t?

_____ 04 H: All righty:::.

_____ 05 E: Bye, Henr.y,

_____ 06 H: Take care. Bye.

3. Conversation 3

_____ 01 P: Thanks a lot. And I'll see you soon.

_____ 02 M: OK, honey.

_____ 03 M: Drive carefully.

_____ 04 P: I will.

_____ 05 M: Bye bye.

_____ 06 P: Bye bye.

4. Conversation 4

_____ 01 S: Nice talking to you, honey. Maybe I'll see you Thursday.

_____ 02 M: Uh, oh, all right. Love to see you.

_____ 03   And, uh, tell, uh, your little girlfriend hello and everything like that.

_____ 04 S: I will, dear.

_____ 05 M: OK.

_____ 06 S: Thank you.

_____ 07 M: Bye bye.

_____ 08 S: Bye bye.

Worksheet 2: Answer Key

1. Conversation 1

	01 H: Let me know what the doctor has to say.
<u>Pre Arr FPP</u>	02 M: Yeah, OK. Well, **I'll call you later,** then.
<u>Pre Arr SPP</u>	03 H: OK.
<u>Pre FPP</u>	04 M: OK, sweetie.
<u>Pre SPP</u>	05 H: OK.
<u>Ter FPP</u>	06 M: Bye bye.
<u>Ter SPP</u>	07 H: Bye.

Lines 02–03: Preclosing arrangements

Lines 04–05: Preclosing

Lines 06–07: Terminal exchange

2. Conversation 2

<u>Pre Arr FPP</u>	01 E: Oh we::ll, **I'll no doubt bump into you next week.**
<u>Pre Arr SPP</u>	02 H: Yeah. I'll see you sometime.
<u>Pre FPP</u>	03 E: All righ::t?
<u>Pre SPP</u>	04 H: All righty:::.
<u>Ter FPP</u>	05 E: Bye, Henr.y,
<u>Sol FPP+Ter SPP</u>	06 H: Take care. Bye.

Lines 01–02: Preclosing arrangements

Lines 03–04: Preclosing signals/sequence

Line 05: Terminal exchange

Line 06: Solicitude/FPP + Terminal exchange/SPP

3. Conversation 3

<u>Pre Arr FPP</u>	01 P: Thanks a lot. And **I'll see you soon.**
<u>Pre Arr SPP</u>	02 M: OK, honey.
<u>Pre Sol FPP</u>	03 M: **Drive carefully.**
<u>Pre Sol FPP</u>	04 P: I will.
<u>Ter FPP</u>	05 M: Bye bye.
<u>Ter SPP</u>	06 P: Bye bye.

Lines 01–02: Preclosing arrangements

Lines 03–04: Preclosing solicitude

Lines 05–06: Terminal exchange

4. Conversation 4

<u>Pre Arr FPP</u>	01 S: Nice talking to you, honey. **Maybe I'll see you Thursday.**
<u>Pre Arr SPP</u>	02 M: Uh, oh, all right. Love to see you.
<u>Pre Sol FPP</u>	03	**And, uh, tell, uh, your little girlfriend hello every-thing like that.**
<u>Pre Sol SPP</u>	04 S: I will, dear.
<u>Pre FPP</u>	05 M: OK.
<u>Pre SPP</u>	06 S: Thank you.
<u>Ter FPP</u>	07 M: Bye bye.
<u>Ter SPP</u>	08 S: Bye bye.

Lines 01–02: Preclosing arrangements

Lines 03–04: Preclosing solicitude

Lines 05–06: Preclosing

Lines 07–08: Terminal exchange

Worksheet 3: Practice Closing Conversations

I. Can you think of other expressions for making arrangements and for showing concern or solicitude? Write them in the spaces provided below.

Expressions for Making Arrangements	Expressions of Concern or Solicitude

II. After checking your list with your teacher, role-play the closing of a conversation with a classmate. Try using some of the expressions that you listed above.

Worksheet 4: Constructing Closings

I. Below is a real telephone closing. The utterances have been scrambled. Read each utterance out loud and make sure you understand all the vocabulary.

> *Lottie: Bye bye.*
>
> *Emma: All right.*
>
> *Lottie: OK, OK. Well, I'll see you in the morning.*
>
> *Emma: Bye bye, dear.*
>
> *Lottie: All right.*
>
> *Emma: Um, sleep well tonight, sweetie.*

II. Now, reorder the utterances in sequence and write the complete closing below.

1. _____

2. _____

3. _____

4. _____

5. _____

6. _____

III. When you have finished, check your answers with your teacher or with a partner. Then read the sequence with a partner, each of you taking the role of one of the speakers.

Worksheet 4: Answer Key

> Emma: Um, sleep well tonight, sweetie.
>
> Lottie: OK, OK. Well, I'll see you in the morning.
>
> Emma: All right.
>
> Lottie: All right.
>
> Emma: Bye bye, dear.
>
> Lottie: Bye bye.

Note to teacher: Emma offers solicitude; Lottie responds with arrangements. The conversation then closes.

Teacher Worksheet: Telephone Closing Strips

To prepare any one of the following three closings for the telephone closing reconstruction task, cut along the dotted lines to create strips for each of the following telephone closings. Each closing is already sequenced appropriately. (Conversations are adapted from Button, 1990, pp. 99, 101, 103.)

Closing 1

✂ -

Wilbur: Well, maybe we will see each other, uh, maybe not Thursday but as soon as you can get down.

✂ -

Lila: Yes.

✂ -

Wilbur: I'm free in the evenings.

✂ -

Lila: Yeah, I'll call you. I've experienced something that I must tell you. I tried to get home before five o'clock since the fog.

✂ -

Closing 2

✂ -

Sam: Nice talking to you, honey. Maybe I'll see you Thursday.

✂ -

Marge: Uh, oh, all right. Love to see you. And, uh, tell your little girlfriend or other little girlfriend hello and everything like that.

✂ -

Sam: I will, dear.

✂ -

Marge: OK.

✂ -

Sam: Thank you.

✂ -

Marge: Bye bye.

✂ -

Sam: B'bye.

Closing 3

✂ -

Mark: ...and, uh, I'll be talking to you Friday.

✂ -

Bob: OK.

✂ -

Mark: Have a happy Thanksgiving, and, uh, may all your dreams come true.

✂ -

Bob: Well, thank you. Thank you. What are you doing tomorrow night? Anything?

✂ -

Mark: hhhhhhhhhhhh Oh uh, well . . .

CHAPTER 11

Responders: Continuers

David Olsher

Responding to others is an important part of everyday conversations and professional interactions. Even in the age of computer-mediated communication (e.g., Internet-based social networking, email, blogs), a lot of our responding to others still occurs in spontaneous talk—in person or via telephone. Therefore, a crucial communication skill is knowing how and when to respond in everyday talk and understanding what may constitute the usual range of expectable responses in various situations. The range of pragmatic and interactional skills required to respond appropriately to any and all conversational utterances is too broad to address in one or even two chapters. With that in mind, this chapter and chapter 12 in this volume introduce a range of responders—brief responses by an addressee or listener to ongoing talk by a speaker—that are widely used in English.

This chapter focuses on one type of responder, *continuers*, which are short listener responses produced during extended talk in progress such as storytelling or various kinds of explaining (e.g., instructions, directions, recipes, reasons). These continuers, which include minimal responses such as *mm-hm, yeah*, and *right,* indicate the listener's understanding that a story or explanation is still in progress, encourage the speaker to proceed, and show that the listener producing them has heard the talk so far and that it is not problematic.

It is important to note that the words or minimal vocalizations used as responders (e.g., *uh-huh, yeah*) can also be used to express meanings and functions or social actions other than those associated with their responder function, depending on the talk to which they are responding. For example, *yeah, right,* and *uh-huh* can be used in their responder function as continuers that invite a speaker to proceed, or in their yes-answer, agreement, or acceptance (nonresponder) functions as a reply to a question, request, invitation, offer, or the like. Examples 1 and 2 provide instances of *uh-huh* functioning as a continuer (responder function) and as a reply to a question (nonresponder function). (Audio for Examples in this chapter is available at www.tesolmedia.com/books /pragmatics2.)

Example 1

Responder Function: *Uh-huh* **as Continuer** (response to ongoing story)

    A: I had the worst experience last night.

    B: Oh really?

    A: Yeah, it was freezing, and I forgot my coat,

→ B: Uh-huh,

    A: And I missed my bus so I had to walk home . . .

Example 2

Nonresponder Function: *Uh-huh* **as Answer** (response to question to which a reply is required)

    A: Had dinner already?

→ B: Uh-huh. How about you?

When listeners respond during stories, explanations, or other kinds of extended talk, they use continuers to display that they are listening and can hear the talk as well as to show that they hear the talk so far as part of an extended speaking turn. Continuers not only indicate that the listener can hear the talk, but also suggest that the talk is following some more or less expected line of progress and is not problematic, at least so far.

CONTEXT

An earlier version of these materials was taught in a class focusing on academic oral skills at an intensive language institute whose mission was to prepare international students with the language skills they needed to enter the university. The activities were presented as part of a focus on language in small-group discussions. Other group discussion skills on the class syllabus included ways to soften disagreements with language such as *I can see your point, but . . . .* These students were aiming to study at universities in the United States and were eager to gain language skills to help with everyday communication in school, so they were quite motivated to learn these pragmatic skills.

The class consisted of 18 high-intermediate-level students primarily from China, Japan, and South Korea. The materials were presented over two class meetings as an addition to the academic language skills the students were studying. Re-recorded versions of the dialogues were used, and these seemed to work well.

Although the formal focus on these pragmatic functions was new to the students, they found the activities meaningful and engaging. Through carefully sequenced activities, the students were able to comprehend the teaching points and were then able to practice the communicative activities successfully as well. After using the materials, the teacher wrote, "[Students] were able to complete all the tasks without any problems. They particularly seemed to enjoy practicing reading the transcripts."

Continuers

As discussed earlier, continuers are responders that are used to show that the listener recognizes that the speaker of an extended unit of talk has not yet finished speaking. The recipient who produces a continuer at a point that might be heard as a place to take a turn passes on the opportunity to take the floor and indicates that the speaker should proceed with a story, explanation, or other kind of extended talk. Thus, a continuer can be heard as passing an opportunity to request clarification, signaling that there are no problems in hearing or understanding so far.

Unexpected uses of continuers can lead to problems. For instance, the use of a continuer instead of a request for clarification when a listener does not understand something in the talk in progress may cause a communication breakdown and can result in a negative evaluation of the listener's English communication skills (He, 1984). Problems can also occur if the listener uses a continuer when the speaker had actually intended the prior turn as a conclusion or solution, rather than as a *telling* or explanation that was still in progress.

Another important consideration is that speakers involved in ongoing, extended storytelling or explanation expect a listener to use a variety of continuers. In fact, there is a danger that several consecutive uses of the same continuer (especially with flat intonation) will be heard as a signal that the listener is not interested and wants the speaker to finish (Schegloff, 1982). Another important caution is that use of repetitions of the same continuer in the same turn with flat or falling intonation (such as *right right right*) can be heard as a sign of impatience and may sound rude.

Functions of Continuers

The three continuer types focused on in this chapter—*uh-huh/mm-hm, yeah,* and *right*—can convey either continuer responder or nonresponder functions. *Uh-huh* (and the similar *mm-hm*) is the prototypical continuer used to show that a listener is following the talk so far and understands that more talk will follow. Although the listener may be deeply involved in the talk, the continuer displays no stance toward the talk in progress. *Uh-huh/mm-hm* usually occurs at the end of a sentence or a phrase that can be heard as a complete idea and is spoken with a slightly rising or flat intonation; it shows that the listener is passing on the opportunity to take a turn. A continuer may occur either immediately or after a brief pause following the speaker's prior talk; it signals, "I am following you, and I know there is more talk to come, so please go on." In other words, these brief responders communicate that the listener has understood and perhaps accepted the talk so far (although acceptance may change as the story or explanation unfolds). Example 3 presents an instance of *mm-hm*, with slightly rising intonation.

Example 3 (adapted from data[1] in Gardner, 1997, pp. 25–26)

1   Mal: I pick it up, from his place at seven o'clock tomorrow morning, I take it

2   down to Motor Italiana, they fix the other things, which need doing, because

3   they're things which I was gonna change anyway,

4 → Ly: Mm-hm,

5   Mal: Or involved with the work which I was gonna get done anyway.

Uh-huh/mm-hm also has nonresponder uses. For example, when produced with falling intonation, it can be used to agree with a statement or answer yes to a question.

Yeah with flat or slightly rising intonation, when responding to an extended turn (e.g., storytelling, explaining), often functions as a continuer in a similar fashion to *uh-huh/mm-hm*. When acting as a continuer, *yeah* may be used with other continuers (e.g., *yeah, uh-huh/mm-hm*), but it does not start a longer turn. Example 4 shows two instances of *yeah*, along with *mm-hm*, as a continuer.

Example 4 (adapted from Raymond, 2004, p. 198)

13   Ger: He's in competition with all the other students,

14 → Shi: Yeah,

15   Ger: doing interviews. [Behind

16 → Shi: [Yeah,

17   Ger: a two-way mirror.

18 → Shi: Mm-hm,

In Example 4, both *yeah* and *mm-hm* are used as continuers. The speaker avoided using the same continuer three times in a row, providing variety by shifting to *mm-hm* in Line 18 (and thus avoiding seeming uninterested or impatient).

Gardner (2001) notes that *yeah* and *yes* with falling intonation can be used to agree and align with prior talk. This agreement function is most common when the speaker is talking about things that the listener also knows about or is expressing an evaluation or assessment the listener can agree with. For instance, in Example 5, Ger is talking about her son's activities in school, activities with which Shi is not familiar, so *yeah* with falling intonation in Line 20 would be quite strange.

Yeah can also be used in a noncontinuer function to begin a longer turn that adds ideas or even at the start of a turn that goes on to disagree.

Right and *all right* are used as continuers not only with slightly rising intonation (signaling recognition that the speaker's talk is still in progress), but also with falling intonation. With falling intonation they confirm receipt and show a provisional acceptance of the unfolding talk (McCarthy, 2003). This use of *right*

---

[1] Conversation excerpts in this chapter are simplified and edited from data of actual conversation in research reports.

or *all right* often follows an explanation or a logical conclusion, as in Excerpt 5, in which Shi uses *right* to confirm receipt after Ger's explanation.

> **Example 5** (adapted from Raymond, 2004, p. 198)
>
> 19   Ger: And he's in the finals, I believe.
>
> 20   Shi: Mm-hm,
>
> 21   Ger: Which means he's doing quite well,
>
> 22 → Shi: Right.

Note that *yeah* followed immediately by *right*, both spoken with falling intonation, can be heard as rude and as doubting the truth of what was said, as in "Yeah. Right." *Yeah* and *uh-huh/mm-hm* with falling intonation tend to occur in different contexts from those in which *right/all right* with falling intonation occurs. In other contexts, *right* and *all right* can be used to agree to a proposal or a request, both of which are nonresponder uses.

Figure 1 summarizes the characteristics and functions of the responders discussed in this section.

CURRICULUM, TASKS, MATERIALS

The materials in this chapter were designed to teach several common forms of continuers: *mm-hm/uh-huh*, *yeah*[2], *right/all right*. This section provides a series of activities designed to raise learners' awareness of the responders typically used in English to acknowledge a speaker's contribution and to invite the speaker to

---

With slightly rising or flat intonation, these responders function as continuers signaling that there is more talk expected. Although less common, *uh-huh, yeah, right,* and *all right* can occur as continuers with falling intonation to show provisional acceptance or alignment. This is especially true of *right*. However, when they occur with falling intonation, these responders are most often used to answer questions or respond to requests, invitations, and the like.

Key: continuer function   [   ]   (usually) noncontinuer function   [▓▓]

Slightly rising or flat intonation	Uh-huh, Mm-hm, Uh-huh Mm-hm	Yeah, Yeah	Right, All right, Right All right
Falling intonation	Uh-huh. Mm-hm.	Yeah.	Right. All right.

Figure 1. Intonation and Meaning of Uh-huh/Mm-hm, Yeah, *and* Right/All right

---

[2] *Yes,* as opposed to *yeah,* is primarily used to answer questions, agree, accept invitations, and agree to comply with a request. So with falling intonation, it is used to agree; with rising intonation, it can be used as a continuer, though it is less usual a choice and sounds more formal.

continue talking. Students are guided to gradually notice the forms and functions of English continuers.

Teachers may want to prepare students for the activities in this chapter by reminding them that effective listeners need to show that they understand what is being said and what it means to the speaker. This is no easy task, because the nature of oral interaction involves a wide range of cultural and social meanings, and it may never be possible to prepare for all possibilities. However, it can be quite useful to increase students' awareness and command of different responses.

Note that in order to understand the intonation in the conversations in the following activities, students will need to be made aware that period (.) represents falling intonation, comma (,) represents slightly rising intonation, question mark (?) represents strongly rising intonation, and no punctuation represents flat intonation.

Activity 1: Raising Awareness of Continuers

In this activity, students receive their first exposure to continuers. They begin by answering some start-up questions, such as the following, designed to encourage them to think about the context of the conversation (buying a ticket to a public performance) in Worksheet 1 (see the Appendix).

1. Have you ever been to a music concert?

2. Was it expensive?

3. Did you have trouble getting the tickets?

4. How did you buy the tickets? At the box office? By phone? Over the Internet?

Once students have completed Worksheet 1, the teacher can point out that the short responses essentially allow the speaker to bypass the opportunity to take a turn and return the floor to the person who had been speaking. At the same time, they indicate at appropriate points in Dave's story that Alan is listening and following what Dave is saying. (Audio of Worksheet 1 is available at www.tesol media.com/books/pragmatics2.)

Activity 2: Understanding Form and Function of Continuers

This activity provides opportunities for students, while completing Worksheet 2 (see Appendix; audio available at www.tesolmedia.com/books/pragmatics2), to notice functions performed by the responders introduced in this chapter, occurring with different intonation contours and associated with different contexts. The teacher may want to remind students that punctuation represents intonation.

As students work their way through the conversations in Worksheet 2, it can be helpful to have them read these aloud. In particular, they should try to reproduce the intonation accurately.

At this point students are ready for a summary of the characteristics of different continuers. Handout 1 (see Appendix; audio available at www.tesolmedia .com/books/pragmatics2) contains an overview of basic characteristics of continuers and can be used throughout the lesson to help guide students and to serve as a reference in future reviews or expansions of the lesson.

Activity 3: Comparing Continuers in Different Languages

By this time students should have developed a general understanding of continuers and their pervasiveness in English. It can be helpful to have learners notice what forms may perform similar functions in their native language. Worksheet 3 (see Appendix) provides an opportunity for students to make such connections.

Students may suggest a variety of discourse particles and demonstrate a range of gestures, such as nodding, eye-gaze direction, and facial expressions, including nonverbal noises. For example, Japanese speakers may nod and use particles such as *ne, so,* and *nn.* It may be useful to show clips from movies or television without sound. The teacher might want to mention differences in frequency of use as well. For instance, according to Clancy, Thompson, Suzuki, and Tao (1996), Japanese speakers use continuers more frequently than English speakers, and English speakers use them more frequently than Chinese speakers.

Activity 4: Indentifying Continuer Intonation

This activity is designed to develop learners' ability to identify the intonation associated with different continuers. Depending on intonation, continuers can convey slight variations in function and meaning. When *yeah, uh-huh,* and *mm-hm* are used with a flat or slightly rising intonation, they have a fairly neutral continuer function—the listener does not express a position or attitude with respect to the preceding talk. The use of *right* and *all right* with a slightly rising or flat intonation indicates that the listener has received and understood the prior talk.

On the other hand, pronounced with a falling intonation, *yeah, uh-huh,* and *mm-hm* can express a stronger alignment with the speaker's prior talk while still returning the floor to the speaker, thus functioning as continuers. And *right* and *all right,* functioning as continuers with falling intonation, signal an acceptance of the talk and information so far (e.g., indicating that they are following an explanation). Students should gain awareness also of how continuers are used for these different functions.

In Worksheet 4 (see Appendix; audio available at www.tesolmedia.com/books /pragmatics2) students first become accustomed to listening for the intonation of continuers. They then identify places in ongoing talk where a continuer would be appropriate.

The teacher might want students to try to produce *mm-hm, uh-huh, yeah,* and *right* with a slightly rising, flat, and falling tone. Student pairs can read the dialogue in Worksheet 4. Another way to draw attention to intonation is to have students practice the intonation while drawing the shape of the intonation contour in the air, as a kinesthetic reinforcement. A final variation is to have students read aloud B's part from Worksheet 4 as a choral reading while the teacher reads A's role, paying attention to the intonation of the continuers used.

Handout 2 (see Appendix; audio available at www.tesolmedia.com/books /pragmatics2) provides an overview of continuers and the functions associated with their intonation. This can be used as a visual aid when practicing hearing and producing the continuers with different intonation patterns.

For additional activities, visit www.tesolbooks.com/books/pragmatics2.

Teachers should be aware that it will take time for students to become fluent at producing appropriate continuers, but if they begin to notice the use of continuers in English conversation (in their lives or in samples of English from electronic media), and if they make some attempts to practice using them, it is likely their interactional skills will improve.

REFLECTIONS

Although the lexical responders that are used to carry out continuer function (e.g., *yeah, right, all right*) are important, they are also challenging because most of them are multifunctional, depending on their delivery and especially their context. It may not be possible for students to master all the variations in form and function easily, but it is possible for them to become familiar with key patterns and learn particular functions that they can recognize, understand, and eventually use with more confidence in spontaneous discourse. The challenges include not confusing students with too much information and providing authentic, meaningful examples of natural language use.

Perhaps the most important point about the use of responders in general and continuers in particular is that they are inseparable from the texture and social action of the talk to which they are responding. Continuers are used in response to extended tellings or explanations of some kind, such as directions (e.g., to school) or instructions (e.g., how to register for classes online, how to tune a guitar).

These responders (as well as those introduced in chapter 12 in this volume) can be heard in a variety of media, such as theatrical dramas and comedies from film, television, or Internet media sources such as YouTube. It may also be useful to point out that responders, in particular continuers, are routinely used in everyday conversation but are also routinely avoided in contexts such as news interviews, talk show interviews, and the like.

To adapt this material for other teaching contexts, it would be good to select communication situations that are familiar to students, such as telling stories and giving directions, that take place in the local area of the school or class. For an extension of these activities, students can do a group project in which pairs or small groups discuss continuers used in their native or other languages and then explain one or two continuers to the class. Another extension is a field observation exercise, during which students go to a public place such as a park or public plaza, a coffee house, or a restaurant and listen in order to overhear the use of continuers and note the continuers they hear. As an in-class practice for the field trip, students could be grouped in threes for small-group practice, taking turns in the role of monitor, or overhearer, who takes notes on intonation and continuers used.

Finally, this field study approach can be carried out with online video of films and television, with students searching for media clips and analyzing them for the use of continuers. Students can bring the media clips to the classroom in some easily shared web format, and these can be jointly analyzed by students and teacher in the classroom. In these ways, students contribute to ongoing talk by adding energy and attention as listener or audience.

ACKNOWLEDGMENTS

I would like to acknowledge the help of San Francisco State University's American Language Institute in piloting materials, particularly teachers Winn Newberry and Sherri Martin. For help with recordings of audio, special thanks go to Andrea Taylor as well as to the students of Amy Kilgard at San Francisco State University: Jared Bosnich, John Calderon, Serena Cutts, Darrell Echiverri, Constance Gordon, Sarah Habache, Cindy Hsu, Alli Logue, Andrea Mas, Jrae Mason, Eva Miekus, Paul Miller, Hobie Owen, Evelyn Rompelman, Jhennifer Thomas, Alfredo Torres, Kyle Voeller, Nicole Wallace, and Amanda Wolff.

David Olsher is an assistant professor in the Department of English Language and Literature at San Francisco State University, in the United States. His research focuses primarily on the discourse of teaching and learning in language classrooms, using conversation analysis to study social action at the microinteractional level of turns and sequences. He has taught English and trained teachers in Japan and the United States.

APPENDIX: WORKSHEETS, HANDOUTS, AND ANSWER KEYS

Worksheet 1: Noticing Continuers

Before the conversation below, the two college students have talked about buying tickets to a concert. Dave has complained that he ordered tickets by telephone from a ticket sales service (Ticketmaster), but they gave him no choice of seats and sold him tickets far from the stage. He is unhappy with the seats.

Part 1

Read and listen to the telephone conversation, then answer the questions that follow.

D: What I hope happens is that I hope that they announce another show like at the Universal <u>A</u>mphitheater or something.

A: → <u>Yea</u>:h,

D: I mean, (0.2) you know 'cause at <u>lea</u>st that'd be a little cl<u>o</u>ser: and

A: Well, then what would you do about these tickets you ordered,

D: We:ll, (.) I don't know. (.) I could probably (.) s<u>e</u>ll them, or maybe I'll go <u>a</u>nyway,

A: → <u>R</u>ight.

D: But (.) I mean I have, like, tw<u>o</u> an' a half months to w<u>o</u>rry about th<u>i</u>s.

A: → Ri:ght.

D: Sooo (0.2) <u>A</u>nyway I'm not really sure what the heck is going on over at (.) at T<u>i</u>cketmaster.

A: Yeah <u>o</u>bviously. umm (.) I guess I'll st<u>i</u>ll go tomorrow morning to the place at the university,

D: → Yeah,

A: An' I'll find out what th<u>e</u>y say,

a. Why does Dave want to buy tickets to a new show if they announce one?

b. What will he do with the tickets he has now if he buys more?

c. What is Alan going to do?

Part 2

Now go back and notice the one-word responses (responders) in the lines with arrows in the conversation—these are all examples of *continuers*. Notice that the punctuation at the end of each utterance represents the way the voice pitch moves at the end of the utterance. A period (.) represents falling intonation and a comma (,) represents slightly rising intonation. No punctuation represents no change in pitch (flat intonation). With this in mind, answer the following questions.

    a.   What words are used as continuers? _____

    b.   How many of the continuers end in falling intonation? _____

    c.   How many of the continuers end in slightly rising intonation? _____

(The conversation in Worksheet 1 is adapted from course materials from Schegloff's Sociology C244A class, University of California, Los Angeles, Fall 2000.)

Worksheet 1: Answer Key

Part 1

    a.   Because the seats would be closer to the stage OR the concert would be closer to his home.

    b.   Dave might sell the tickets or he might go to both shows.

    c.   Alan will go to the university "place" (ticket office) to get more information.

Part 2

    a.   *yeah, right*

    b.   2

    c.   2

Worksheet 2: Identifying Forms and Functions of Continuers

Part 1

Read and listen to the following brief excerpts of conversations, then answer the question that follows each one.

Conversation 1: G is instructing F on where to go; F is looking at a map

    1 G: So when you turn

    2 F: → Uh-huh

    3 G: South southwest,

    4 F: → Yeah,

    5 G: A little bit, or when I say a little bit I suppose a few centimeters down,

    6 F: → All right.

    7 G: Um:: and then turn um:: west. (0.8) directly

What is G doing? __ (a) telling a story __ (b) giving reasons __ (c) giving directions

Conversation 2: G is instructing F on where to go; F is looking at a map

    1 G: So you head east::. and you go AROUND Millstream (0.5) so it's like-

    2 F: Go around Millstream?

    3 G: Yeah, like, um, over the top of Millstream and back down again.

    4 F: → Right,

    5 G: OK?

    6 F: Right,

    7 G: So you head (1.0) ah:: south to …

What is G doing? __ (a) telling a story __ (b) giving reasons __ (c) giving directions

Conversation 3: M and T are talking about their son's travels

    1 M: So I took him to the airport, but he couldn't buy a ticket. He could only

    2   get on standby.

    3 T: → Uh-huh,

    4 M: And I left him there at about noon.

What is M doing? __ (a) telling a story __ (b) giving reasons __ (c) giving directions

Conversation 4: A is explaining why Harriet is low on cash

    1 A: Harriet's got some money invested,

    2 B: → Mm-hm,

    3 A: But it's not easily accessible.

What is A doing? __ (a) telling a story __ (b) giving reasons __ (c) giving directions

Conversation 5: M is talking about his plans for the next day

    1 M: I pick it up, from his place at seven o'clock tomorrow morning, I take it

    2   down to Motor Italiana, they fix the other things, which need doing, because

    3   they're things which I was gonna change anyway,

    4 L: → Mm-hm,

    5 M: Or involved with the work which I was gonna get done anyway.

What is M doing? __ (a) telling a story __ (b) giving reasons __ (c) giving directions

Part 2

Answer the following questions about Conversations 1–5.

    a.   When is the continuer used?

        ___ in the middle of the other speaker's turn or sentence

        ___ at the end of a completed turn or turn segment

    b.   What is the intonation or change in pitch of each continuer?

        ___ slightly rising   ___ flat   ___ falling

    c.   What social actions are carried out by the use of the continuer? (You may select one or more than one of the following for each conversation.)

        ____ invites or allows speaker to continue

        ____ recognizes speaker is not finished

        ____ claims to be following the speaker so far

(The sources of the conversations in Worksheet 2 are as follows: Conversation 1, Filipi & Wales, 2003, p. 436; Conversation 2, Filipi & Wales, 2003, p. 441; Conversation 3, Schegloff, 2007, p. 232; Conversation 4, Gardner, 1997, p. 19; Conversation 5, Gardner, 1997, pp. 25–26.)

Worksheet 2: Answer Key

Part 1

    1. Giving directions

    2. Giving directions

    3. Telling a story

    4. Giving a reason

    5. Telling a story (of a future plan, but using present tense); at the moment this continuer occurs, the storyteller has started giving a reason for his plan.

Part 2

Conversation 1

    a.   at the end of each piece of information ("when you turn"; "south southwest"; "a few centimeters down")

    b.   intonation or change in pitch at the end of the continuer: line 2, flat; line 4, slightly rising; line 6, falling

    c.   social action—allows or invites the speaker to continue; suggests that the speaker is following successfully on the map

Conversation 2

    a.   at the end of a complete piece of information ("over the top of Millstream and back down again")

    b.   line 4, slightly rising

    c.   social action—allows or invites the speaker to continue; suggests that the speaker is following the directions so far

Conversation 3

    a.   at the end of a complete piece of the story ("he could only get on standby")

    b.   line 3, slightly rising

    c.   social action—allows or invites the speaker to continue; recognizes that the speaker hasn't finished her story

Conversation 4

    a.   at the end of a complete piece of information ("Harriet's got some money invested.")

    b.   line 2, slightly rising

    c.   social action—allows or invites the speaker to continue; recognizes that the speaker hasn't finished making his point

Conversation 5

    a.   at the end of a story followed by a "because" clause sentence, after the final "which I was gonna get done anyway"

    b.   line 4, slightly rising

    c.   social action—allows or invites the speaker to continue; recognizes that the speaker hasn't finished explaining his plans

Handout 1: Functions of Different Continuers

This handout presents an overview of the functions of the responders that are often used to (a) encourage the speaker to continue talking, (b) acknowledge what the speaker has said so far, or (c) align/agree with the speaker's prior utterance.

Forms and Functions of Continuers

Continuing	Confirming receipt	Aligning with prior statement	Accepting prior statement
mm-hm, uh-huh, yeah, *mm-hm uh-huh yeah*	*right, all right,* *right all right*	*yeah.* *uh huh.*	*right.* *all right.*

-----*slightly rising or flat intonation*----------------------*falling intonation*---------------

Continuers usually follow a phrase or sentence that is heard as complete. They show that the listener, who produces the responder, expects more talk to follow.

Worksheet 3: Thinking About Continuers Across Languages

This worksheet focuses on continuers used in different languages. Discuss your answers in pairs.

1. What languages do you speak other than English? _____

2. What languages does your partner speak other than English? _____

3. Below are some examples of continuers used in different languages. Do you recognize any of these?

so, ne, nn [Japanese]	*da* [Russian]	*nu* [Hebrew]
jah [Estonian]	*si si* [Spanish]	*oui* [French]
shi ma [Chinese]	*joo* [Finnish]	*ja* [German]

    What words or sounds do you use in your first language to let a speaker know you are listening and to invite him or her to continue?

    You _____

    Partner _____

4. What kinds of body positions, gestures, and facial expressions do you use to show you are listening and interested when speaking your first language? Demonstrate this by play-acting with a partner.

Worksheet 3: Answer Key

Answers will vary. Answers to Question 4 may include nodding, looking at speaker, and eye gaze toward speaker.

Worksheet 4: Practice Listening for Intonation

Part 1

Listen to the following continuers and mark the intonation you hear as slightly rising (↗), flat (→), or falling (↘) on the lines provided. Begin by listening to the first four examples.

E1: *mm-hm* ↗	E2: *uh-huh* ↘	E3: *mm-hm* →	E4: yeah ↘
1. *all right* ___	2. *mm-hm* ___	3. *yeah* ___	4. *right* ___
5. *yeah* ___	6. *uh-huh* ___	7. *right* ___	8. *mm-hm* ___
9. *uh-huh* ___	10. *right* ___	11. *mm-hm* ___	12. *yeah* ___

Part 2

Listen to the following dialogue. Fill in the blanks with the continuers, and mark the intonation used in the dialogue.

1 A: You know, Jim is a good jazz guitar player.

2 B: Absolutely.

3 A: Well, last night he was playing at the bar down the street,

4 B: _____

5 A: And these two guys from out of town asked to join him on stage.

6 B: _____

7 A: So, one took out a saxophone and the other had a bass guitar,

8 B: _____

9 A: And at first they didn't sound too good together, but then they started

10   playing this old ballad, *Autumn Leaves*, you know?

11 B: _____

12 A: And then, wow, they suddenly found this amazing jazz rhythm and sounded great!

13 B: Hey, cool!

14 A: And everyone stopped talking and we were all just listening, really amazed

15   at their sound . . .

Worksheet 4: Answer Key

Part 1

1. *all right* ↗	2. *mm-hm* ↗	3. *yeah* ↘	4. *right* →
5. *yeah* ↗	6. *uh-huh* →	7. *right* ↘	8. *mm-hm* ↗
9. *uh-huh* ↘	10. *right* ↘	11. *mm-hm* ↗	12. *yeah* →

Part 2

4 B: Uh-huh ↗

6 B: Mm-hm ↗

8 B: Yeah ↗

11 B: Yeah ↗

Handout 2: Intonation and Meaning/Function of Responders

Intonation

With slightly rising or flat intonation, these responders function as continuers signaling that there is more talk expected. Although less common, *uh-huh, yeah, right,* and *all right* can occur as continuers with falling intonation to show acceptance or alignment. However, when they occur with falling intonation, they are most often used with a nonresponder function to answer questions or respond to elicitations such as requests or invitations.

Key: continuer function ☐   (usually) noncontinuer function ▨

Slightly rising or flat intonation	Uh-huh, Mm-hm,	Yeah,	Right, All right,
	Uh-huh Mm-hm	Yeah	Right All right
Falling intonation	Uh-huh. Mm-hm.	Yeah.	Right. All right.

Three Cautions

1. Multiple sayings of *yeah* or *right* may sound rude. For example, *Right, right, right* may sound impatient or may suggest that the prior statement is obvious or unimportant, especially if spoken quickly, with falling intonation on each word.

2. The phrase *yeah, right* can have different meanings depending on how it is said. If used with falling intonation, it can be heard as a sarcastic form of disagreement that sounds rude.

3. Variation in the choice of continuer is important. Use of the same continuer in more than two separate responses in a row (following different points in the speaker's talk) makes the listener sound bored or impatient. From one response to the next, avoid repeating the same continuer too often (e.g., use *mm-hm / yeah / mm-hm*, but avoid *yeah / yeah / yeah*).

CHAPTER 12

Responders: Change-of-State Tokens, News Markers, and Assessments

David Olsher

Responders such as continuers are part of everyday talk in a wide variety of contexts and activities. Adult English language learners (ELLs) already use these kinds of responses as part of their competence in other languages, and speakers at all levels generally rely on short responses, head nods, and so on. However, greater control over English language responders and their functions can help ELLs more effectively engage with the speaker of an extended turn. Responders such as the continuers *uh-huh, yeah,* and *right* are quite useful in responding to an extended turn, but when a speaker tells important, surprising, or interesting news, a listener needs to reply by expressing a stance toward the information with responders such as the change-of-state token *oh,* the news markers *really?* and *oh really?,* and assessments (e.g., *not bad, amazing*) that show the hearer's understanding of the prior talk.

This chapter expands the range of responders beyond continuers (see chapter 11 in this volume). Continuers display the speaker's awareness that the prior speaker has not finished what he or she intended to say or, in some cases, suggest provisional acceptance of the talk so far. The responders in this chapter mark the prior talk as informative, as something newsworthy that invites further talk, or as something assessable. As discussed in chapter 11, responders are short responses of single words or short phrases that are offered by a listener to show that he or she is following and understanding a speaker who is taking an extended turn at talk (e.g., telling a story, giving an explanation). Responders encourage the speaker to continue and at the same time may take a stance with regard to the just-prior segment of talk. The responders in chapter 11 mark an orientation to the prior talk as part of an unfinished longer turn (e.g., *mm-hm, uh-huh*), or they agree with or acknowledge a prior point (e.g., *yeah, right*).

This chapter introduces responders that can add to a richer and more complete repertoire of short responses, that is, responses that show an orientation to the previous turn as (a) informative (something that the hearer did not know or understand before, but now does as a result of the prior turn), (b) newsworthy (something notable enough to focus on as a topic for further talk), or (c) worth assessing (e.g., good news). By broadening their awareness of this range of responder resources and functions, ELLs will be able to experiment, notice their occurrence in English, and work toward acquisition of these English interactional resources and an understanding of appropriate ways to use them.

CONTEXT

The materials in this chapter were designed for international students studying in an intensive English language institute at a U.S. university, many aiming to enter the university as undergraduates. Earlier versions of these materials were used in an English as a second language oral skills class. A revised version of activities was developed with a refined linguistic focus.

The sessions with the revised materials were conducted in a different set of classes designed to promote academic skills. Teachers integrated the activities into a content-based academic oral skills curriculum with a focus on small-group discussions and peer-to-peer presentations. They motivated students by letting them know that these skills are also used in a wide variety of everyday speaking situations. Teachers used a set of activities as a stimulus to create a model dialogue for students who were preparing to discuss their research projects. The students worked with examples of responders from the teacher-generated dialogue to raise their awareness. After working through the dialogue, students worked in groups to share their own stories of doing their research, and partners were instructed to listen attentively and use responders.

This chapter focuses on three types of stance-taking responders: the change-of-state-of-awareness marker *oh*, the news markers *really?* and *oh really?*, and assessments such as *good*.*

Oh as a responder with falling intonation indicates that the speaker is in the process of becoming aware of new information or has understood a repair of a problem of hearing or understanding. This *oh* has been referred to as a change-of-state token (Heritage, 1984). In Example 1, *oh* marks the successful understanding of a word that hadn't been heard or understood, in this case the repeated word *Me* (line 4) that followed *Probably what?* (line 3). Simplified recordings of the original conversations in the following examples are available at www.tesol media.com/books/pragmatics2.

---

*A period following responders represents falling intonation, a question mark represents a strong rise, and a comma represents a mild rise.

Example 1 (Schegloff, 2007, p. 120)

1 A: Uh, that's probably Bea you hear.

2   (0.5)

3 B: Probably what?

4 A: Me.

5   (.)

6 B: → Oh.

7   (0.8)

Oh provides a way for recipients to align themselves to prior talk and confirm that a prior turn was informative (Heritage, 1984). Furthermore, by the addition of specific types of turn components, such as assessments or requests for further information, recipients can treat the informing as complete (with assessments such as *Oh good.*) or incomplete (with requests for further information, such as *Oh, how did that happen?*). Schegloff (2007) notes that a common composite of response particles is *Oh. Okay.* which is regularly associated with accepting prior talk and moving toward sequence closure. Special emphasis is possible with *oh* when spoken with a stretch and a strong rise–fall intonation (↗oh::↘), marking the prior talk not only as informing but as something surprising or of special interest.[1]

Oh also functions as something other than a responder, for instance, as the preface to a turn. In this role it can mark some special personal, subjective stance, such as rejection of an assumption conveyed by the previous turn (e.g., A: *I heard you were pretty angry at Jeff* / B: *Oh not really*). Or an *Oh yes* response to a question, produced with finality, treats what was just said as obvious and "indicates a problem about a question's relevance, appropriateness, or presuppositions" (Heritage, 1998, p. 295). *Oh* as a change-of-state token also has a nonresponder use when it is used to mark a noticing or remembering of something that involves a change of state of awareness, such as noticing a friend's new haircut (e.g., *Oh, you got your hair cut*) or remembering something such as an upcoming appointment (e.g., *Oh, I just remembered I've got to meet Sue in a half hour*).

News markers such as *really?* or *oh really?*[2] with rising (or occasionally falling) intonation are brief responses that mark the prior talk as something of special

---

[1] Note that *ah* can also function like *oh* in marking receipt of new information, as can *ah ha*, which carries the added sense that the news either was suspected or resolves some existing question. The responder *ah ha* can take on a special meaning with a rise on *ah* and a strong fall on the *ha*; this in effect indicates that the new information is something the listener had suspected was true before or that suddenly makes clear some existing situation or prior issues in a way not previously explained.

[2] News markers may include partial repeats uttered with rising intonation, such as *He is?* or *A new car?* The *oh* preface can also be found in front of news markers that are intonational questions, such as *Oh, ya do?* or *Oh, she has?* (Heritage, 1984, pp. 303–304). Intonational questions, often without the *oh*, can also be used to perform other, non-news-marker functions, targeting a problem of hearing, speaking, or understanding, or to signal a yet-to-be-expressed disagreement.

interest, worth further talk. The use of news markers invites confirmation and added talk on the topic by the prior speaker. What follows the news marker may be a simple confirmation and brief expansion of the telling or even a more extended story. The use of a news marker shows surprise or some sort of special interest in the news, ideas, or information that was just conveyed; in other words, it treats the prior talk as newsworthy in some way. In Example 2, the news is that the sister of someone both A and B know has recently had a baby. Once a problem in hearing is repaired (lines 2–3), A treats this announcement as newsworthy with a news marker (line 4).

Example 2 (Schegloff, 2007, pp. 39–40)

1 B: Oh, Sibbie's sister had a ba:by bo:y.

2 A: Who?

3 B: Sibbie's sister.

4 A: →   Oh really?

5 B: Yeah, she had it yesterday. Ten:: pou:nds.

While both *really?* and *oh really?* are regularly used as news markers, they are not exactly the same. The *oh* preface can be seen as a kind of upgrade that adds a sense of personal stance or involvement, depending on the context. When spoken with stress and stretched or lengthened vowel or consonant sounds, but with relatively flat intonation, *really* and *oh really* can also be used to perform non-news-marker functions such as expressing disbelief or signaling a potential challenge or disagreement to follow. (For more on teaching these responders used in response to announcements, see Wong & Waring, 2010).

Assessments are used to respond to news or descriptions of things or events that are easy to evaluate positively (as interesting or exciting) or negatively (as unfortunate or distressing). To assess news or ideas, the hearer needs to understand their importance to the speaker. Assessments are often expected. For instance, if one speaker gives an assessment of something that the hearer is also familiar with, such as the food at a local restaurant, then a second assessment (e.g., *that's/that sounds good, great, fantastic, cool, awful, bad*) is due as a response. Example 3 includes two responder assessments.

Example 3 (Schegloff, 2007, p. 124)

1 A: How've you been?

2 B: Oh::, survi:ving I guess, hh

3 A: →   That's good,

4   how's Bob,

5 B: He's fine,

6 A: →   Tha::t's goo:d,

7 B: Goo:d an how's school going?

As mentioned previously, assessments as responders can follow news or information, or they can follow assessments of something known to both speaker and hearer, as second assessments. In Example 3, good news—that B is doing relatively well ("surviving") and that Bob is fine—is positively assessed by the use of *That's good* (lines 3, 6), an evaluation that shows A's appreciation of the good news. It can be seen in the example as part of a series of related *How are you* sequences, but it could follow any informing that is hearable as good news.

Another type of assessment, second assessments, can follow a first assessment of something that both participants have knowledge of or experience with. Pomerantz (1984) writes that these second assessments need to be upgraded to be heard as agreeing or aligning (e.g., A: *Nice day* / B: *Beautiful*). A same evaluation may be heard as a sign of possible disagreement (e.g., A: *Nice day* / B: *Nice, yes, but . . .*).

Responses that are assessments but are not responders can be produced in response to a question (e.g., A: *How was the movie?* / B: *Not bad*).

CURRICULUM, TASKS, MATERIALS

The materials in this chapter can be used over several class meetings. The lesson includes awareness-raising, identification, and optional application activities, each of which can take 30 minutes to an hour of class time. Between lessons an optional homework activity to help students notice this type of responder in both English and their native language can be included as part of a broader pragmatics awareness-raising approach.

Activity 1: Raising Awareness of *Oh, Really* and Assessments

Activity 1 (Worksheet 1, see the Appendix) is designed to get students thinking about the stance-taking responders *oh* and *oh really* and assessments. Students are instructed to answer questions on the talk preceding the responder and then to determine the difference in meaning among *oh*, *oh really*, and assessments. (Audio available at www.tesolmedia.com/books/pragmatics2.)

When the students have completed the activity, the teacher can point out that Sherry's reply in Line 3 is surprising, because it was not what Mark seemed to recall from prior conversations, a change in the plan he had asked about. Thus, Mark produced a news marker indicating his surprise. Karen's turn in line 8 is new information but does not seem as surprising. Therefore he used the change-of-state *oh*, indicating that this is new information, but not particularly surprising. A speaker might say *oh really?* here, but because it is not such big news, *oh* works fine. In line 14, Mark is adding to his own earlier assessment in line 12 (which is more substantive but essentially fulfills the same function as a responder) as providing an upgraded positive assessment. Notice that this assessment closes down the current sequence.

Once students have been introduced to *oh really?* and assessments, the teacher may want to provide an overview of the characteristics of these responders. Handout 1 (see the Appendix) contains a summary of some of the basic characteristics of the responders focused on in this chapter and can be used throughout the lesson as a guide as well as a reference in future reviews or expansions of the lesson.

Handout 1 can also be used for practice with producing and identifying these responders versus their prosodic upgrade with the whole class and in groups. (Audio available at www.tesolmedia.com/books/pragmatics2.) Or the teacher can instruct students to work in pairs to create examples of turns that could come before different responders. Pairs can share their examples with the class and let others try to guess which responder could follow each example.

Activity 2: Identifying Functions of *Oh, Really?* and Assessments

During this activity, learners read and listen to an extended dialogue (Worksheet 2, see the Appendix) in order to notice the targeted responders' forms and functions in context. The transcription symbols include comma (,) for mild rise in intonation, question mark (?) for strong rise in intonation, and period (.) for falling intonation. One or more colons (:::) convey sounds that are stretched, and pauses are indicated with parentheses as brief [(.)] or longer, in seconds [(1.8)]. (See the Transcription Conventions at the beginning of this volume.) Students who cannot hear the intonation can use the punctuation as a guide. (Audio available at www.tesolmedia.com/books/pragmatics2.)

Activity 3: Interpreting Effect of *Oh, Really?* and Assessments on Following Text

This activity includes questions that review the functions of the responders and focus on what happens after responders are used—in other words, the kinds of turns that follow them. Students first read and listen to an example and then, as a class, discuss the answers to the questions on the example item from Worksheet 3 (see the Appendix). They should then have time to read and listen to the dialogues one by one, with the teacher answering any questions they have after each dialogue. After this, students work alone or in pairs answering the questions about the dialogues. It may be useful to replay the audio as students work on the task. After they complete the task, students can listen again and then practice reading the dialogues aloud. (Audio available at www.tesolmedia.com/books/pragmatics2.)

The teacher may want to point out that the freestanding *oh* in Line 3 and the *oh* followed by an assessment in Line 8 in Dialogue 1 both close down the current sequence, whereas the two instances of *really?* in Dialogue 2 (Line 3) and Dialogue 3 (Line 2) both invite more discussion of the topic. For more detailed explanation of this sequence, see the Suggested Answers for Worksheet 3 in the Appendix.

Students may find it useful and engaging to practice these dialogues by reading them out loud, practicing the intonation, and then performing them for the class. For a creative extension of this activity, pairs can imagine the continuation of one of these dialogues, write two more turns for each speaker, and share this with the class.

Activity 4: Comparing Change-of-State Tokens, News Markers, and Assessments With Responders in Other Languages

This activity (Worksheet 4, see the Appendix) provides a chance for students to talk about responders in their first language (L1) with roughly equivalent functions to those being introduced in English. The worksheet provides brief dialogues in English to provide context for the English examples. Students may have more than one possible translation for some responders. To get the most out of this, students should think about how well the English responders fit the meaning and function of their L1 translations. Even though there may not be exact translations, it is valuable for students to begin to reflect on their L1 pragmatic language use while learning similar resources in English. (Audio available at www.tesolmedia .com/books/pragmatics2.)

Activity 5: Recognizing Prosodic Features of Change-of-State Tokens, News Markers, and Assessments

An important point about responders is that their delivery (e.g., short versus stretched, rising versus flat versus falling intonation) can affect their pragmatic meaning. Activity 5 provides both information on (Handout 2) and practice listening to (Worksheet 5) short and stretched occurrences of one high-involvement responder (*oh*) with various intonation contours (see the Appendix for both of these resources). If teachers would like to prepare students with information on how *oh* may be upgraded to ↗*oh::*↘ prosodically, they can distribute Handout 2. (Audio for handout and worksheet available at www.tesolmedia.com/books /pragmatics2.)

With intermediate-level classes, it may be best to focus primarily on the points summarized on Handout 1 (which was introduced during Activity 1). Worksheet 5 and Handout 2 can be used as optional activities for more advanced-level students once Handout 1 has been mastered and students seem fairly comfortable with *oh really?* and assessments.[3]

For an additional activity, visit www.tesolmedia.com/books/pragmatics2.

---

[3] Note that these kinds of intonation are often exploited in television situation comedies such as *Friends*, and it may be possible to identify additional examples in videos of episodes of such programs.

REFLECTIONS

Students reported that the activities were entertaining and fun to do. Regarding reading the transcripts aloud, one student commented, "We can copy Americans if we have this activity, and that's something I want to do. I want to sound like an American, so I'm trying to copy" (from a Japanese student). Students felt this kind of pragmatic information is good to know because they're "not used to the way people talk here." Students said that they would use responders with Americans in the future "because it's part of the culture."

On the other hand, some students felt uncomfortable when they were asked to produce typical American responders, saying that the responders felt unnatural. For students such as these, an awareness of and ability to identify and comprehend the meaning of responders and their use in English may be all that should be required. The activity available at www.tesolmedia.com/books/pragmatics2 provides an opportunity for those students who wish to practice producing *oh really?* and assessments.

Teachers may also want to mention that the responders in chapter 12 are part of a wider repertoire of responders speakers use; others include forms such as *uh-huh, yeah,* and *right* (discussed in chapter 11 in this volume).

ACKNOWLEDGMENTS

I would like to acknowledge the help of San Francisco State University's American Language Institute in piloting materials, particularly teachers Winn Newberry and Sherri Martin. For help with recordings of audio, special thanks go to Andrea Taylor as well as to the students of Amy Kilgard at San Francisco State University: Jared Bosnich, John Calderon, Serena Cutts, Darrell Echiverri, Constance Gordon, Sarah Habache, Cindy Hsu, Alli Logue, Andrea Mas, Jrae Mason, Eva Miekus, Paul Miller, Hobie Owen, Evelyn Rompelman, Jhennifer Thomas, Alfredo Torres, Kyle Voeller, Nicole Wallace, and Amanda Wolff.

David Olsher is an assistant professor in the Department of English Language and Literature at San Francisco State University, in the United States. His research focuses primarily on the discourse of teaching and learning in language classrooms, using conversation analysis to study social action at the microinteractional level of turns and sequences. He has taught English and trained teachers in Japan and the United States.

APPENDIX: WORKSHEETS, ANSWER KEYS, AND HANDOUTS

Worksheet 1: Awareness of Responders in Interaction

Read the following dialogue, and look at the list of responders at the end. Look at the lines with arrows (→). Then answer these questions:

1. Which of the following does the word or phrase with the arrow indicate about the prior turn?

    a. The content of the prior turn is informative.

    b. The content of the prior turn is surprising.

    c. The content of the prior turn is worthy of assessment.

2. What is the difference in meaning between the three words/phrases?

Dialogue

Context of the conversation: Three friends are visiting. Mark, Karen, and Sherry are talking about plans for Sherry's wedding.

1 Mark:		hh What about the outside candlelight routine? Is that still
2		gonna go on?
3 Sherry:		No, you can't have outside candlelight. It's a fi:re hazard.
4		(0.5)
5 Mark:	→	Oh, really?
6		(·)
7 Sherry:		Yes::.
8 Karen:		You could have it inside, though.
9 Mark:	→	Oh.
10 Sherry:		Yeah, but who wants to get married inside in the middle of the
11		summer when it's still light till nine o'clock.
12 Mark:		It's going to be beautiful outsi:de.
13 Sherry:		Ye:ah.
14 Mark:	→	That sounds fantastic.
15.		(0.2)
16. Mark:		So have you called any other hotels or anything?

(This dialogue is adapted from Schegloff, 2007, pp. 156–157.)

Handout 1: Change-of-State Tokens, News Markers, and Assessments

At times speakers indicate that the prior turn has provided new information by showing their own change of state of awareness (e.g., with *oh*). At other times they show surprise or interest with news markers that invite more talk on the topic (e.g., *really?*). They show that they recognize normal, everyday good news with mild positive assessments (e.g., *good*) and particularly good news with strong positive assessments (e.g., *fantastic*). Using these responders can contribute to smooth and engaged talk.

	Change-of-State Tokens	News Markers	Brief Assessments
Examples	*oh*↘	*really?*↗ *oh really?*↗	*cool* ↘ *fantastic* ↘ *good* ↘ *amazing* ↘ *too bad* ↘ *terrible* ↘
Intonation	Falling Can also be rising (oh?↑) or mild rise (oh, ↗), which adds a sense of surprise or doubt	Rising Can also be falling (really. ↘) or mild rise (really, ↗), which adds a sense of surprise or doubt	Falling Can also be rise–fall (c↗o:ol.↘)
Function	*Recognizes prior talk as informative *When produced as freestanding *oh*, with falling intonation, can close a sequence *Shows speaker's change of state of knowledge or awareness	*Indicates prior talk as newsworthy *Invites more talk on the topic *Caution:* Can be heard to express doubt, to challenge, or to show disagreement	*Responds to something assessable in the prior talk *Ranges from mild to strong *Can take phrasal and clausal formats (e.g., *that's/that sounds*) Examples: *Cool, That's cool, Sounds cool*

Worksheet 2: Identifying the Functions of *Oh, Really?* and Assessments

I. Read and listen to the dialogue.

II. Answer the following questions about each of the arrowed (→) turns:

1. Prior turn's action? ___ telling/informing ___ asking a question

2. Arrowed turn's final intonation? ___ falling ___ flat ___ rising

3. Arrowed turn's action?

___ treats prior turn as informative (but not particularly surprising)

___ treats prior turn as surprising or newsworthy

___ gives an assessment of something in the prior turn

If the arrowed turn gives an assessment of something in the prior turn, what is it?

Dialogue

Context of the conversation: In this telephone conversation, Sue and Jane, two friends, are catching up on recent events, including recent visits with friends.

1 Sue:		So Tim and Leslie ca:me dow:n for dinne:r,
2 Jane:		Was it good?
3 Sue:		Oh yeah, the salmon was delicious[s,
4 Jane:		[Oh ↓ goo:d.
5 Sue:		Mm. (.5) What's new with you:.
6		(0.7)
7 Jane:		↑ No:thi:ng,
8 Sue:	→	Reall[y?
9 Jane:		[Except I: had Bill over. (.)
10 Sue:		Ye:ah,
11 Jane:		Yea:h, he drove
12		You know his sister wrote a book?
13 Sue:	→	Oh, really?
14 Jane:		Yeah, it's her own travel story
15 Sue:	→	Oh::.
16 Jane:		About her year in (.) Malaysia and Indonesia. (.)
17 Sue:	→	Ve::ry co:ol.
18 Jane:		It's uh::: (.) she's gonna have a book party when it comes out.

Worksheet 2: Suggested Answers

Line 8

1. Prior turn's action? *telling/informing*

2. Arrowed turn's final intonation? *rising*

3. Arrowed turn's action? *treats prior turn as newsworthy*

Line 13

1. Prior turn's action? *telling/ informing*

2. Arrowed turn's final intonation? *rising*

3. Arrowed turn's action? *treats prior turn as newsworthy*

Line 15

1. Prior turn's action? *telling/informing*

2. Arrowed turn's final intonation? *falling*

3. Arrowed turn's action? *shows information receipt*

Line 17

1. Prior turn's action? *telling/ informing*

2. Arrowed turn's final intonation? *falling*

3. Arrowed turn's action? *gives an assessment* (Sue assesses the topic of Bill's sister's book.)

Worksheet 3: Interpreting *Oh Really?* and Assessments

I. Read and listen to each dialogue.

II. Answer the following questions about the arrowed (→) turns:

1. Prior turn's action?   ___ telling/informing   ___ asking a question

2. Arrowed turn's final intonation?   ___ falling   ___ flat   ___ rising

3. Arrowed turn's action?

> ___ treats prior turn as informative (but not particularly surprising)

> ___ treats prior turn as surprising or newsworthy

> ___ gives an assessment of something in the prior turn

4. If arrowed turn gives an assessment, what is it assessing?

5. What follows?

> ___ more talk by same speaker   ___ talk by another speaker   ___ pause

6. If more talk from same speaker follows, what kind of talk?

> ___ explanation   ___ assessment   ___ question

III. Now listen again, and then work with a partner to practice reading the dialogues out loud.

Example Dialogue

1 Jeff: Hello there. I rang you earlier but ya were out,

2 Ken: Oh, I musta been at Dave's house

3 Jeff: → O::h.

4   (1.0)

Suggested Answers for Line 3

1. Prior turn's action? *telling/informing*

2. Arrowed turn's final intonation? *falling*

3. Arrowed turn's action? *treats prior turn as informative (but not particularly surprising)*

4. If arrowed turn gives an assessment, what is it assessing? *not applicable*

5. What follows? *pause*

6. If more talk from same speaker follows, what kind of talk? *none*

Dialogue 1
(Nancy and Hyla are talking about Hyla's old boyfriend, whom Hyla recently called)

1 Nancy:		Does he have his own apartment?
2 Hyla:		Yeah,
3 Nancy:	→	Oh,
4		(1.0)
5 Nancy:		How did ya get his number,
6		(.)
7 Hyla:		I called information in San Francisco
8 Nancy:	→	Oh:::::.
9	→	Very clever,
10 Hyla:		=Thank you: I-ˑ hh-ˑhhhhh
11 Nancy:		What's his last name,
12		(0.2)
13 Nancy:		So is he …

Dialogue 2
(Two students are chatting about prices for tickets for a hockey game)

1 A:		But who's willing to pay that much money. That you know.
2 B:		Every game's sold out.
3 A:	→	Really?
4 B:		Yeah. This one is worth like (1.0) It's worth like
5		a hundred dollars. These are on the glass. Front row
6		on the glass. Center ice.
7 A:	→	Wow.
8 B:		Best seats you can get . . .

Dialogue 3
(Two friends are talking on the telephone about a friend of theirs, Jim)

    1 A: Hey, did you hear Jim got a new car?

    2 B: → Rea::lly?

    3 A: Yeah, it's an all-electric car.

    4 B: → Sounds great.

    5   (0.2)

    6 B: Eh (.) what kind.

    7 A: It's a NEw one, a sports car.

    8 B: → Amazing. (.) Ve:ry coo:l.

    9 A: Yeah, he just showed up in it last <u>night</u>

    10   at the party…

Dialogue 4
(Ava and Bea are talking on the telephone; the conversation is already in progress)

    1 Ava: Anyway. How've you been.

    2 Bea: O:::h, surviving I guess,

    3 Ava:→ That's good,

    4   How's Bob,

    5 Bea: He's fine,

    6 Ava:→ That's good,

    7 Bea: Goo:d, an' how's school going.

Dialogue 5
(B = travel agent; C = customer; B is explaining some options for package trips)

    1 B: But there is availability there. It's just a matter of deciding where you

    2   want to go. And really how much you want to spend. But this

    3   weekend they start at a hundred 'n forty-nine Euros.

    4 C: → Great. That's brilliant.

    5 B: So you've got some very nice options here . . .

(Dialogues in Worksheet 3 are from the following sources: Example, Heritage, 1984, p. 301; Dialogue 1, Schegloff, 2007, p. 119; Dialogue 2, McCarthy, 2003, p. 51; Dialogue 3 (original); Dialogue 4, Schegloff, 2007, p. 124; Dialogue 5, McCarthy, 2003, p. 37.)

Worksheet 3: Suggested Answers

Dialogue 1

Line 3

1. Prior turn's action? *telling/informing*

2. Arrowed turn's final intonation? *mildly rising*

3. Arrowed turn's action? *treats prior turn as informative (but not particularly surprising)*

4. If arrowed turn gives an assessment, what is it assessing? *NA*

5. What follows? *more talk by same speaker*

6. If more talk from same speaker follows, what kind of talk? *question*

Line 8

1. Prior turn's action? *telling/informing*

2. Arrowed turn's final intonation? *falling*

3. Arrowed turn's action? *receives new information*

4. If arrowed turn gives an assessment, what is it assessing? *NA*

5. What follows? *more talk by responder*

6. If more talk from same speaker follows, what kind of talk? *assessment*

Line 9

1. Prior turn's action? *telling/informing*

2. Arrowed turn's final intonation? *mildly rising*

3. Arrowed turn's action? *assesses information from prior speaker's turn*

4. If arrowed turn gives an assessment, what is it assessing? *Hyla's idea to call information to get her old boyfriend's number*

5. What follows? *more talk by same speaker (after a brief response by Hyla)*

6. If more talk from same speaker follows, what kind of talk? *questions about the person being discussed*

Dialogue 2

Line 3

1. Prior turn's action? *telling/informing*

2. Arrowed turn's final intonation? *rising*

3. Arrowed turn's action? *treats information in prior turn as newsworthy*

4. If arrowed turn gives an assessment, what is it assessing? *NA*

5. What follows? *other speaker continues, elaborates*

6. If more talk from same speaker follows, what kind of talk? *NA*

Line 7

1. Prior turn's action? *telling/informing*

2. Arrowed turn's final intonation? *falling*

3. Arrowed turn's action? *treats information in prior turn as surprising news*

4. If arrowed turn gives an assessment, what is it assessing? *the ice hockey tickets that B is discussing*

5. What follows? *other speaker continues, elaborating on the tickets*

6. If more talk from same speaker follows, what kind of talk? *NA*

Dialogue 3

Line 2

1. Prior turn's action? *telling/informing*

2. Arrowed turn's final intonation? *rising*

3. Arrowed turn's action? *treats information in prior turn as newsworthy*

4. If arrowed turn gives an assessment, what is it assessing? *NA*

5. What follows? *other speaker continues, elaborating on the car*

6. If more talk from same speaker follows, what kind of talk? *NA*

Line 4

1. Prior turn's action? *telling/informing*

2. Arrowed turn's final intonation? *falling*

3. Arrowed turn's action? *positive assessment*

4. If arrowed turn gives an assessment, what is it assessing? *the information that Jim's new car is all electric*

5. What follows? *same speaker continues after a brief pause*

6. If more talk from same speaker follows, what kind of talk? *question about the car*

Line 8

1. Prior turn's action? *telling/informing*

2. Arrowed turn's final intonation? *falling*

3. Arrowed turn's action? *assesses information positively*

4. If arrowed turn gives an assessment, what is it assessing? *information about Jim's car—that it's a new sports car*

5. What follows? *other speaker continues, explaining when he saw the car*

6. If more talk from same speaker follows, what kind of talk? *NA*

Dialogue 4

Line 3

1. Prior turn's action? *telling/informing*
2. Arrowed turn's final intonation? *mildly rising*
3. Arrowed turn's action? *assesses information positively*
4. If arrowed turn gives an assessment, what is it assessing? *information about Bea's health*
5. What follows? *same speaker continues*
6. If more talk from same speaker follows, what kind of talk? *asks about another person's health*

Line 6

1. Prior turn's action? *telling/informing*
2. Arrowed turn's final intonation? *mildly rising*
3. Arrowed turn's action? *assesses information positively*
4. If arrowed turn gives an assessment, what is it assessing? *information about Bob's health*
5. What follows? *other speaker asks question about Ava*
6. If more talk from same speaker follows, what kind of talk? *NA*

Dialogue 5

Line 4

1. Prior turn's action? *telling/informing*
2. Arrowed turn's final intonation? *falling*
3. Arrowed turn's action? *assesses information positively*
4. If arrowed turn gives an assessment, what is it assessing? *information about the price and availability of vacation package trips*
5. What follows? *other speaker continues talking about the package trips*
6. If more talk from same speaker follows, what kind of talk? *NA*

Some points that the teacher may want to make with students

In discussing the effect of the responder on the next turn, the teacher might point out that the next turn may open a new sequence with a question, as in Dialogue 1 (Line 11, after assessment in Line 9), Dialogue 3 (Line 6, after assessment in line 4), and Dialogue 4 (Line 4, after assessment in Line 3; line 7, after assessment in Line 6). Or the next turn may provide additional information to that in the previous sequence, as in Dialogue 3 (Line 9, which begins a new sequence on the same topic, after the assessment in Line 8) or Dialogue 5 (Line 5, in which B moves on to a discussion of C's options after C's positive assessment of prices in Line 4).

Worksheet 4: Change-of-State Tokens, News Markers, and Assessments in Your Language

Read the example dialogues on the left. Each has one responder with a box around it. In the column on the right, please write one or more possible translations of each boxed responder in your first language or another language you speak. Work independently, then compare your answers with a partner. Explain why your translations seem to fit the meaning and function of the boxed English responders.

Dialogue 1 B: So:: we thought that ya know if you wanna come over early. Come on over. M: Ah::: hh for dinner ya mean? B: No, not for dinner. M: Oh.	Language: _____ Translation: _____
Dialogue 2 Deb: I don't think I ever sent Monica a birth- a present for her birthday, did I? = Or did we buy something together, (0.3) Deb: Mo:m, Mom: Yeah, I think we d:id. Deb: Oh:, good. (1.2)	Language: _____ Translation: _____
Dialogue 3 Emm: Hey, that was the same spot where we took off for Honolulu (0.3) Emm: Where they put Jim o:n, (0.6) Emm: at that chartered place, Nan: Oh:, really? Emm: Ye::ah, Nan: Oh, for heaven's sakes. Emm: Exactly the same spot. And that's the hangar where we waited . . .	Language: _____ Translation: _____

(These dialogues were adapted from the following sources: Dialogue 1, Heritage, 1984, p. 319; Dialogue 2, Schegloff, 2007, p. 131; Dialogue 3, Schegloff, 2007, p. 158.)

Handout 2: Prosodic Upgrades to Responders

The following chart summarizes two more ways of adding special emphasis to change-of-state tokens and assessments: using a rise–fall intonation (↗ ↘) and stretching the length of the responders.

	Change-of-State Token	Assessment		News Marker
Responders	↘ oh	↘ cool	↘ fan<u>tas</u>tic	↑ really?
		↘ good	↘ am<u>az</u>ing	↗ oh really?
Upgraded responders	↗ ↘ o::h	↗ ↘ ↗ ↘ go::od ama::zing		↑ ↘ oh really

Worksheet 5: Practice With Meaning and Prosody

1. Review the following lines and listen to the example pronunciation of these responders.

   Falling intonation can signal receipt of information or agreement

   > *Oh.* ↘   *Really.* ↘

   Mildly rising intonation can signal curiosity or doubt about the new information.

   > *Oh,* ↗   *Really,* ↗

   Strongly rising (often produced with stretch) usually signals news marker (curiosity)

   > *Oh::?* ↑   *Rea::lly?* ↑

   Strong rise–fall (usually produced with stretch) usually signals news marker (surprise)

   > ↗ *Oh:::.* ↘   ↗ *Rea::lly.* ↘

2. Now listen and answer the following questions for each set of choices (**Oh/Oh:::**) below.

   a. For Lines 2, 5, and 7, circle the *oh* you hear as either short falling or stretched falling/rise–falling.

   b. Mark the intonation of each *oh* in the dialogue between V and J as falling (.), rising (?), slight rise(,), or flat (no punctuation). (Note: Rise–fall can be considered a type of falling intonation.)

   Dialogue

   1 V: And she's got the application forms.=

   2 J: **Oh/Oh:::** __ so when is her interview, did she say

   3 V: She didn't, well, she's gotta send their form back

   4   She didn't know when

   5 J: **Oh/Oh:::** __

   6 V: the interview is yet.

   7 J: **Oh/Oh:::** __ it's just the form

Worksheet 5: Suggested Answers

Line 2: **Oh,** so when is her interview, did she say

Line 5: **Oh.**

Line 7: **Oh:::** it's just the form [realizes the situation, that no interview scheduled yet]

CHAPTER 13

Developing Students' Language Awareness

Maria Dantas-Whitney

This chapter describes a set of activities that I have labeled the Language Research Project, an assignment developed for advanced-level English as a second language (ESL) students in a university-based intensive English program in the United States in preparation for entering degree programs in their majors. The project was designed to foster the type of consciousness-raising processes advocated by van Lier (1996). The tasks and activities comprising the Language Research Project encourage students to perform ethnographic activities and to become language researchers. Furthermore, the project is designed to move students from noticing the language, to engaging with it, and then to using it effectively.

The aim of the project is to integrate linguistic and sociocultural learning as students investigate the nature of discursive practices within the university community (Hall, 1999). The intention is not to transform students into ethnographers; rather, it is to encourage them to develop a critical and analytical stance toward their own communicative performances and those of others.

Through their participation in the Language Research Project, students start to grasp the complexities of communicative practices in the university discourse community. They become aware of the social forces surrounding their own participation and seek to improve their performance in academic interactions.

CONTEXT

The Language Research Project was designed to give students the experience they needed to communicate comfortably within the wider university community. Typically, many of the students in the class were concurrently attending university courses in their major fields of study. Even though these students had exposure to the academic discourse of their disciplines, most of them did not feel competent, comfortable, or welcome to engage in academic interactions, and they reported difficulty establishing meaningful academic relationships with classmates and professors.

The set of activities presented here was developed to provide guided opportunities to participate in communicative interactions outside the environment of an ESL classroom. Activities such as listening to radio reports, videos, and guest lectures or giving oral presentations and engaging in group discussions and debates were important for the development of students' language and interactional skills. However, because these activities were performed within the ESL classroom, students lacked the sociocultural elements that affect communication in mainstream academic settings. The impetus for designing the Language Research Project came from this need to create a structure for students to notice, analyze, and reflect critically on the language being used around them within the academic community.

The Language Research Project proved to be a successful curricular innovation. Students formulated research questions, generated hypotheses, and conducted ethnographic observations of interactions in the community. Based on their analyses of communicative exchanges, students built theories about social and academic uses of language in the community, reflected on their current language abilities, and made plans for future self-development (Dantas-Whitney, 2003, 2007).

CURRICULUM, TASKS, MATERIALS

The Language Research Project combines the techniques of ethnography and action research. The project is organized around several tasks that build upon each other. Students are guided through a research cycle involving the following components:

- Planning: formulating a research question and making arrangements for observations (Activities 2, 3, 4)

- Observation: observing interactions and taking field notes on different aspects of talk (Activity 5)

- Interpretation: analyzing field notes and drawing conclusions about communicative patterns (Activity 6)

- Reflection: reflecting on findings collaboratively through a web discussion board and individually through an audio journal (Activity 7)

- Action: thinking about actions to improve future participation in interactions (Activity 7)

These tasks guide students to make choices about topics to explore and methods to use in their explorations. They also encourage students to examine critically their own beliefs, assumptions, and skills and to observe ordinary events in the university community through different perspectives and points of view.

Activity 1: Introduction to the Project

The introduction to the project is perhaps the most important step because it sets the tone for the entire research process (see Handout 1, Appendix A). Because this is a long-term project, typically lasting approximately 8 weeks, students must perceive their research endeavors as a legitimate and serious enterprise, rather than as a trivial class assignment. By adopting the identity of researchers/ethnographers, students gain confidence in their ability to communicate in English and are motivated to continue their process of exploration. They are empowered to engage with their own realities from a position of strength (Norton, 2000).

At the center of the project are the students' ethnographic observations conducted in academic settings such as classes, workshops, and advising meetings. The reflection tasks (e.g., audio journals, web discussions) are important to help students articulate their findings and plan subsequent steps. To illustrate each step of the project, sample handouts are provided with detailed instructions for students to follow.

Before beginning the project, most students need basic training in data collection techniques in order to conduct effective observations and to benefit fully from the project. They also need to be acquainted with research terminology (e.g., *participant observation, field work, data*) so they have a common metalanguage when discussing research methods and procedures. Short clips from movies can be an effective resource for practicing data collection techniques in class and for introducing research vocabulary in context.

When analyzing movie clips, it is helpful to use a think-aloud strategy to model research procedures. Interactive think-aloud is a step-by-step process of problem solving that enables teachers to share expertise with students. While watching a movie clip, students are instructed to take field notes using the SPEAKING framework (developed by Hymes, 1972, to account for the various components that comprise a *speech event*; see Figure 1), which will later be used for data collection.

After watching the clip several times and consulting in small groups, the class may engage in a whole-group think-aloud guided by the teacher, as exemplified by the transcription of a real teacher-initiated discussion in Example 1, in which the teacher models the kinds of information that students will want to take notice of (e.g., participants' roles, gender, age).

Example 1

T: Now the participants, how many participants . . . ?

Ss: (Students respond)

T: Maybe six or seven. Who are they? . . . The board of a company, maybe all the vice presidents and the president of the company. So, this is their role. When you talk about role, that's what we mean . . . they are the vice presidents and the president of the company. If we were describing this setting here, the role would be students and teacher, OK? . . . If you are describing a study meeting situation, the roles, classmates. Right? They are all . . . in a class together. OK? Sometimes it could be just friends; that's a role.

T: Uhm . . . gender, gender is very important in this conversation, isn't it?

Ss: (Students respond)

T: Only one woman and six men. So, this idea that who is more talkative, a man or a woman . . . maybe it depends on how many men and how many women there are. . . . It depends on the setting, it depends on the topic of conversation, right?

T: OK. How old? How old do you think they are?

As shown in this transcript, the teacher (T) first asked the students to consider the number of participants ("how many participants") and their roles ("the vice presidents and the president of the company"). She took this opportunity to give

---

○ **Situation** (setting and scene): Here the students are asked to describe the physical aspects of the setting where their observation is taking place. For example, they should record the size of the room, the arrangement of the seats, any objects, decorative elements, and so on. It is also a good idea to tell them to draw a map.

○ **Participants** (age, roles, gender, ethnicity): Here the students should describe the people participating in the interaction in as much detail as possible. For example, they should describe the participants' gender, ages, roles, relationships, nationalities, native languages, and so on.

○ **Ends** (goals and outcomes): Here the students should explain the goals and motivations of each participant. For example, the students and the teacher in a class will have different goals and motivations for the same event. Students are encouraged to consider other components of the SPEAKING framework to determine the goals of other participants (e.g., participants' roles, act sequence, genre).

○ **Act sequence** (message form and message content): In most cases, it is impossible for the students to transcribe the whole interaction, unless they use an audio recorder. Nevertheless, it is important to tell them to capture the main sequence of speech acts in the interaction. For example, a class observation could be described in this way: "The teacher started the class by announcing that there would be a quiz the next day, and one student asked if they could have time in class for review. The teacher agreed and told the class to open the books to chapter 4. . . ."

○ **Key** (tone, manner, spirit of the communication): Here the students describe the tone of the interaction (e.g., formal or informal).

○ **Instrumentalities** (channels and forms of communication): Here the students describe the different forms of communication that are present. Are the interlocutors using oral or written language, or a combination of both?

○ **Norms** (of interaction and of interpretation): Here the students should try to figure out the rules for the interaction. Certain events have particularly clear norms of interaction. For example, students in class usually raise their hands when wanting to ask a question. However, some rules of interaction may be more obscure and are only noticed when they are broken, for example, when a speaker stands too close and the interlocutor backs away.

○ **Genre** (type of event): Here the students simply record the type of event they are observing, for example, a lecture, dinner conversation, or party.

Figure 1. Adaptation of Hymes's (1972) SPEAKING Framework for Analyzing Speech Events

an explicit explanation of the meaning of the word *role*. She knew that students would conduct their observations in university classes, in study groups, and in more informal settings such as a university dining hall, so she referred to these contexts as examples to model the description of participants' roles ("students and teacher," "classmates," "friends"). The teacher then asked students to consider the gender of the participants, and she pointed out that gender may have had a significant impact on the outcomes of this particular interaction, because there were "only one woman and six men." (The students had noted previously that the woman had stayed quiet during the whole meeting.)

By modeling the analysis of movie clips, the teacher encourages students to consider the dynamic and interdependent relationship among different components of the SPEAKING framework: the participants, the situation (setting), and the act sequence (message content).

Activity 2: Self-Observation

The first observation activity involves a self-observation log (Handout 2, see Appendix A), which students use to record all their interactions in English for 2 days. It is important to tell students that the goal of this activity is to help them explore different aspects of these interactions and to identify topics of interest for an initial research question.

Worksheet 1 (see Appendix A) is a sample data entry sheet designed to help students organize their self-observation logs. This worksheet can be reproduced several times, depending on the number of interactions each student participates in on a given day.

Activity 3: Web Discussion 1

The first web discussion is carried out soon after students complete their self-observation logs. Students reflect on their own communicative abilities in English, engage in dialogue with each other, and start identifying topics for their investigations.

The teacher may want to provide a set of prompts to guide students on their initial postings (Handout 3, see Appendix A). After everyone has posted a reflection to the web board, the students and the teacher can respond to each other.

To ensure that every student receives a reply from a peer, students draw each other's names from an envelope and respond to the person whose name they picked. It is important to encourage responses that give as much feedback as possible to the partner (making additional comments, raising questions, and making parallels to their own observations and experiences).

Activity 4: Audio Journal 1

The audio journals and the web discussions are tools used to extend learning beyond the classroom walls, to encourage reflection, and to provide meaningful opportunities for practice in the four language skills. Unlike the web discussions, the audio journals foster private dialogue between individual students and the teacher.

The purpose of the first audio journal is to guide students to formulate their research questions (Handout 4, see Appendix A). Students are told to record their reflections using a conversational style. They can prepare notes with key words and main ideas, but they cannot read from a prepared script. The teacher listens to the journals and records his or her feedback on the same audiocassette or digital audio file, thus engaging in dialogue with the students. In large classes, it can be quite time-consuming for teachers to record individual responses. It is also possible to provide responses in short written notes, which saves a great deal of time because the notes are written while the teacher is listening to the student's recording. When students do not own a tape or digital recorder, the school may make a few recorders available for student use in a public space such as a language lab.

Teachers return the recordings to students, and students are told to listen to responses and to address any concerns or suggestions the teacher has expressed. When students have completed this activity, they should have a reasonable research question, such as the following, that will guide the next activities: "What kinds of examples do students give in a seminar?" "How are disagreements expressed in English?" "How do students interrupt a teacher in class?" "How are hand gestures used in interactions in English?"

Activity 5: Observation

Students conduct two types of observations—nonparticipant and participant. During the nonparticipant observation, they act solely as observers, simply taking field notes during the interactions, but not participating. During the participant observation, they observe and participate in an interaction. The goal is for students to analyze speaking practices related to their research question first (through nonparticipant observation) and then to attempt to participate in some of these practices (through participant observations).

Hymes's (1972) SPEAKING framework provides a helpful structure for analysis and observation (refer back to Figure 1). This framework gives students a rich range of components to focus on when conducting observations and analyzing data, guiding them to make connections between linguistic and sociocultural aspects of communication. The framework is intended to guide description of a particular speech event by focusing on eight components.

Worksheet 2 (see Appendix A) provides a template that can be used multiple times by students for both participant and nonparticipant observation. (For a sample data collection worksheet completed by a student, see Appendix B at www.tesolmedia.com/books/pragmatics2.)

Activity 6: Web Discussion 2

The second web discussion takes place after both observations have been conducted. Students are instructed to summarize their findings and then respond by commenting on each other's research results. Handout 5 (see Appendix A) provides guidelines for participating in this discussion.

Activity 7: Audio Journal 2

The second audio journal is the final task of the project. Students are told to evaluate the Language Research Project as a whole and to articulate their plans for future action. Handout 6 (see Appendix A) presents guidelines for the audio journal.

Each task in the Language Research Project is carefully tailored to encourage students to integrate knowledge acquired from previous tasks and to expand their inquiry using prior experiences. After students complete their self-observation logs, they discuss their self-observations in the first web discussion. They then reflect on the ideas shared on the web board in their first audio journal, trying to identify an initial research question. Once a research question has been formulated, they conduct their participant and nonparticipant observations. They discuss findings from these observations in the second web discussion, and they finally assess the whole project in their second audio journal.

REFLECTIONS

Through the Language Research Project students become familiar with the process of systematic inquiry. Most students who have participated in the process had no previous experience with the techniques of ethnography or action research. However, through questioning, reflecting, observing, and discussing with others, they were able to develop sophisticated understandings about the nature of interactions in U.S. classrooms, their own abilities to communicate in English, and the process of conducting empirical research itself. Learning was meaningful to them because they were able to make choices based on personal experiences. They observed real language use in a context that is directly relevant to their future needs.

At the same time, students needed basic training in data collection techniques in order to conduct effective observations and to benefit fully from the project. The practice in data collection through the use of movie clips has proved helpful. Also, using more specialized terms to describe research procedures (e.g., *field work*, *data*) and communication processes (e.g., *genres*, *channels of communication*, *interlocutors*) inspired students to use these words as well. These terms gave students a common language to discuss research experiences and findings with each other. In addition, the use of this specialized vocabulary served to legitimize and formalize students' research procedures.

During the course, it was also helpful to build connections between students' research projects and other activities being carried out in class. For example, Hymes's (1972) SPEAKING framework was used when discussing a lecture by a guest speaker, a workshop the class attended, and a seminar conducted by the students. This enabled the teacher to model data collection and analysis procedures in a contextualized way, giving students several chances to practice using the framework in preparation for their observations.

The Language Research Project is not limited to teachers with a research background. It can be adapted by other classroom teachers, regardless of their familiarity with research methods. Teachers who are particularly interested in guided-inquiry tasks and who are willing to help students conduct their own investigations will likely find the Language Research Project to be a valuable activity.

This project was conducted with advanced-level students in a university ESL setting. Younger students or those at lower proficiency levels would benefit from a more structured project. One way to adapt the project would be for the teacher to assign the same research question for the whole class to investigate. For example, the whole class could be instructed to collect data on disagreements and then compare their observations and analyses as a group. In English as a foreign language settings, teachers can use movie clips or segments from TV shows (e.g., talk shows, news reports) for similar purposes.

Maria Dantas-Whitney is associate professor of ESOL/bilingual education at Western Oregon University, in the United States. Her professional interests include language teacher education, critical reflective practice, and ethnographic classroom-based research. She has taught and conducted research in the United States, Mexico, Cyprus, and Brazil.

APPENDIX A: HANDOUTS AND WORKSHEETS

Handout 1: Overview of the Language Research Project

This project is designed to heighten your awareness about the cultural rules that govern interactions within the academic community. In this project, you will assume the role of a *language researcher*. You will observe speakers as they engage in interactions in English. You will also observe your own interactions and reflect on your own communicative performance. The project consists of two threads:

> **Thread I: Nonparticipant Observations**—You will observe and analyze discussions by English speakers in a university setting (e.g., classroom, group study setting, meeting).

> **Thread II: Participant Observation**—You will observe and analyze your own interactions with English speakers in the university community.

Based on your observations, you will reflect on speakers' behaviors and make hypotheses about conversational patterns and rules that operate in different contexts. You will also reflect on actions you can take to improve your participation in group discussions within the university community. The project follows a cycle that looks like this:

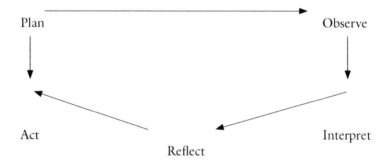

Plan: First, you will formulate a *research question* based on what you would like to learn about interactions in English. You will also *make arrangements* for your observations (i.e., location, date, time) ahead of time.

Observe: As you observe the interaction, you will carefully *take notes* on different aspects of the conversation, focusing on your research question.

Interpret: You will carefully analyze your observation notes individually and in groups and *make conclusions* about conversational patterns occurring within the interactions.

Reflect: You will reflect on your findings in an *audio journal* and on a *web discussion board*.

Act: Based on your observations, you will think about actions you can take to improve your own participation in discussions.

Handout 2: Self-Observation Log

The purpose of this activity is to help you build awareness of your own communicative performance in natural settings (outside of the ESL classroom). You will record details of all the interactions you have with English speakers outside of your ESL class **during the course of 2 days**.

Please write down details about the **setting**, the **participants**, the **purposes** of the interaction, and the **language used** by you and the other speakers. You may want to use Worksheet 1, the Data Entry Sheet, to record your data.

At the end of the 2 days, reflect on all the interactions you have had during these 2 days and answer the following questions. Give concrete examples from specific conversations to support your answers.

1. Did you understand all the speakers' words and meanings? Did they understand you? Explain any difficulties experienced during the interactions.

2. How important was the setting of the conversations? Did some visual facts (e.g., clothes, appearance) affect the interactions?

3. How did you feel before/during/after the conversations? Why?

Worksheet 1: Data Entry Sheet

Day 1: _____

Interaction 1:

Setting	
Participants	
Purposes	
Language used (try to re-create the dialogue)	

Handout 3: Web Discussion 1

Please reflect on your own participation in interactions in English. Post these refl[
on the assigned web page. After everyone has posted his or her own reflections, you will
be assigned a partner. Read your partner's reflections, and then post your comments
about them.

- What **type** of conversations/discussions do you usually participate in? **Where** do the interactions take place? **With whom?**

- How do you **feel** when you participate in interactions with other English speakers? What type of communicative interactions do you feel most and least comfortable with?

- Do you consider yourself an effective participant in English interactions? What **strategies** do you use when you discuss in groups?

- What have you observed about oral interactions in English that might be **different from or similar to** oral interactions in your native language?

- In your opinion, what types of **communicative behaviors** (besides accent) identify speakers as nonnative?

- What would you like **to learn** about oral interactions in English?

- How would you like **to improve** your participation in interactions in English?

Handout 4: Audio Journal 1

The purpose of this audio journal is to help you **identify a topic and formulate a research question** for your Language Research Project. Please address the following points in your audio journal.

1. Reflect

Refer to your self-observation log and to our web discussion. Can you identify some topics or themes that you would like to explore further? What intrigues you about the way English speakers communicate? About the way you communicate with other English speakers? What types of interactions would you like to observe/analyze/learn more about? What do you hope to learn from this project?

2. Plan
Choosing the speech situation

In this project you will be required to observe and analyze interactions in an academic setting (e.g., classroom, group study setting, meeting). What type of setting would you like to observe? Do you have access to this setting? Would it be easy for you to observe interactions and take notes? Explain how you plan to arrange your observations.

Formulating the research question

Now that you have had a chance to reflect on aspects that affect interactions in English, take a moment to formulate your initial research question for your Language Research Project. This research question will guide your observations. Make sure you focus on an aspect of communication that can be observed.

Worksheet 2: Data Collection for Observations

Research question: _____?

Date of observation: _____ Duration: _____

Location of observation: _____ Number of participants: _____

1. Note as many details as you can about the following components of the scene. Use the **SPEAKING framework** (adapted from Hymes, 1972) to guide your analysis.

S **Situation** Description of the place: seating arrangements, size of room, objects, etc. Good idea to draw a map.	
P **Participants** Description of the people: gender, age, educational level, role, ethnic background, native country, etc.	
E **Ends** Purpose of the event: goals and motivations of each participant	
A **Act sequence** Sequence of speech acts and topics of conversation	
K **Key** Tone or spirit of communication: Serious? Formal? Informal?	
I **Instrumentalities** Written language? Oral language?	
N **Norms of interaction** Rules for participation	
G **Genre** Type of activity: Class? Meeting? Seminar?	

2. Now it is time for you to **reflect on your research question**. Try to provide answers based on your observation notes. Give several examples from your data in order to support your statements.

Handout 5: Web Discussion 2

Now it is time for you to summarize the findings of your research and draw conclusions based on your observations. Based on your notes for your two observations (nonpartici- pant and participant), write a short analysis of the oral interactions you have observed. Please include the following points in your analysis:

1. Describe and compare some of the components of the scenes you observed (set- ting, participants, ends, act sequence, etc.). What are some interesting things you noticed about some of these components?

2. Discuss what surprised you about the interactions. Did you notice anything going on that you had not noticed before conducting this research project?

3. State your research question, and try to provide answers based on your field notes. Give several examples from your data in order to support your statements. Again, try to compare and contrast your observations.

4. Reflect on your personal experiences during the participant observations. How do you usually participate in interactions with other English speakers? Again, please mention specific examples/situations.

Handout 6: Audio Journal 2

Your second audio journal should have two parts: **your assessment of the project** and **your plans for future action**. Before you start preparing your audio journal, please take a moment to think about all the steps of the Language Research Project. Here are a few questions for you to consider:

1. How and why did you choose your research question? Did you change your research question during the project? If so, why? How did you evolve in the process of researching your question? Describe your progress through different phases of the project.

2. How did you choose the settings for your observations? How did you feel during each observation? How did you collect your data? Did you use a tape recorder? Did you take notes during the observations? After the observations? Did you talk with other classmates about your field notes?

3. You engaged in several dialogues about communicative practices in English throughout the term (in class, out of class, through the web discussions). How did these conversations impact your perceptions and interpretations? Please give specific examples to illustrate your answers.

4. Go back to our web discussion board and reread the comments you wrote in the beginning of the term about your own participation in interactions (web discus- sion 1). Now, review and revise your answers based on what you have learned from this project.

5. In your opinion, what was the most valuable aspect of the project?

6. How do you plan to use the information you learned about interactions for your own language development in the future?

Once you have your answers in mind and a clear idea of what you are going to say, record your responses and submit the recording to your teacher.

References

Agar, M. (1994). *Language shock: Understanding the culture of conversation.* New York, NY: William Morrow.

Bardovi-Harlig, K. (2001). Evaluating the empirical evidence: Grounds for instruction in pragmatics? In K. Rose & G. Kasper (Eds.), *Pragmatics in language teaching* (pp. 13–32). Cambridge, England: Cambridge University Press.

Bardovi-Harlig, K. (2006). On the role of formulas in the acquisition of L2 pragmatics. In K. Bardovi-Harlig, C. Félix-Brasdefer, & A. S. Omar (Eds.), *Pragmatics and language learning* (Vol. 11, pp. 1–28). Honolulu: University of Hawai'i at Manoa, Second Language Teaching and Curriculum Center.

Bardovi-Harlig, K. (2008). Recognition and production of formulas in L2 pragmatics. In Z.-H. Han (Ed.), *Understanding second language process* (pp. 205–222). Clevedon, England: Multilingual Matters.

Bardovi-Harlig, K. (2009). Conventional expressions as a pragmalinguistic resource: Recognition and production of conventional expression in L2 pragmatics. *Language Learning, 59,* 755–795. doi:10.1111/j.1467-9922.2009.00525.x

Bardovi-Harlig, K. (2010). Recognition of conventional expressions in L2 pragmatics. In G. Kasper, H. T. Nguyen, D. R. Yoshimi, & J. K. Yoshioka (Eds.), *Pragmatics and language learning* (Vol. 12, pp. 141–162). Honolulu: University of Hawai'i, National Foreign Language Resource Center.

Bardovi-Harlig, K., Bastos, M.-T., Burghardt, B., Chappetto, E., Nickels. E. L., & Rose, M. (2010). The use of conventional expressions and utterance length in L2 pragmatics. In G. Kasper, H. T. Nguyen, D. R. Yoshimi, & J. K. Yoshioka (Eds.), *Pragmatics and language learning* (Vol. 12, pp. 163–186). Honolulu: University of Hawai'i, National Foreign Language Resource Center.

Bardovi-Harlig, K., & Dörnyei, Z. (1998). Do language learners recognize pragmatic violations? Pragmatic vs. grammatical awareness in instructed L2 learning. *TESOL Quarterly, 32,* 233–259.

Bardovi-Harlig, K., Hartford, B. A. S., Mahan-Taylor, R., Morgan, M. J., & Reynolds, D. W. (1991). Developing pragmatic competence: Closing the conversation. *ELT Journal, 45*, 4–15.

Bardovi-Harlig, K., & Mahan-Taylor, R. (Eds.). (2003). *Teaching pragmatics.* Washington, DC: U.S. Department of State, Office of English Language Programs. Retrieved from http://exchanges.state.gov/englishteaching/resforteach/pragmatics.html

Barnlund, D. C., & Araki, S. (1985). Intercultural encounters: The management of compliments by Japanese and Americans. *Journal of Cross-Cultural Psychology 16*, 9–26. doi:10.1177/0022002185016001002

Bergman, M., & Kasper, G. (1993). Perception and performance in native and nonnative apology. In G. Kasper & S. Blum-Kulka (Eds.), *Interlanguage pragmatics* (pp. 82–107). Oxford, England: Oxford University Press.

Bernsten, S. (2002). Using conversation analysis to evaluate pre-sequences in invitation, offer, and request dialogues in ESL textbook (Unpublished master's thesis). University of Illinois, Urbana-Champaign.

Billmyer, K. (1990). "I really like your lifestyle": ESL learners learning how to compliment. *Penn Working Papers in Educational Linguistics, 6*(2), 31–47.

Blum-Kulka, S., House, J., & Kasper, G. (1989a). The CCSARP coding manual. In S. Blum-Kulka, J. House, & G. Kasper (Eds.), *Cross-cultural pragmatics: Requests and apologies* (pp. 273–294). Norwood, NJ: Ablex.

Blum-Kulka, S., House, J., & Kasper, G. (1989b). Investigating cross-cultural pragmatics: An introductory overview. In S. Blum-Kulka, J. House, & G. Kasper (Eds.), *Cross-cultural pragmatics: Requests and apologies* (pp. 1–34). Norwood, NJ: Ablex.

Bodman, J., & Eisenstein, M. (1988). May God increase your bounty: The expression of gratitude in English by native and non-native speakers. *Cross Currents, 15*, 1–21.

Bowles, H. (2006). Bridging the gap between conversation analysis and ESP: An applied study of the opening sequences of NS and NNS service telephone calls. *English for Specific Purposes, 25*, 332–357. doi:10.1016/j.esp.2005.03.003

Bowles, H., & Seedhouse, P. (Eds.). (2007). *Conversation analysis and language for specific purposes.* Bern, Switzerland: Peter Lang.

Boxer, D., & Pickering, L. (1995). Problems in the presentation of speech acts in ELT materials: The case of complaints. *ELT Journal, 49*, 44–58. doi:10.1093/elt/49.1.44

Button, G. (1987). Moving out of closings. In G. Button & J. Lee (Eds.), *Talk and social organization* (pp. 101–151). Clevedon, England: Multilingual Matters.

Button, G. (1990). On varieties of closings. In G. Psathas (Ed.), *Interaction competence* (pp. 93–148). Washington, DC: University Press of America.

Button, G. (1991). Conversation-in-a-series. In D. Boden & D. H. Zimmerman (Eds.), *Talk and social structure: Studies in ethnomethodology and conversation analysis* (pp. 251–277). Berkeley: University of California Press.

Carroll, D. (2000). Precision timing in novice-to-novice L2 conversations. *Issues in Applied Linguistics, 11,* 67–110.

Carroll, D. (2005). Vowel-marking as an interactional resource in Japanese novice ESL conversation. In K. Richards & P. Seedhouse (Eds.), *Applying conversation analysis* (pp. 214–234). Houndsmills, England: Palgrave Macmillan.

Carroll, D. (2006). Co-constructing competence: Turn construction and repair in novice-to-novice second language interaction (Unpublished doctoral dissertation). University of York, England.

Chomsky, N. (1959). Review of B. F. Skinner's "Verbal behavior." *Language, 35,* 26–58.

Clancy, P., Thompson, S., Suzuki, R., & Tao, H. (1996). The conversational use of reactive tokens in English, Japanese, and Mandarin. *Journal of Pragmatics, 26,* 355–387. doi:10.1016/0378-2166(95)00036-4

Coulmas, F. (1981). "Poison to your soul": Thanks and apologies contrastively viewed. In F. Coulmas (Ed.), *Conversational routine: Explorations in standardized communication situations and prepatterned speech* (pp. 69–91). The Hague, Netherlands: Mouton.

Dantas-Whitney, M. (2003). *ESL students as ethnographers: Co-researching communicative practices in an academic discourse community* (Unpublished doctoral dissertation). Oregon State University, Corvallis.

Dantas-Whitney, M. (2007). ESL students as ethnographers: Examining academic interactions. In H. M. McGarrell (Ed.), *Language teacher research in the Americas* (pp. 55–67). Alexandria, VA: TESOL.

Drummond, K., & Hopper, R. (1993). Some uses of yeah. *Research on Language and Social Interaction, 26,* 203–212. doi:10.1207/s15327973rlsi2602_6

Dulay, H., Burt, M., & Krashen, K. (1982). *Language two.* New York, NY: Oxford University Press.

Eisenstein, M., & Bodman, J. W. (1986). "I very appreciate": Expressions of gratitude by native and non-native speakers of American English. *Applied Linguistics, 7,* 167–185. doi:10.1093/applin/7.2.167

Eisenstein, M., & Bodman, J. (1993). Expressing gratitude in American English. In G. Kasper & S. Blum-Kulka (Eds.), *Interlanguage pragmatics* (pp. 64–81). New York, NY: Oxford University Press.

Ellis, N. C. (1996). Sequencing in SLA: Phonological memory, chunking, and points of order. *Studies in Second Language Acquisition, 18*, 91–126.

Ellis, N. C. (2007). The associative-cognitive CREED. In B. VanPatten & J. Williams (Eds.), *Theories in second language acquisition* (pp. 77–95). Mahwah, NJ: Lawrence Erlbaum.

Ellis, R. (2009). *Handout from a lecture on interlanguage pragmatics.* Temple University Japan.

eslandcateaching. (2009, August 30). Teaching ESL or EFL with conversation analysis [Web log post]. Retrieved from http://eslandcateaching.wordpress.com/2009/08/

Filipi, A., & Wales, R. (2003). Differential uses of *okay, right*, and *alright*, and their function in signaling perspective shift or maintenance in a map task. *Semiotica, 147*, 429–455. doi:10.1515/semi.2003.102

Gardner, R. (1997). The listener and minimal responses in conversational interaction. *Prospect, 12*(2), 12–32.

Gardner, R. (2001). *When listeners talk: Response tokens and listener stance.* Amsterdam, Netherlands: John Benjamins.

Grant, L., & Starks, D. (2001). Screening appropriate teaching materials: Closings from textbooks and television soap operas. *International Review of Applied Linguistics, 39*, 39–50. doi:10.1515/iral.39.1.39

Griswold, O. (2003). How do you say good-bye? In K. Bardovi-Harlig & R. Mahan-Taylor (Eds.), *Teaching pragmatics.* Washington, DC: U.S. Department of State.

Hall, J. K. (1999). A prosaics of interaction: The development of interactional competence in another language. In E. Hinkel (Ed.), *Culture in second language teaching and learning* (pp. 137–151). Cambridge, England: Cambridge University Press.

He, A. (1984). Answering questions in LPIs: A case study. In R. Young & A. He (Eds.), *Talking and testing: Discourse approaches to the assessment of oral proficiency* (pp. 101–116). Amsterdam, Netherlands: John Benjamins.

Hellerman, J. (2008). *Social actions for classroom language learning.* Clevedon, England: Multilingual Matters.

Herbert, R. K. (1989). The ethnography of English compliments and compliment responses: A contrastive sketch. In W. Oleksy (Ed.), *Contrastive pragmatics* (pp. 3–35). Philadelphia, PA: John Benjamins.

Herbert, R. K. (1990). Sex-based differences in compliment behavior. *Language in Society, 19*, 201–224. doi:10.1017/S0047404500014378

Herbert, R. K. (1991). The sociology of compliment work: An ethnocontrastive study of Polish and English compliments. *Multilingua, 10*, 381–402. doi:10.1515/mult.1991.10.4.381

Heritage, J. (1984). A change-of-state token and aspects of its sequential placement. In J. M. Atkinson & J. Heritage (Eds.), *Structures of social action: Studies in conversation analysis* (pp. 299–344). Cambridge, England: Cambridge University Press.

Heritage, J. (1998). Oh-prefaced responses to inquiry. *Language in Society, 27,* 291–334. doi:10.1017/S0047404598003017

Holmes, J. (1988). Paying compliments: A sex-preferential politeness strategy. *Journal of Pragmatics, 12,* 445–465. doi:10.1016/0378-2166(88)90005-7

Holmes, J., & Brown, D. F. (1987). Teachers and students learning about compliments. *TESOL Quarterly, 21,* 523–546. doi:10.2307/3586501

House, J. (1996). Developing pragmatic fluency in English as a foreign language: Routines and metapragmatic awareness. *Studies in Second Language Acquisition, 17,* 225–252. doi:10.1017/S0272263100014893

Houtkoop-Steenstra, H. (1991). Opening sequences in Dutch telephone conversations. In D. Boden & D. Zimmerman (Eds.), *Talk and social structure* (pp. 232–250). Berkeley: University of California Press.

Hutchby, I., & Barnett, S. (2005). Aspects of the sequential organization of mobile phone conversation. *Discourse Studies, 7*(2), 147–172. doi:10.1177/1461445605050364

Hymes, D. (1972). Models of the interaction of language and social life. In J. Gumperz & D. Hymes (Eds.), *Directions in sociolinguistics: The ethnography of communication* (pp. 35–71). Cambridge, England: Cambridge University Press.

Jefferson, G. (1973). A case of precision timing in ordinary conversation: Overlapped tag-positioned address terms in closing sequences. *Semiotica, 9,* 47–96. doi:10.1515/semi.1973.9.1.47

Jefferson, G. (1984). Notes on a systematic deployment of the acknowledgement tokens "yeah" and "mm hm." *Papers in Linguistics, 17,* 197–216.

Jefferson, G. (1986). Notes on "latency" in overlap onset. *Human Studies, 9,* 153–183. doi:10.1007/BF00148125

Kasper, G. (2006). Beyond repair: Conversation analysis as an approach to SLA. *AILA Review, 19,* 83–99. doi:10.1075/aila.19.07kas

Kasper, G., & Rose, K. R. (2002). Pragmatic development in a second language. *Language Learning, 58*(Suppl. 1).

Knapp, M. L., Hopper, R., & Bell, R. A. (1984). Compliments: A descriptive taxonomy. *Journal of Communication, 34,* 12–31. doi:10.1111/j.1460-2466.1984.tb02185.x

Lee, S.-H. (2006). Second summonings in Korean telephone conversation openings. *Language in Society, 35,* 261–283. doi:10.1017/S0047404506060118

Leech, G. N. (1983). *Principles of pragmatics.* London, England: Longman.

Lerner, G. (1996). On the "semi-permeable" character of grammatical units in conversation: Conditional entry into the turn space of another speaker. In E. Ochs, E. Schegloff, & S. Thompson (Eds.), *Interaction and grammar* (pp. 238–276). Cambridge, England: Cambridge University Press.

Liddicoat, A. (2007). *An introduction to conversation analysis.* New York, NY: Continuum.

Lieske, C. (2010). Bumping into someone: Japanese students' perceptions and observations. *ELT Journal, 64,* 194–204. doi:10.1093/elt/ccp023

Lindstrom, A. (1994). Identification and recognition in Swedish telephone conversation openings. *Language in Society, 23,* 231–252. doi:10.1017/S004740450001784X

Luke, K. K. (2002). The initiation and introduction of first topics in Hong Kong telephone calls. In K. K. Luke & T.-S. Pavlidou (Eds.), *Telephone calls: Unity and diversity in conversational structures across languages and cultures* (pp. 171–200). Amsterdam, Netherlands: John Benjamins.

Mackiewicz, J. (2006). The functions of formulaic and nonformulaic compliments in interactions about technical writing. *IEEE Transactions on Professional Communication, 49,* 12–27. doi:10.1109/TPC.2006.870461

Manes, J., & Wolfson, N. (1981). The compliment formula. In F. Coulmas (Ed.), *Conversational routine: Exploration in standardized communication situations and prepatterned speech* (pp. 115–132). The Hague, Netherlands: Mouton.

McCarthy, M. (2003). Talking back: "Small" interactional response tokens in everyday conversation. *Research in Language and Social Interaction, 36,* 33–63. doi:10.1207/S15327973RLSI3601_3

McHoul, A. (1978). The organisation of turns at formal talk in the classroom. *Language in Society, 19,* 183–213.

Mori, J. (2002). Task design, plan and development of talk-in-interaction: An analysis of a small group activity in a Japanese language classroom. *Applied Linguistics, 23,* 323–347. doi:10.1093/applin/23.3.323

Mori, J. (2007). Border crossings? Exploring the intersection of second language acquisition, conversation analysis and foreign language pedagogy. *Modern Language Journal, 91,* 849–862.

Mursy, A. A., & Wilson, J. (2001). Towards a definition of Egyptian complimenting. *Multilingua, 20,* 133–154. doi:10.1515/MULTI.2001.006

Nattinger, J. R., & DeCarrico, J. S. (1992). *Lexical phrases and lexical teaching.* Oxford, England: Oxford University Press.

Nelson, G. L., El Bakary, W., & Al Batal, M. (1996). Egyptian and American compliments: Focus on second language learners. In S. M. Gass & J. Neu (Eds.), *Speech acts across cultures* (pp. 109–128). Berlin, Germany: Mouton de Gruyter.

Norton, B. (2000). *Identity and language learning: Gender, ethnicity and educational change*. Harlow, England: Pearson Education.

Olshtain, E. (1989). Apologies across languages. In S. Blum-Kulka, J. House, & G. Kasper (Eds.), *Cross-cultural pragmatics: Requests and apologies* (pp. 155–173). Norwood, NJ: Ablex.

Omar, A. (1993). Closing Kiswahili conversations: The performance of native and non-native speakers. *Pragmatics and Language Learning, 4,* 104–125.

Parisi, C., & Wogan, P. (2006). Compliment topics and gender. *Women in Language, 29*(2), 21–28.

Pawley, A., & Syder, F. H. (1983). Two puzzles for linguistic theory: Nativelike selection and nativelike fluency. In J. C. Richards & R. W. Schmidt (Eds.), *Language and communication* (pp. 91–226). London, England: Longman.

Pillet-Shore, D. (2008). Coming together: Creating and maintaining social relationships through the openings of face-to-face interactions (Unpublished doctoral dissertation). University of California, Los Angeles.

Placencia, M. E. (1997). Opening up closings—the Ecuadorian way. *Text, 17*(1), 53–81. doi:10.1515/text.1.1997.17.1.53

Pomerantz, A. M. (1984). Agreeing and disagreeing with assessment: Some features of preferred/dispreferred turn shapes. In J. M. Atkinson & J. Heritage (Eds.), *Structures of social action: Studies in conversation analysis* (pp. 57–101). Cambridge, England: Cambridge University Press.

Raymond, G. (2004). Prompting action: The stand-alone "so" in ordinary conversation. *Research on Language and Social Interaction, 37,* 183–218. doi:10.1207/s15327973rlsi3702_4

Regents of the University of Minnesota. (2010). *Lesson plan for teaching compliments.* Retrieved from http://www.carla.umn.edu/speechacts/compliments/lessonplan.html

Rose, K. R. (2001). Compliments and compliment responses in film: Implications for pragmatics research and language teaching. *International Review of Applied Linguistics in Language Teaching, 39,* 309–326. doi:10.1515/iral.2001.007

Rose, K. R., & Kasper, G. (Eds.). (2001). *Pragmatics in language teaching.* Cambridge, England: Cambridge University Press.

Rose, K. R., & Ng Kwai-fun, C. (2001). Inductive and deductive teaching of compliments and compliment responses. In K. R. Rose & G. Kasper (Eds.), *Pragmatics in language teaching* (pp. 200–222). Cambridge, England: Cambridge University Press.

Sacks, H. (1975). Everyone has to lie. In M. Sanches & B. Blount (Eds.), *Sociocultural dimensions of language use* (pp. 57–80). New York, NY: Academic Press.

Sacks, H. (1987). On the preference for agreement and contiguity in sequences in conversation. In G. Button & J. Lee (Eds.), *Talk and social organisation* (pp. 54–69). Clevedon, England: Multilingual Matters.

Sacks, H., Schegloff, E. A., & Jefferson, G. (1974). A simplest systematics for the organization of turn-taking for conversation. *Language, 50,* 696–735. doi:10.2307/412243

Saito, H., & Beecken, M. (1997). An approach to instruction of pragmatic aspects: Implications of pragmatic transfer by American learners of Japanese. *Modern Language Journal, 81,* 363–377. doi:10.2307/329311

Salsbury, T., & Bardovi-Harlig, K. (2000). Oppositional talk and the acquisition of modality in L2 English. In B. Swierzbin, F. Morris, M. E. Anderson, C. A. Klee, & E. Tarone (Eds.), *Social and cognitive factors in second language acquisition: Selected proceedings of the 1999 Second Language Research Forum* (pp. 57–76). Somerville, MA: Cascadilla Press.

Saville-Troike, M. (1997). The ethnographic analysis of communicative events. In N. Coupland & A. Jaworski (Eds.), *Sociolinguistics: A reader and a coursebook* (pp. 126–144). New York, NY: St. Martin's Press.

Scarcella, R. C. (1979). Watch up! *Working Papers in Bilingualism, 19,* 79–88.

Schauer, G. A., & Adolphs, S. (2006). Expressions of gratitude in corpus and DCT data: Vocabulary, formulaic sequences, and pedagogy system. *System, 34,* 119–134.

Schegloff, E. A. (1967). The first five seconds (Unpublished doctoral dissertation). University of California, Berkeley.

Schegloff, E. A. (1968). Sequencing in conversational openings. *American Anthropologist, 70,* 1075–1095. doi:10.1525/aa.1968.70.6.02a00030

Schegloff, E. A. (1979). Identification and recognition in telephone conversation openings. In G. Psathas (Ed.), *Everyday language studies in ethnomethodology* (pp. 23–78). New York, NY: Irvington.

Schegloff, E. A. (1982). Discourse as an interactional achievement: Some uses of "uh huh" and other things that come between sentences. In D. Tannen (Ed.), *Analyzing discourse: Text and talk* (pp. 71–93). Washington, DC: Georgetown University Press.

Schegloff, E. A. (1986). The routine as achievement. *Human Studies, 9,* 111–151. doi:10.1007/BF00148124

Schegloff, E. A. (1990). On the organization of sequences as a source of "coherence" in talk-in-interaction. In B. Dorval (Ed.), *Conversational organization and its development* (pp. 51–77). Norwood, NJ: Ablex.

Schegloff, E. A. (2007). *Sequence organization in interaction: A primer in conversation analysis. Volume 1.* Cambridge, England: Cambridge University Press.

Schegloff, E., Jefferson, G., & Sacks, H. (1977). The preference for self-correction in the organization of repair in conversation. *Language, 53*, 361–382. doi:10.2307/413107

Schegloff, E. A., Koshik, I., Jacoby, S., & Olsher, D. (2002). Conversation analysis and applied linguistics. *Annual Review of Applied Linguistics, 22*, 3–31. doi:10.1017/S0267190502000016

Schegloff, E. A., & Sacks, H. (1973). Opening up closings. *Semiotica, 8*, 289–327. doi:10.1515/semi.1973.8.4.289

Schmidt, R. (1983). Interaction, acculturation, and the acquisition of communicative competence: A case study of an adult. In E. Judd & N. Wolfson (Eds.), *Sociolinguistics and language acquisition* (pp. 137–174). Rowley, MA: Newbury House.

Schmidt, R. (1995). Consciousness and foreign language learning: A tutorial on the role of attention and awareness in learning. In R. Schmidt (Ed.), *Attention and awareness in foreign language learning* (pp. 1–63). Honolulu: University of Hawai'i at Manoa, Second Language Teaching and Curriculum Center.

Schmidt, R., & Frota, S. (1986). Developing basic conversational ability in a second language: A case study of an adult learner of Portuguese. In R. Day (Ed.), *Talking to learn* (pp. 237–326). Rowley, MA: Newbury House.

Searle, J. R. (1969). *Speech acts: An essay in the philosophy of language*. Cambridge, England: Cambridge University Press.

Seedhouse, P. (2004). *The interactional architecture of the language classroom: A conversation analysis perspective*. Oxford, England: Blackwell.

Seedhouse, P. (2005). Conversation analysis and language learning. *Language Teaching, 38*, 165–187. doi:10.1017/S0261444805003010

So'o, A., & Liddicoat, A. (2000). Telephone openings in Samoan. *Australian Review of Applied Linguistics, 23*(1), 95–107.

Suszczynska, M. (1999). Apologizing in English, Polish and Hungarian: Different languages, different strategies. *Journal of Pragmatics, 31*, 1053–1065. doi:10.1016/S0378-2166(99)00047-8

Taleghani-Nikazm, C. (2002). A conversational analytic study of telephone conversation openings between native and nonnative speakers. *Journal of Pragmatics, 34*, 1807–1832. doi:10.1016/S0378-2166(02)00049-8

Tatsuki, D. (2005). Telephone call behavior in films and language textbooks. *Kobe Gaidai Ronso, 56*(2), 59–82.

Tatsuki, D., & Nishizawa, M. (2005). A comparison of compliments and compliment responses in television interviews, film and naturally occurring data. In D. Tatsuki (Ed.), *Pragmatics in language learning, theory, and practice* (pp. 87–98). Tokyo: Japan Association of Language Teachers.

Thornbury, S., & Slade, D. (2006). *Conversation: From description to pedagogy.* Cambridge, England: Cambridge University Press.

van Lier, L. (1996). *Interaction in the language curriculum: Awareness, autonomy and authenticity.* Harlow, England: Longman.

Vellenga, H. (2004). Learning pragmatics from ESL and EFL textbooks: How likely? *TESL-EJ, 8*(2). Retrieved from http://tesl-ej.org/

Wieland, M. (1995). Complimenting behavior in French/American cross-cultural dinner conversations. *The French Review, 68,* 796–812.

Wilson, T. P., Wiemann, J. M., & Zimmerman, D. H. (1984). Models of turntaking in conversational interaction. *Journal of Language and Social Psychology, 3,* 159–183. doi:10.1177/0261927X8400300301

Wolfson, N. (1981). Compliments in cross-cultural perspective. *TESOL Quarterly, 15,* 117–124. doi:10.2307/3586403

Wolfson, N. (1989). The social dynamics of native and nonnative variation in complimenting behavior. In M. R. Eisenstein (Ed.), *The dynamic interlanguage: Empirical studies in second language variation* (pp. 219–236). New York, NY: Plenum.

Wong, J. (1984). Using conversational analysis to evaluate telephone conversations in English as a second language textbooks (Unpublished master's thesis). University of California, Los Angeles.

Wong, J. (2002). "Applying" conversation analysis in applied linguistics: Evaluating dialogue in English as a second language textbooks, *International Review of Applied Linguistics in Language Teaching, 40,* 37–60. doi:10.1515/iral.2002.003

Wong, J. (2003). Telephone openings. In K. Bardovi-Harlig & R. Mahan-Taylor (Eds.), *Teaching pragmatics.* Washington, DC: U.S. Department of State, Office of English Language Programs.

Wong, J. (2007). Answering my call: A look at telephone closings. In H. Bowles & P. Seedhouse, *Conversation analysis and language for specific purposes* (pp. 271–304). Bern, Switzerland: Peter Lang.

Wong, J., & Waring, H. Z. (2010). *Conversation analysis and second language pedagogy: A guide for ESL/EFL teachers.* New York, NY: Routledge.

Wray, A. (2002). *Formulaic language and the lexicon.* New York, NY: Cambridge University Press.

Wright, M. (2004). *The phonetic properties of multi-unit first closing turns in British-English telephone call closing sequences.* Cambridge, England: Colloquium of the British Association of Academic Phoneticians.

Yorio, C. (1989). Idiomaticity as an indicator of second language proficiency. In K. Hyltenstam & L. K. Obler (Eds.), *Bilingualism across the lifespan* (pp. 55–72). Cambridge, England: Cambridge University Press.

Yu, M. (2004). Interlinguistic variation and similarity in second language speech act behavior. *Modern Language Journal, 88*, 102–119. doi:10.1111/j.0026-7902.2004.00220.x

Yu, M. (2005). Sociolinguistic competence in the complimenting act of native Chinese and American English speakers: A mirror of cultural value. *Language & Speech, 48*, 91–119. doi:10.1177/00238309050480010501

Index

Page numbers followed by an *f* indicate figures and a *t* indicate tables.

A

Acceptance, 106, 111–112. *See also* Preference organization
Adjacency pair, 106, 136. *See also* Preference organization
Agreement, 106, 110, 115–117. *See also* Preference organization
Apologies
context of, 42–44
curriculum, tasks, and materials for, 44–49, 44*t*
overview, 3–4, 41
reflections regarding, 49–50
worksheets, answer keys, and handouts regarding, 50–60
Appreciation. *See* Thanking expressions
Arrangement sequences, 139–140
Assessment
conventional expressions and, 10
overview, 7–8
students' current knowledge regarding compliments, 64–65
Assessments in conversations. *See also* Responders
context of, 172–175
curriculum, tasks, and materials for, 115–117, 175–177
overview, 171–172
preference organization and, 110
reflections regarding, 177–178
worksheets, answer keys, and handouts regarding, 179–191
Awareness, language. *See* Language Research Project

B

Bumping into someone
apology sequence for, 43–44
curriculum, tasks, and materials for, 44–49, 44*t*

C

Change-of-state tokens. *See also* Responders
context of, 172–175
curriculum, tasks, and materials for, 175–177
overview, 171–172
reflections regarding, 177–178
worksheets, answer keys, and handouts regarding, 179–191
Closings, telephone. *See* Telephone conversation closings
Compliments
context of, 61–64, 79–80
curriculum, tasks, and materials for, 64–67, 80–83
male and female complimenting behavior, 79–89
overview, 4, 61
reflections regarding, 68–69, 83
thanking expressions as, 24

Compliments *(continued)*
worksheets, answer keys, and handouts
regarding, 69–78, 84–89
Conditional relevance, 106. *See also* Preference
organization
Continuers. *See also* Responders
context of, 154–157, 157*f*
curriculum, tasks, and materials for,
157–160
overview, 153–154
reflections regarding, 160–161
worksheets, answer keys, and handouts
regarding, 162–169
Conventional expressions. *See also* Apologies;
Compliments; Familiarity with natural
conventional expressions; Thanking
expressions
assessing students' knowledge of, 10
characteristics of, 11*t*
list of, 17, 19–20
versus modified expressions, 10, 11*t*
overview, 1–2, 3, 9–10
Conversation analysis system, 92–94
Conversation closings, telephone. *See*
Telephone conversation closings
Conversation openings, telephone. *See*
Telephone conversation openings
Conversational turn-taking. *See* Turn-taking
Curriculum
apologizing and, 44–49, 44*t*
compliments and, 64–67, 80–83
continuers and, 157–160
evaluating familiarity with conventional
expressions and, 11–15, 13*t*
Language Research Project and, 194–199,
196*f*
male and female complimenting behavior,
80–83
preference organization and, 111–117, 113*f*
responders and, 157–160, 175–177
telephone conversation closings and,
142–144
telephone conversation openings and,
124–127, 126*f*
thanking expressions and, 27–28
turn-taking and, 94–102

D

Delaying a response, 108
Disagreement, 106, 110. *See also* Preference
organization
Discourse completion test (DCT), 43–44

E

Evaluating familiarity
context of, 8–10, 11*t*
curriculum, tasks, and materials for, 11–15,
13*t*
list of conventional and modified expressions
for, 17, 19–20
listening-based assessment task, 11–15, 13*t*,
18, 20–22
overview, 7–8
reflections regarding, 15–16
Explicit apology, 42. *See also* Apologies
Explicit compliments, 62. *See also* Compliments
Expressions. *See* Conventional expressions
Expressions of gratitude. *See* Thanking
expressions

F

Familiarity with natural conventional
expressions. *See also* Conventional
expressions
context of, 8–10, 11*t*
curriculum, tasks, and materials for, 11–15,
13*t*
list of conventional and modified
expressions, 17, 19–20
listening-based assessment task and, 11–15,
13*t*, 18, 20–22
overview, 7–8
reflections regarding, 15–16
Female complimenting behavior. *See also*
Compliments
context of, 79–80
curriculum, tasks, and materials for, 80–83
overview, 79
reflections regarding, 83
worksheets, answer keys, and handouts
regarding, 84–89

G

Gaps in conversations, 108
Gender differences, 79–89
Granting, 106. *See also* Preference organization
Gratitude, expressions of. *See* Thanking expressions
Greeting sequence, 120–121, 122–123, 131–132. *See also* Telephone conversation openings

H

How are you sequence, 120–121, 123–124, 131–132. *See also* Telephone conversation openings

I

Identification/recognition sequence, 120–121, 122, 131–132. *See also* Telephone conversation openings
Inappropriate responses, 67. *See also* Responders
Indebtedness expressions, 25
Initiations, 2. *See also* Interaction
Instructional goal, 12
Interaction, 2. *See also* Initiations; Interactional sequences; Responders; Turn-taking
Interactional sequences, 2. *See also* Interaction
Interactive think-aloud strategy, 195–196
Intonation
    continuers and, 156–157, 158, 159–160, 169
    responders and, 173

L

Lack of necessity/obligation expressions, 25
Language awareness, 5. *See* Language Research Project
Language Research Project
    context of, 193–194
    curriculum, tasks, and materials for, 194–199, 196*f*
    overview, 193, 201
    reflections regarding, 199–200
    worksheets, answer keys, and handouts regarding, 201–205
Linguistic learning, 193
Listening-based assessment task
    evaluating familiarity with conventional expressions and, 11–15, 13*t*
    scoring, 20–22
    student answer sheet for, 18
Listening-based exercises, 30–40

M

Making arrangements, 139–140
Male complimenting behavior. *See also* Compliments
    context of, 79–80
    curriculum, tasks, and materials for, 80–83
    overview, 79
    reflections regarding, 83
    worksheets, answer keys, and handouts regarding, 84–89
Materials
    apologizing and, 44–49, 44*t*
    compliments and, 64–67, 80–83
    continuers and, 157–160
    evaluating familiarity with conventional expressions and, 11–15, 13*t*
    Language Research Project and, 194–199, 196*f*
    male and female complimenting behavior, 80–83
    preference organization and, 111–117, 113*f*
    responders and, 157–160
    telephone conversation closings and, 142–144
    telephone conversation openings and, 124–127, 126*f*
    thanking expressions and, 27–28
    turn-taking and, 94–102
Mm-hm continuer. *See* Continuers
Modified expressions
    characteristics of, 11*t*
    versus conventional expressions, 10, 11*t*
    evaluating familiarity with conventional expressions and, 14
    list of, 17, 19–20

N

News markers. *See also* Responders
    context of, 172–175
    curriculum, tasks, and materials for,
        175–177
    overview, 171–172
    reflections regarding, 177–178
    worksheets, answer keys, and handouts
        regarding, 179–191

O

Openings, telephone. *See* Telephone
    conversation openings

P

Phone closings. *See* Telephone conversation
    closings
Phone openings. *See* Telephone conversation
    openings
Phono-logical Phone Game, 119, 124–127,
    126*f*, 133–134. *See also* Telephone
    conversation openings
Preannouncements, 108–109. *See also*
    Preference organization
Preclosing signals. *See also* Telephone
    conversation closings
    curriculum, tasks, and materials for,
        142–144
    overview, 137–141, 138*f*, 139*f*
    worksheets, answer keys, and handouts
        regarding, 145–152
Preference organization
    context of, 105–110
    curriculum, tasks, and materials for,
        111–117, 113*f*
    overview, 4, 105
    reflections regarding, 117–118
Preinvitations, 108–109. *See also* Preference
    organization
Prerequests, 108–109. *See also* Preference
    organization
Presequences, 108–110, 114–115. *See also*
    Preference organization
Promises to repay/reciprocate, 25
Prosody, 190–191

R

Reassuring, 24
Recognition of natural conventional
    expressions
    context of, 8–10, 11*t*
    curriculum, tasks, and materials for, 11–15,
        13*t*
    list of conventional and modified
        expressions, 17, 19–20
    listening-based assessment task and, 11–15,
        13*t*, 18, 20–22
    overview, 7–8
    reflections regarding, 15–16
Refusals, 106. *See also* Preference organization
Rejection, 106, 112–114, 113*f*. *See also*
    Preference organization
Responders. *See also* Interaction
    beyond continuers, 171–191
    to compliments, 63–64, 66–67, 71–75
    context of, 154–157, 157*f*, 172–175
    continuers, 153–169
    curriculum, tasks, and materials for,
        157–160, 175–177
    delaying, 108
    overview, 2, 4–5, 153–154, 171–172
    preference organization and, 107–108
    reflections regarding, 160–161, 177–178
    worksheets, answer keys, and handouts
        regarding, 162–169, 179–191
Responsibility taking, 42. *See also* Apologies
Right continuer. *See* Continuers
Role-plays
    apologizing and, 49
    compliments and, 68, 74

S

Self-observation
    Language Research Project and, 197
    worksheets, answer keys, and handouts
        regarding, 202
Sensitive subjects, 67
Sequence organization, 4. *See also* Turn-taking
Sequences in telephone openings, 120–124,
    131–132. *See also* Telephone
    conversation openings
Signaling the end of a presentation, 24

Signaling the end of a service encountered, 24
Silence, 108
Situation-specific apology strategies, 43. *See also* Apologies
Social functions of expressions, 65
Sociocultural learning, 193
Solicitude preclosing, 140–141. *See also* Preclosing signals
Speaker characteristics, 62–63
Speaker selection, 93
Speaker transitions, 92, 93–94. *See also* Turn-taking
SPEAKING Framework for Analyzing Speech Events, 196*f*, 197, 198, 200
Summons-answer sequence, 120–121, 131–132. *See also* Telephone conversation openings
Surprise/delight expressions, 25

T

Taboo subjects, 67
Taking on responsibility, 42. *See also* Apologies
Taking turns in conversations. *See* Turn-taking
Tasks
    apologizing and, 44–49, 44*t*
    compliments and, 64–67, 80–83
    continuers and, 157–160
    evaluating familiarity with conventional expressions and, 11–15, 13*t*
    Language Research Project and, 194–199, 196*f*
    male and female complimenting behavior, 80–83
    preference organization and, 111–117, 113*f*
    responders and, 157–160, 175–177
    telephone conversation closings and, 142–144
    telephone conversation openings and, 124–127, 126*f*
    thanking expressions and, 27–28
    turn-taking and, 94–102
Telephone conversation closings. *See also* Telephone conversation openings
    context of, 136–141, 138*f*, 139*f*
    curriculum, tasks, and materials for, 142–144
    overview, 4, 135

reflections regarding, 144–145
worksheets, answer keys, and handouts regarding, 145–152
Telephone conversation openings. *See also* Telephone conversation closings
    context of, 119–124
    curriculum, tasks, and materials for, 124–127, 126*f*
    overview, 4, 119
    reflections regarding, 127–128
    worksheets, answer keys, and handouts regarding, 129–134
Terminal exchange sequence, 136–137, 145–152. *See also* Telephone conversation closings
Textbook dialogue, 2–3
Thanking expressions. *See also* Conventional expressions
    context of, 23–27
    curriculum, tasks, and materials for, 27–28
    overview, 23
    reflections regarding, 28–29
    responding to compliments and, 63–64
    worksheets, answer keys, and handouts regarding, 30–37, 76
Think-aloud strategy, 195–196
Transitions, speaker, 92, 93–94. *See also* Turn-taking
Turn-taking. *See also* Interaction; Sequence organization
    context of, 91–94
    curriculum, tasks, and materials for, 94–102
    overview, 2, 4, 91
    preference organization and, 106, 107–108
    reflections regarding, 102–103
    telephone conversation closings and, 136

U

Uh-huh continuer. *See* Continuers

W

Wong's Phono-logical Phone Game, 119, 124–127, 126*f*, 133–134. *See also* Telephone conversation openings

Worksheets, answer keys, and handouts
apologizing, 50–60
compliments and, 69–78, 84–89
continuers and, 162–169
evaluating familiarity with conventional
expressions, 20–22
Language Research Project and, 201–205
male and female complimenting behavior,
84–89
responders and, 162–169, 179–191

telephone conversation closings and,
145–152
telephone conversation openings and,
129–134
thanking expressions, 30–37

Y

Yeah continuer. *See* Continuers

Also Available From TESOL

TESOL Classroom Practice Series
Maria Dantas-Whitney, Sarah Rilling, and Lilia Savova, Series Editors

Authenticity in the Classroom and Beyond: Children and Adolescent Learners
Maria Dantas-Whitney and Sarah Rilling, Editors

Language Games: Innovative Activities for Teaching English
Maureen Snow Andrade, Editor

Authenticity in the Classroom and Beyond: Adult Learners
Sarah Rilling and Maria Dantas-Whitney, Editors

Adult Language Learners: Context and Innovation
Ann F. V. Smith and Gregory Strong, Editors

Applications of Task-Based Learning in TESOL
Ali Shehadeh and Christine Coombe, Editors

Explorations in Second Language Reading
Roger Cohen, Editor

Insights on Teaching Speaking in TESOL
Tim Stewart, Editor

Multilevel and Diverse Classrooms
Bradley Baurain and Phan Le Ha, Editors

Pragmatics: Teaching Speech Acts
Donna Tatsuki and Noël Houck, Editors

Effective Second Language Writing
Susan Kasten, Editor

Integrating Language and Content
Jon Nordmeyer and Susan Barduhn

Using Textbooks Effectively
Lilia Savova, Editor

Classroom Management
Thomas S. C. Farrell, Editor

Teaching Listening: Voices From the Field
Nikki Ashcraft and Anh Tran, Editors

❈ ❈ ❈ ❈ ❈

Language Teacher Research Series
Thomas S. C. Farrell, Series Editor

Language Teacher Research in Africa
Leketi Makalela, Editor

Language Teacher Research in Asia
Thomas S. C. Farrell, Editor

Language Teacher Research in Europe
Simon Borg, Editor

Language Teacher Research in the Americas
Hedy McGarrell, Editor

Language Teacher Research in the Middle East
Christine Coombe and Lisa Barlow, Editors

Language Teacher Research in Australia and New Zealand
Jill Burton and Anne Burns, Editors

✳ ✳ ✳ ✳ ✳

Collaborative Partnerships Between ESL and Classroom Teachers Series
Debra Suarez, Series Editor

Helping English Language Learners Succeed in Pre-K–Elementary Schools
Jan Lacina, Linda New Levine, and Patience Sowa

Helping English Language Learners Succeed in Middle and High Schools
Faridah Pawan and Ginger Sietman, Editors

✳ ✳ ✳ ✳ ✳

CALL Environments: Research, Practice, and Critical Issues, 2nd ed.
Joy Egbert and Elizabeth Hanson-Smith, Editors

Learning Languages through Technology
Elizabeth Hanson-Smith and Sarah Rilling, Editors

Global English Teaching and Teacher Education: Praxis and Possibility
Seran Dogancay-Aktuna and Joel Hardman, Editors

Local phone: (240)646-7037
Fax: (301)206-9789
E-Mail: tesolpubs@brightkey.net
Toll-free: 1-888-891-0041
Mail Orders to TESOL, P.O. Box 79283, Baltimore, MD 21279-0283
ORDER ONLINE at www.tesol.org and click on "Bookstore"